FROM THE EDITORS OF MILITARY HISTORY MAGAZINE

DESERT STORM

FOREWORD BY
COL. HARRY G. SUMMERS, JR.

ROBERT ELLIOTT, U.S. ARMY

The men of 3rd Platoon, A Company, 1st Battalion, 327th Infantry Regiment, 1st Brigade Airborne Division, who defeated a division-size Iraqi element during fighting in southern Iraq, celebrate the coalition victory on March 1, 1991.

ACKNOWLEDGMENTS

Empire Press would like to extend its deep appreciation to the following military units and individuals whose invaluable assistance made this book a reality: 1st Marine Division; 2nd Marine Air Wing; 82nd Airborne Division; 24th Mechanized Infantry Brigade; 197th Infantry Brigade; 1st Infantry Division; 11th Air Defense Artillery Brigade; 3rd Armored Cavalry Regiment; 3rd Marine Air Wing; the Darien, Conn., VFW Post 6933; the 27th Tactical Fighter Squadron, "the oldest squadron in the U.S. Air Force"; Sgt. 1st Class Mike Bachand, USA; Sgt. Brian Baker, USA; Lt. William Barrentine, USA; Captain Mike Beguelin, USMC; Captain Jim Braden, USMC; Captain Christopher Burnham, USMC; Captain Ray Coia, USMC; Sgt. Sean Combs, USA; Col. Ralph Cossa, USAF; Richard Curtiss; Cpl. Carl "Randy" Davis, USMC; Captain Joseph DeAntona, USA; Cpl. Rob Detherow, USMC; Lt. W. Ebert, USA; Sharon Fenton; Spc. 4 Lisa Foster, USA; Skip Freeman; Rear Adm. Vance Fry, USNR; Col. Carl Fulford, USMC; Pfc Jeff Gilley, USA; Captain Sal Granata, USA; 2nd Mate Robert Guttman, merchant marine; Sgt. 1st Class Anthony Harper, USA; Keith Hock, USMC; Bob Hornlein; Captain Tim Hoyle, USMC; Sgt. William James, USA; Rocky Jay; Captain Matt Johnson, USA; Captain Mike Kenny, USMC; Janet Krueger; Senator Joseph I. Lieberman (D-Conn.); Sgt. William Limb, USMC; Monica Manganaro; Captain Mark A. Melin, USMC; Lisa Michaelis; Chief Warrant Officer Jim Millard, USMC; Sgt. 1st Class Erie Miller, USA; Captain John Millestad, USA; Captain Steve Olds, USAF; Pfc Theodore Phillips, USA; Spc. 4 Angela Rooney, USA; Captain Russell A. Sanborn, USMC; Captain Stephen Sicinski, USA; James Sparrow; Max Springer; Staff Sgt. Daniel Stice, USA; Lt. Gen. Bernard Trainor, USMC (Ret.); Captain Roger Vincent, USAF; and Captain Mary Jane Wordel, USA.

CREDITS

Edited by William M. Vogt and Carl A. Gnam, Jr.
Consulting Editors: Harry G. Summers, Jr., C. Brian Kelly
Associate Editors: Jon Guttman, Greg Lalire
Project Manager/Picture Research: Kenneth H. Phillips
Project Coordinator: Roberta S. Phillips
Composition by Ralph U. Scherer
Copy Assistants: Mary Lou Witmer and Delinda Hanley
Color separations and pre-press by Graphic Color Systems, Lanham, Maryland

Library of Congress Catalog Card Number 91-073213
ISBN 0-943231-46-9

Published by Empire Press, 602 S. King St., Suite 300, Leesburg, Virginia 22075
Telephone: (703) 771-9400   Fax: (703) 777-4627
Vice President/General Manager: Carl A. Gnam, Jr.
Vice President/Business Manager: Mark Hintz
Empire Press is an affiliate of Cowles Media Company, 6405 Flank Drive, Harrisburg, Pennsylvania 17112
FIRST PRINTING

Distributed exclusively to the trade by Howell Press, Inc.
1147 River Road, Bay 2, Charlottesville, Virginia 22901
Telephone: (804) 977-4006   Toll-Free 1-800-868-4512   Fax: (804) 971-7204

Printed and bound in the USA by Arcata Graphics

Staff Sergeant Daniel Stamaris salutes during the playing of the National Anthem at Andrews Air Force Base during a ceremony for returning American prisoners of war on March 10, 1991.

DEDICATION

To those who served in the Persian Gulf, the men and women who were the thunder and lightning of Desert Storm, and to the memory of the coalition troops who fell—among them, 352 Americans: 46 in the air war, 28 from Scud attack, 77 in the ground war, and 201 non-combat deaths, by Central Command's count.

RIGHT: A Fairchild A-10 Thunderbolt II attack plane armed with a Maverick missile prowls the Kuwaiti desert in search of armored Iraqi prey. BELOW LEFT: The battleship USS Wisconsin fires one of her 16-inch guns in support of Operation Desert Storm. BELOW RIGHT: M1 Abrams tanks of the VII Corps' 3rd Armored Division move up to their forward assembly point in western Saudi Arabia prior to the commencement of the ground war.

CHRISTOPHER MORRIS/BLACK STAR

BRUCE MORRIS, U.S. NAVY

C O N T E N T S

D.W. HOLMES, U.S. NAVY

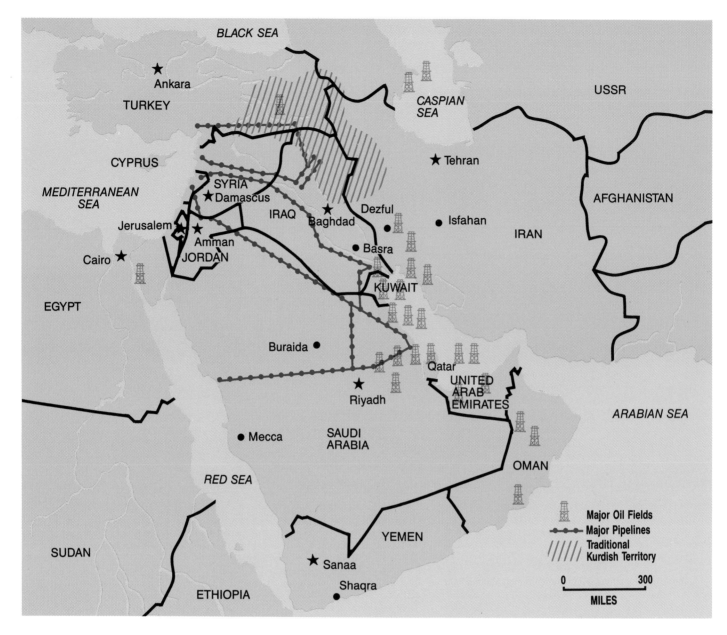

Mixed blessing: The major oil fields that dot the landscape are the principal source of the Persian Gulf's wealth—and of many of its troubles. Complicating the situation, artificial borders and events left Kurds, like Palestinians, aliens in their own homeland. Iraq's despotic leader, Saddam Hussein, coveted tiny Kuwait's port and several important oil fields, and invaded to claim them— earning the enmity of Western nations and other Arab countries, and touching off the Persian Gulf War: Operation Desert Storm.

The faces of Saddam Hussein's soldiers seemed to reflect confident dedication in January 1991. By February, however, Saddam's veteran troops behaved more "battle weary" than "battle hardened."

FOREWORD

Desert Storm was the most massive application of U.S. military power since World War II. Making good on President George Bush's promise that this time we would not fight with one hand tied behind our backs, the full fury of American arms was unleashed on Iraqi dictator Saddam Hussein's army, navy and air force and on his ability to wage war—including his chemical, nuclear and military plants and installations.

The results were devastating, almost beyond belief. First, a spectacular 38-day air war cut Iraq's lines of command, control and communications to ribbons and crippled its forces in the field as well. Next, the resounding victory of the 100-hour ground war astounded everyone, including the U.S. commander in the Persian Gulf, General H. Norman Schwarzkopf, who had stockpiled 609 days of ammunition and supplies in the desert for his assault divisions in anticipation of a slugging match with the "battle-hardened" Iraqi army.

It surprised the rest of the world as well, considering doubts raised in Vietnam about America's capability and will to fight. Such doubts were groundless. America had both the will to fight and a military trained and ready to do so. In retrospect, Saddam's fighting force might seem to have been a pushover, but few believed so before the battle was joined. Lost in the postwar euphoria was the fact that, according to intelligence reports, Iraq's million-man army, 5,000 tanks and 3,500 artillery pieces actually outnumbered those of the allied coalition. And some of Saddam's weaponry—the South African-supplied G-5 155mm gun/howitzers, for example, with their 45-kilometer range—were superior to those of the allies.

In not only military but in political, diplomatic and psychological terms as well, it was a remarkable achievement. How did it happen? Answering that question is the central theme of this book. Various political, diplomatic, psychological and military aspects of allied and Iraqi power are amplified by firsthand accounts of the fighting there to provide a unique perspective on the war, by a roster of distinguished and knowledgeable contributors.

The book gives a factual, readable account of America's war in the Persian Gulf, in clear and understandable terms. How did it happen? Read on and find out.

Colonel Harry G. Summers, Jr. (USA, ret.)
Editor, *Vietnam* Magazine
Distinguished Fellow, Army War College.

7

BRIEF, VIOLENT WAR

82ND AIRBORNE

A coalition soldier moves out on signal. In the final assault, the most crucial stage of Operation Desert Storm, sophisticated weapons could not entirely replace troops on the ground.

JUMP-OFF TIME. Ground war against Iraq. February 23, 1991.

Up and down the long desert line, separated from the Iraqi enemy by berms of sand, the troops stood ready. The armada of vehicles, too. Including a U.S. Marine Corps tank fondly called "Scumdog."

"The sky over Kuwait on the other side was pitch black from our aerial bombardment and the burning oil fields," recalled one of the awaiting onlookers later. "One particularly enormous, bright flash lit up the entire night sky. I suspected it was from a 15,000-pound 'Daisy Cutter' FAE [fuel-air-explosive] bomb."

That one explosion was "incredible." But there were many more on the far side of the 12-foot-high barrier of desert sand marking the border. "During that moonlit night we could see other flashes and hear the long drawn-out rumble of a B-52 raid some 40 kilometers away."

At the signal to burst through, various elements of the 1st Marine Division were stacked up and ready to go—infantry plus light armored vehicles, mobile artillery, amphibious tractors (amtracs) and M60 tanks. Including Scumdog.

These were Task Forces Ripper, Grizzly, Papa Bear and Taro. Task Force Ripper alone had "seven thousand Marines and one thousand vehicles of various types—everything from motorcycles to M60 tanks," said its commander, Colonel Carl Fulford.

Ripper, in fact, was beyond the border, 12 "clicks" (kilometers) into Kuwait, hours before the go signal. The word was: Don't do anything

"irreversible" and be prepared to pull back if the ground war were delayed or called off.

But no such word came, and at the appointed hour, the Marines, the U.S. Army—the entire coalition force arrayed against Iraq's Saddam Hussein—launched the final and most crucial stage of Operation Desert Storm, the ground war against hundreds of thousands of Iraqis lodged in occupied Kuwait.

After plunging through, over and across the berm, the spearhead forces had to deal with the minefields—but high tech was ready for this job, just as it had been since Day One of the short but violent war against Iraq. Lumbering ahead, the miracle machines spat out their "giant vipers"—explosive lines that set off the hidden mines in front. Next would come a plow tank shoving through the furrow and setting off any further mines.

The time consumed by the American-led war in the Persian Gulf was very short—a matter of days. Many a historical battle has been decided in minutes or hours, but few wars are settled so quickly or so *efficiently* as was the recent Persian Gulf War.

High-tech weapons played their crucial role, true. So did the massive and incredibly fast buildup depicted in the early chapters of this book.

Determination also played *its* role, however.

The Americans leading this campaign once were junior officers in another war—Vietnam. They saw—and suffered—a war that their nation would only fight half-heartedly.

"Never Again" may well have been their motto.

General H. Norman "Bear" Schwarzkopf made his determination clear many times before the war broke out in January. The Americans and other forces he commanded would go for broke, no holds barred—and no faintheartedness about the job ahead, either. To a group of veterans from the Battle of the Bulge in World War II (the 87th Infantry Division), he wrote that, like that great battle, "another may be just around the corner in the Middle East."

It was the day after Christmas 1990 when he wrote the Bulge vets and added: "Hopefully, we can end this crisis peacefully, but if not, you can be proud to know that today's armed forces in Operation Desert Shield are fully prepared to fight and win in order to uphold our nation's interests."

Fight and win!

Just weeks, days, later, they did. *Fought and won.*

How they did it, how it all came about, and how it came to a fast end is what this book is all about.

The editors at Empire Press hope you, the reader, will agree that our team of writers has captured the flavor and the essence, the who, what, where...the how and the why. The short, dramatically illustrated history of Desert Shield and Desert Storm.

As the book was being prepared, we had the advantage of hindsight: later reports of intelligence lapses that overestimated the enemy's strength (not all a bad thing during a war), heretofore unpublicized commando actions, and controversies over how fully high tech was able to compensate for the inaccuracy of "dumb" weaponry. Details that later came to light included sorties by Navy SEALs and Special Operations teams to locate Scud launchers, give the Iraqis false impressions of coalition intentions, and blast a hole in enemy air defenses to give the mighty armada of aircraft the element of surprise over Baghdad.

In the end, of course, it was a lopsided victory for the American-led coalition forces. Our history here cannot go much beyond the immediate aftermath of the war itself, nor is the proverbial crystal ball yet available for prognosticating the political future of the always-volatile Middle East.

Still, a couple of related thoughts are worth pondering. On the one hand, the largely Free West weaponry and its application would seem so efficient, so effective, that in the future even a superpower such as the Soviet Union surely must hesitate before embarking upon adventures that would incur the same violent wrath—even in a conventional war in which the Soviet equipage presumably would outnumber that of its Western adversaries.

APWIDE WORLD PHOTOS

Such thinking is a possible comfort to traditional Cold Warriors and may indeed be entirely valid, in the event a Cold War scenario should set in again.

On the other, more chilling hand, however, the Free World's great victory raises uncomfortable visions of future conflicts, a great power opposed to the United States and its allies, would be all the more tempted to consider a bludgeoning first strike in the event of war.

Likewise, the Iraqs of the future and even punier Third World troublemakers may be all the more likely to resort from the outset to the "no-no" weapons that Iraq in this case never did use—nukes, chemicals, biological agents.

The victory over a ruthless dictator and aggressor was great, even though tempered by his continuance in power. It was great, and while it should intimidate the bullies of the future, we of the Free World—keepers, apparently, of the new world order that President Bush has urged—must remain ever vigilant against those who will use any means to win their objectives.

Whatever the case, U.S. Army General Colin Powell, chairman of the Joint Chiefs of Staff, had it right when he said the coalition's strategy against the Iraqi army would be "very, very simple." Said Powell: "First we're going to cut it off, and then we're going to kill it."

Done, done and done.

C. Brian Kelly
Editor
Military History Magazine

Under a pall of toxic smoke from burning oil wells, the remains of an Iraqi tank stands as testimony to U.S. Army General Colin Powell's summation of coalition strategy against the Iraqi army: ''First we're going to cut it off, and then we're going to kill it.''

CHAPTER ONE

BATTLEFIELD OF SAND

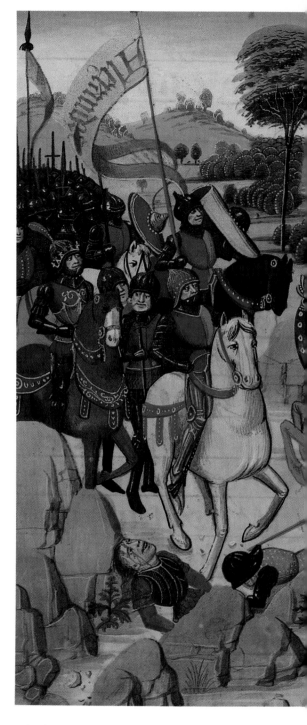

JOHN WALLER

Sargon of Akkad, the first of many empire-builders in the Middle East.

IT IS A CAPRICE of history that the lands now occupied by Iraq and Kuwait, ravaged by conflict throughout history and now again rent by war, gave birth to the world's first civilization. An advanced culture flourished in the Mesopotamian city-states of Sumer as early as the 4th millennium BC, but despite all their achievements, the Sumerians could not keep peace among themselves. Sumerian cities such as Kish, Uruk and Ur fought for supremacy but ultimately succumbed to stronger, more unified invaders such as Sargon the Great, who led his people out of the deserts during the early part of the 3rd millenium BC to invade Sumeria and establish the Semitic kingdom of Akkad.

And so it would go for millennia to come; in a rondo of history, stronger people would conquer those who were weaker. Causes and conquerors would come and go, some leaving only footnotes in history, a few leaving behind a substantial legacy to some degree. Many antagonisms of the past continue to affect relations of Middle Eastern countries in the present, while the protagonists of the Gulf War purported to find inspiration in notable figures from the past—Iraq's Saddam Hussein, for example, tried to liken himself, somewhat ironically, to Saladin, while U.S. General H. Norman Schwarzkopf expressed admiration for Alexander the Great.

The first recorded battle in history—the record still exists—was the Battle of Megiddo in 1469 BC between the Egyptians, under their ambitious and brilliant Pharaoh Thutmose III, and a coalition of Assyrians and Palestinians,

which occurred in the Palestine fortress city of Megiddo, gateway to Mesopotamia, the Iraq of today. (A second battle of Megiddo was waged in 609 BC, when it was prophesied that Megiddo would be the site of the final Battle of Armageddon between good and evil at the end of the world.)

The Fertile Crescent, enveloping the deserts in an arc stretching from the Nile Valley to the valleys of the Tigris and Euphrates rivers in Mesopotamia, was fertile ground not only for providing the sustenance of life but sadly for the seeds of war. An uneasy equilibrium of power existed in the Fertile Crescent until the Assyrians forged an empire in the 9th century

Alexander the Great's army is ambushed in a mountain pass by 25,000 rock-throwing Persians—a setback that failed to prevent him from conquering a vast, cosmopolitan empire. This anachronistic rendering illustrated a book of Alexander's life, written in 1463 for the Duke of Burgundy, who—like General H. Norman Schwarzkopf— was inspired by the Macedonian's exploits.

BC through superior force of arms. Marching under the standard of the man-headed winged bull, symbol of the storm god Adad, they perfected the art of the siege and used, in perfect coordination, archers, heavy infantry and cavalry to defeat their enemies—foreshadowing the artistry of Desert Storm's joint operations some 3,000 years later. The Assyrian Empire achieved its greatest size under Tiglath-pileser III in 732 BC.

In the 6th century BC, Nebuchadnezzar II built a magnificent new capital at Babylon on the banks of the Euphrates, but a Persian juggernaut from the east under Cyrus I (the Great) conquered Babylon in 539 BC, defeating the weakened Assyrians. Then, the greatest in the parade of conquerers, Alexander III of Macedon, swept eastward some 300 years before the Christian era in fulfillment of his destiny to rule the known world, defeating the mighty Persian Empire in 334 BC, and razing its ceremonial capital, Persepolis.

The lion's share of Alexander's empire, inherited by his Macedonian general Seleucus, embraced the Anatolian Plateau, Mesopotamia, Persia and the lands eastward to the edges of India. The Seleucid dynasty left the stamp of Hellenistic culture before its rule was ended by Parthian predators. Although the Parthians seized most of the Seleucid realm, the Roman conquerer Pompey took Syria, center of the

Seleucid kingdom, and Jerusalem, holy city of the Jews.

The Jews were of unique significance; their testament, the history of their people, would provide the basis of the other great religions of the Book, Christianity and Islam. Descended from the patriarch Abraham, venerated alike by Christians and Moslems, the Jewish tribes produced such great early leaders as Saul, David and Solomon, but then for centuries they were inundated by foreign conquerors with roots in the Western world, including Alexander the Great, the Ptolemaic kings of Egypt and the Hellenistic Seleucids, whose attempts to outlaw all religions but the Greek pantheon of gods caused a Jewish revolt in 164 BC that eventually led to a revival of Jewish independence in 141 BC.

With the decline of the Seleucids, a civil conflict among the Jews was settled by Roman intervention when Pompey occupied Jersualem in 63 BC after a three-year siege. Israel became the Roman province of Judea, and it was Roman rule that sat heavily upon the Jews. It was, of course, the Roman Pontius Pilate who presided uneasily over the Jews at the time of the Crucifixion and has since lived in the chronicles of Christendom for his infamous contributing role in Christ's martyrdom.

In 66 AD, Jewish zealots revolted against the Romans, but on August 29, 70 AD, the Romans under Titus destroyed the Great Temple of the Jews and forbade them to visit Jerusalem except once a year to mourn on the anniversary of the Temple's destruction.

When in 132 AD Roman Emperor Hadrian outlawed Judaism, the Jews, under Simon Bar Kokhba, again rose in rebellion and fought for three years before hope for freedom was finally extinguished. Hadrian's "final solution" to the problem of Jewish restiveness was to drive most of the Jews out of their land and scatter them throughout the empire, in what is known as the Diaspora, or dispersion. Homeless, they made their way in an inhospitable world, absorbing new cultures while preserving their own and cherishing dreams of returning one day to Jerusalem.

In the early 7th century, an Arab named Mohammed of the Qoreishi family, inspired by an angel, wrote his testament, the Koran, and preached its doctrine to those who would listen. Islam proclaims the unity of an all-powerful God: "There is no God but Allah; Mohammed is the Messenger of Allah." It calls for prayer five times a day, almsgiving to the poor, daytime fasting during the holy month of Ramadan and pilgrimage to Mecca, heart of Islam and site of the shrine of the sacred Kaaba stone. Mohammed was at first harassed by non-believers and forced to flee from his home in Mecca in

622 AD and take refuge in nearby Medina. This signal event, called the Hegira, or flight to new life, is revered by Moslems as the beginning of Islam, the date from which the Moslem calendar is calculated.

Mohammed's teaching continued to attract followers who revered him as the prophet of Allah. The movement survived his death; within a century Islam had spread with the speed of a brush fire. *Jihads*, or holy wars, brought the Middle East, North Africa and Spain within the Empire of Islam.

In the 11th, 12th and 13th centuries, Christendom made repeated efforts to "rescue" the holy city of Jerusalem from Islam with its Christian shrines—some hallowed by Islam and Judaism as well. On July 15, 1099, the crusaders succeeded in taking Jerusalem, and for some centuries thereafter they and their successors clung to Latin kingdoms that they had carved out of the Holy Land. But the Holy Sepulchre would not remain in their possession for long.

On July 4, 1187, the Moslems, reunited and resurgent under a charismatic and gifted warrior-statesman of Kurdish descent named Salah-ad-Din Yusuf ibn-Ayyub, routed the crusaders at the Horns of Hattin and retook Jerusalem. The Moslems came to refer to their leader as Al Nasir ("the Victorious") but remarkably, he became equally renowned in Christian annals under the Europeanized name of Saladin.

Europe was not long in responding to Jerusalem's fall. Numerous kings and nobles converged on Palestine, but few stayed long before abandoning the Third Crusade and returning to domestic business in their respective lands. The great exception was King Richard I of England who, with the help of his rival-turned-ally King Philip II (Augustus) of France, relieved the besieged Christian-held fortress at Acre and, in September 1191, won a victory over Saladin at Arsuf which demonstrated that he had a tactical acumen equal to the courage that immortalized him to posterity as Richard the Lion-Hearted. The negotiated peace that was concluded between Richard and Saladin a year later, however, left Jerusalem in Moslem hands, although it did permit all "people of the Book"—Christian, Jewish or Moslem—free and peaceful access to the city's sacred places.

Later Crusades varied in zeal and Christian devotion. The Fourth Crusade, for reasons quite unchristian, sacked the Byzantine capital of Constantinople on April 13, 1204, further inflaming the schism between the Eastern and Roman Catholic churches. King Louis IX of France, leader of the Seventh Crusade and destined for sainthood, was defeated at the Battle of El Mansûrah on the Nile Delta on February 9, 1250. Not until 1291 when the Crusader port of Acre fell

to the Moslems, did Europe finally abandon its fruitless efforts to gain Jerusalem.

In 1251, the rivalry between European Christian and Turkic Moslem was complicated by the incursion of a third power into the Middle East—the Asiatic Mongols. The Great Khan Möngke called a *quriltay,* or gathering of the chiefs, at his capital of Korakorum to discuss the administration of the vast Mongol Empire. Among other things, he gave Hülegü, grandson of Genghis Khan, responsibility for enforcing Mongol rule over Persia. One of Hülegü's first assignments was to eliminate once and for all the Shiite sect known as the Ismailis, whose notoriously efficient network of assassins had terrorized the Moslem world.

Hülegü and his Mongols proved more than a match for the Ismailis, taking their mountain fortresses one after the other—including the supposedly impregnable cave fortress of Maymun-Diz in the Elburz Mountains, which Hülegü captured in only a fortnight, along with the Ismaili Grand Master, Ruknh al Din. Hülegü then turned his attention westward, taking Baghdad in 1258, followed by Aleppo and Damascus in 1261.

The Mongols were not destined to remain for long, however. The Mamluks, a class of warrior-slaves who had risen to a position of political dominance in Egypt, moved to challenge the Mongol army (which, depleted by the overconfident Hülegü, only numbered 20,000 men). The forces met at Ayn Jalut (the Spring of Goliath) on September 3, 1261, with the result being a resounding victory for the Mamluks under Baybars I. After another defeat at Hims on December 10, Mongol power in the Middle East quickly waned, leaving behind little more than a legacy of destruction that exceeded even the atrocities of the Crusades.

European intrusions into the Near and Middle East would in modern times find other motives: competition for trade, empire and strategic advantage. English and Portuguese merchant fleets vying for mastery of the sea lanes to India often found themselves at swords' points in the Persian Gulf during the 17th century. But by the 18th century, the Gulf was an English preserve. When Napoleon invaded Egypt in 1798, the British once again felt that their ocean lifeline to India might be threatened, although British Admiral Horatio Nelson's stunning defeat of the French fleet off of Alexandria on August 2, 1798, and the French withdrawal from Egypt in 1801 lessened the threat. But when the Russians, after conquering their way down through the Caucasus, gained pre-eminence in Persia in 1828 and coveted the Gulf as its answer to a warm-water port, the British had another, more dangerous imperial rival to concern them.

A somewhat exaggerated European view of the Crusades depicts mailed knights making short shrift of unarmored Moslems. Under leaders such as Saladin and Baybars, the Moslem forces could and did win decisive victories against both Christian and Mongol invaders.

13

The Battle of Sediman, one of several engagements and sieges during Napoleon Bonaparte's unsuccessful adventure in Egypt and Palestine.

Toward the latter part of the 19th century, France and Great Britain's scramble for imperial trophies again made them rivals. British Prime Minister Benjamin Disraeli's master stroke in purchasing controlling interest in the Suez Canal from the heavily mortgaged khedive of Egypt for 4,000,000 English pounds in 1875 stole a march on the French. But it was the Battle of Tel el-Kebir on September 13, 1882, handily won by British General Sir Garnet Wolseley, that gave Egypt to the British. Twenty-two thousand British troops made short work of the xenophobic Egyptian revolutionary, Achmet Arabi, who by threatening the Ottoman khedive had put British control of the Suez Canal at risk. The result of meticulous planning, this victory was a high point in Wolseley's career. The general's name had already become synonymous with total efficiency; plans working well were "all Sir Garnet" in the British slang of the day. And Tel el-Kebir became his ultimate accomplishment in the field.

Tel el-Kebir was as valuable for what it did for British prestige in the Arab world as for what it accomplished in securing Egypt and the Suez Canal.

In 1884, a self-proclaimed messiah of Islam named Mohammed Ahmad, styling himself the Mahdi (chosen one) of Allah, raised the Sudanese tribes against Turkish-Egyptian rule. As a climax to this revolution, the Mahdi's hordes under the black standard of their leader captured the Sudan's capital, Khartoum, on January 26, 1885, and murdered its governor, the legendary Charles "Chinese" Gordon, who had been sent by British Prime Minister William Gladstone to evacuate the beleaguered Egyptian garrisons in the Sudan. Although the Mahdi died shortly after the fall of Khartoum, British prestige suffered in the Arab world until 13 years later, when General Horatio Herbert Kitchener led an army of retribution to retake the Sudan from the Mahdi's successor, Khalifa Abdullah Ibn Mohammed, and avenge Gordon's murder at the Battle of Omdurman on September 2, 1898. The Mahdi's revolt foreshadowed 20th century eruptions of Islamic fundamentalism such as the Moslem Brotherhood and, more recently, Ayatollah Ruhollah Khomeini's revolution in Iran, whose targets have been the intrusion of Western influence at the expense of Islamic purity and power.

World War I, fought to preserve Europe's balance of power and Britain's and France's imperial empires in the face of German aggression, was important to the Near and Middle East as well. Germany nursed dreams of a Berlin-to-Baghdad colonial empire, while Britain and France considered the decaying remnants of the Turkish Empire theirs for the taking. The adventures of T.E. Lawrence "of Arabia," that intrepid though eccentric British officer who led Arab tribes to desert victories over their Turkish masters in World War I, are the stuff of romance. More substantial were the eventual victories of British arms in 1917, as General Frederick Maude marched into Baghdad and General Sir Edmund Allenby became the first European to occupy Jerusalem since the Second Crusade.

More significant were the behind-the-scenes negotiations between the French and English as to how the two countries would draw new boundaries in the Near East and split the territorial spoils as the Turkish Empire collapsed. Most of the Arabs of the Near East, for all their contribution to the Allied war effort, would still find themselves subject people, exchanging Turkish masters for French or English rulers. Following the Armistice on November 11, 1918, and the treaties signed in its wake, the British occupied Palestine, Transjordan and Mesopotamia (Iraq), while the French occupied Syria and Lebanon.

The artificial borders they established failed to take the ethnic, linguistic or religious differences of the indigenous peoples into consideration, creating—intentionally or not—a regional time bomb of instability. The foundations for further bitterness were also laid by British promises made to the Arab Hashimite leader Sharif Hussein that an independent kingdom would be awarded him in return for his aid against the Turks—and the breaking of those promises after 1918. Still another was the Balfour declaration of 1917, promising the creation of a "national home for the Jews" in part of Palestine. The Arabian Peninsula would be torn by a tribal dispute between Hussein, sherif of Mecca, and Abdulazziz Al-Saud, heading a Wahabbi tribal coalition. Abdulazziz, more commonly referred to in the United States as Ibn Saud, came out on top to found the Arab kingdom of Saudi Arabia.

The British and French were still trying to preserve their Near and Middle East interests a generation later during World War II. Iraq, worrisome because of the pro-Axis leanings of its ardently nationalist prime minister, Rashid Ali el Gailani, provoked the British to occupy Basra and the air base at Habbaniyah on April 29, 1941. Pressed by greater demands elsewhere, the British could ill afford a big effort in Iraq.

On May 18, a British column en route to relieve Habbaniyah was strafed by a Messerschmitt Bf-110D fighter-bomber—one of a number of Bf-110Ds and Heinkel He-111 bombers flying from air bases in Vichy French-held Syria to Mosul in Iraq, wearing Iraqi markings but flown by German air crews. With Nazi commitment to the upcoming invasion of the Soviet Union,

however, Adolf Hitler's assistance to Rashid's cause was limited only to this token gesture. On June 1, 1941, the British took Baghdad, despite a spirited defense by its inhabitants. Rashid fled to Iran and spent the rest of the war in Germany. Meanwhile, the main focus of conflict was in the North African desert. In June 1940, Italy entered the war as an Axis power and its army invaded Egypt from its colony of Libya—only to be ignominiously routed in a brilliant British counteroffensive in January-February 1941.

On February 12, 1941, the first contingents of German troops arrived in Tripoli as Hitler sought to bolster his Italian allies with the smallest commitment of men and materiel possible. The most potent weapon Hitler sent was the force's commander, *Generalleutnant* Erwin Rommel. Ordered to defend Tripoli, Rommel did so by taking the offensive against what he judged to be a logistically stretched and weary enemy. His calculated risk paid off, as his small German force—known as the *Afrika Korps*—and its Italian allies drove the British back to the Egyptian border by early April 1941.

There followed a remarkably fluid, mobile war in which one or the other of the opposing forces alternately attacked, only to be driven back in turn as it reached the limits of its supply lines. Finally, in June 1942, Rommel won a breakthrough at Gazala, the momentum of which carried him forward to overrun the long-embattled bastion of Tobruk. Rommel then swept into Egypt, in a serious bid to seize the vital Suez Canal, but was finally stopped in a series of savage armored encounters at and around El Alamein, where the British, commanded by General Claude Auchinleck, made a determined stand. At the end of October 1942, the British Eighth Army, now under the command of Lt. Gen. Bernard Law Montgomery, retook the offensive and by the end of November had driven Rommel's Axis forces 500 miles back into Libya, never to return. The Battles of El Alamein marked a turning point in the war.

In another action of World War II, combined British and Free French forces liberated Syria from the pro-Axis Vichy French on July 12, 1941 (the Allied casualties including the loss of an eye by a Palestinian Jewish soldier named Moshe Dayan). The British also invaded the Gulf ports of southern Iran, vital transfer areas for American war supplies destined for the beleaguered Soviet Union, on August 25. On the same day, to avoid trouble with Iran's pro-German strongman, Reza Shah Pahlavi, and to secure their lines of supply, the Soviets invaded Iran from the Caucasus and Transcaspia while the British moved into their southern Iran oil fields and refineries from Basra—sinking Iran's tiny fleet at its moorings in the Gulf while

NATIONAL ARMY MUSEUM, LONDON

NATIONAL ARMY MUSEUM, LONDON

TOP: Achmet Arabi Pasha failed to oust the Ottoman Turks from Egypt, but it took British intervention to stop him. ABOVE: Arabi's nemesis and W.S. Gilbert's "very model of a modern major general," Sir Garnet Wolseley (seen here as a field marshal in 1895) served British imperial interests around the world from 1852 to 1900.

An insect-class gunboat, designed for use in Mesopotamia, in action on the Tigris River near Kut-al-Amara, where the British suffered a humiliating setback at the hands of the Turks in 1916.

they were at it. On September 16, Reza Shah was driven from Iran's throne and sent into exile on the island of Mauritius by the British, abdicating in favor of his 22-year-old son, Mohammed Reza Pahlavi.

At this point, the United States entered Middle Eastern affairs as well. Thirty thousand soldiers of the U.S. Persian Gulf Command occupied southern Iran to handle the forwarding of supplies to the Soviet Union. This would begin a fateful involvement in an area scarcely known by Americans before the war, but one which would soon loom as vital to the United States and much of the industrialized world.

Incubator of civilization, strategic crossroads where three continents meet, and birthplace of religions, the Fertile Crescent had now become a principal source of the world's energy.

Following World War II, not only was oil vital to fuel America's burgeoning economy but also the cold war with the Soviet Union made it impossible to ignore the strategic and political importance of Iran as buffer to the Gulf. Cold war meant denying to the USSR advantage in every way possible short of hot war. To avoid Soviet domination of northern Iran, the United States prodded the U.N. to oppose Moscow's aggressive tactics in Iran's Azerbaijan province which, contiguous to Soviet Azerbaijan, had fallen under Soviet control (although the puppet regime curiously chose as its marching song the rousing melody of that Allied war favorite, "The Beer Barrel Polka"). Iran was also cajoled into retrieving the Kurdish Mahabad Republic, another hastily erected Soviet puppet state south of Azerbaijan. Desperate to protect their Iranian

Allen W. Dulles, and Middle East expert Kermit Roosevelt—rushed to his majesty's rescue by encouraging massive counterdemonstrations against Mossadegh. The Shah's throne was saved and its legitimacy preserved. This was quintessential cold war: political intervention justified on the grounds of preventing a disintegration of postwar Iran before it had a chance to resist Soviet pressure and survive as a viable nation friendly to the United States. The battlefields were the streets of Tehran, not the sands of Kuwait and Iraq, but with the Iranian linchpin in hostile hands, the oil-rich sands of the Gulf otherwise would also have been in jeopardy.

While Iran became a cold-war battlefield between the United States and the Soviets, Palestine had become a battlefield for a hotter kind of war between the Jews and Arabs. In the twilight of World War II, clandestine Jewish rescue missions to save their people in Nazi Europe from genocidal extinction landed boatloads of refugees in British-occupied Arab Palestine. While illegal, the British could find no humane way to stop the flow. Although seen by the Jews as acts of brave desperation, the Arabs of the area saw this as an illegal invasion of their lands by European Jews, whose claim to the biblical lands of antiquity did not seem valid in the 20th century.

With the end of British rule in Palestine after the war, the state of Israel came into being, a dream fulfilled, but a dream for which the Jews found they must fight. In 1948, the Jews won their first contest, the "War of Independence," against the Arabs after bitterly contested battles that left intense enmity between the two peoples and a displaced Palestinian population.

In October 1956, the Jews, in alliance with Great Britain and France, attacked Egypt in response to Gamal Abdel Nasser's nationalization of the Suez Canal, the most ambitious of the Egyptian premier's exhibitions of nationalism. When the United States forced a halt to the war, neither the British, who were still denied the canal, nor their allies had gained by their ill-considered act. The 1967 "Six Day War," in which Egypt blockaded the Straits of Tiran to deny Israel access to the Gulf of Aqaba, resulted in an Israeli land-air offensive of astonishing speed and brilliant execution that seized Syria's Golan Heights, the Gaza Strip and the West Bank of Jordan—a source of bitterness to this day. The 1969-70 "War of Attrition" saw Israel entrenched across the Suez Canal in their Bar-Lev Line bunkers lobbing shells into Cairo.

On October 6, 1973, the "Yom Kippur War," informally called for the Jewish Holiday in which it occurred, erupted when Egypt and Syria launched simultaneous surprise attacks against Israel. Caught unaware and unprepared, Israel had a close call. But in the Golan

oil fields from Soviet encroachment, the British played their own game in the south by inciting tribes to rise against the Iranian central government in protest to its plans for granting the Soviets an oil concession in the north. The cold war in Iran was astonishingly similar to the "Great Game" of intrigue and political maneuver played between British and Russian imperial rivals throughout the 19th century in Persia (Iran).

In August 1953, when Iranian nationalist Prime Minister Mohammed Mossadegh nationalized Iranian oil and found common cause with the Communist Tudeh Party to drive the young Shah, Mohammed Reza Pahlavi, from Iran by street uprisings, the United States—mainly through the actions of the Central Intelligence Agency under the direction of its chief,

Heights, the Israelis stopped the Syrian assault in an epic defense, then launched a swift counterattack that carried them to the outskirts of Damascus, leaving a trail of wrecked Syrian armor in their wake. After crossing the Suez Canal and overrunning Israel's vaunted Bar-Lev Line, the Egyptians fought with unexpected skill and élan to repulse armored counterattacks and air attacks with heavy casualties to the Israelis. Finally, however, Israeli General Ariel Sharon managed to achieve a breakthrough on October 15, which carried his forces back over the Canal to split and encircle two Egyptian armies before a cease-fire was declared.

Meanwhile, the United States rushed armaments to Israel from its forces in Europe and warned the USSR against entering the fray on the Arab side. Some feared a serious confrontation between the two superpowers, but cooler judgment prevailed on both sides.

In 1982, another battleground came to the world's attention. Lebanon, considered one of the most stable countries in the Middle East, was in fact a volatile hotbed of religious and factional rivalries whose delicate balance of power was upset by the increasing presence of the Palestinian Liberation Organization (PLO), members of which, mostly exiled from Jordan and Israel, had been settling there and often conducting terrorist raids over Lebanon's border with Israel.

On June 6, 1982, Israeli forces crossed the Litani River and linked up with Lebanese Christian Phalangist forces, with the intention of annihilating the PLO in Lebanon. The Israeli offensive quickly overran Tyre and Sidon, and trapped PLO leader Yasser Arafat and 14,000 of his men in West Beirut, but in the Bekaa Valley of eastern Lebanon, Israeli forces came into violent contact with another foreign instrument of intervention—the Syrian 1st Armored Division, with the support of the Syrian air force. In the sharp encounters that followed, Israel's new, indigenously designed Merkava tanks proved superior to the latest Soviet-built T-72s in the Syrian arsenal, while in one day's air battle the Israeli air force downed a staggering 89 Syrian aircraft for the loss of only one.

In the long run, foreign intervention only served to escalate Lebanon's multifactional rivalries into a long and bloody civil war. The Ayatollah Khomeini's Islamic regime in Iran sent clandestine aid to Shiite Moslem factions, while the Syrians alternately aided and fought with the PLO. In a move that left Israel dumbfounded, the United States intervened on behalf of Arafat, helping to arrange for him and his men to be evacuated out of Beirut on August 19, under the supervision of a "peace-keeping force" of American, British, French and Italian troops.

SIGNAL

LEFT: German Messerschmitt Bf-110D fighters return to Tripoli after escorting a Mediterranean convoy to North Africa.
BELOW: A truckload of Afrika Korpsmen passes British prisoners on the road to Tobruk in June 1942. Rommel's drive to the Suez Canal was finally halted at El Alamein.

Israeli Merkava (chariot) tanks with M-113 "Zelda" armored personnel carriers in close attendance. First seeing action in Lebanon in 1982, the indigenously designed Merkava was the product of wartime experience. So were Israel's improved combined-arms battle tactics.

ISRAELI DEFENSE FORCE

Although President Ronald Reagan believed that the U.S. intervention in the volatile Lebanese situation was justified, it proved to be signally unsuccessful in bringing peace to the country. In a disastrous climax, terrorist suicide bombers attacked both the U.S. Marine and French Foreign Legion paratroop barracks in Beirut on October 23, killing 240 Americans and 78 French. In February 1984, the various foreign contingents began withdrawing from Lebanon, leaving behind them a devastated country with an unresolved problem.

Despite this misstep, the United States was still concerned about the Arab-Israeli conflict. It was then, and still is, a problem difficult to ignore. While the area may no longer be a cockpit of a cold war with the Soviet Union, it is nonetheless a dangerous flash point in its own right, as the war with Iraq has just demonstrated. Certainly the complications and intricacies of the Arab-Israeli conflict do not suggest easy solutions.

In the specific Palestinian problem there is a strong motive for conflict: a striving for a homeland by homeless people. Not always fully understood by nations well-entrenched in their territory and secure in their identity is the passion aroused among those denied the land of their fathers. Both the Jews and Palestinians have known this passion, but unfortunately both claim the same homeland.

Islam has also been plagued by factionalism within its own ranks, particularly the centuries-

old schism between the Sunni and Shiite sects, and conflicts which have arisen between the followers of pan-Islamic union and the secular nationalists who exhalt their own country. The 20th century, an age of oil, brought with it a division of the Arab states into haves and have nots—those with oil and those without. This has created tensions when the oil riches of one state have been used to the detriment of others. Here the finger points at the late Ayatollah Khomeini, whose oil profits funded Shiite fundamentalist agitation and terrorism beyond Iran's borders.

Terrorism is often as effective as it is despicable. It is a cheap way for the small and weak to strike back at the large and powerful. Khomeini used this weapon with great effect when on November 4, 1979, he seized and held hostage the entire U.S. Embassy in Tehran and soon afterward inspired the kidnapping of individual American hostages in Lebanon.

It is interesting to note that Persia was the birthplace of organized terrorism used for political/religious purposes. In the 11th century, Hassan es-Sabbah, known as "the old man of the mountain" because of his remote redoubt in the Elburz highlands northwest of Tehran, was grand master of the Ismaili sect of Islam which considered the murder of its opponents a religious obligation. Called the *Hashashin* because of the widely held, but probably erroneous, belief that they braced themselves with hashish before setting out to commit their foul

deeds to earn martyrdom, they inspired abject terror among the statesmen of the Abbasid Khalifate in Baghdad who were among their favorite targets. Not until Mongols under Hülegü wiped out the sect's stronghold in 1256 could the Middle East breathe easily. The name *Hashashin* survives in English as the word assassin. The Ismaili sect itself, now devoted to good works, survives under the benign leadership of the Agha Khan.

Khomeini's neighbor, Iraq's Saddam Hussein, plays the lead in another cautionary tale—the drama of a leader whose country is blessed with enormous natural wealth—oil reserves perhaps second only to those of Saudi Arabia; and a fertile valley of two great rivers to provide abundant food. Yet this leader's nation is in disarray and he has doomed a generation of his country's manhood who gave their lives for no useful cause.

The Shatt al Arab, having gathered the waters of the Tigris and Euphrates rivers, flows 120 miles before emptying into the Gulf. Vital to Iraq as its only access to the Gulf and important as a natural riverine boundary between Iraq and Iran, the Shatt al Arab has long been an object of intense dispute as it was on September 22, 1980, the date when Iraq invaded Iran. Following Ayatollah Khomeini's Iranian revolution of 1979, Iraq's Saddam Hussein accused Iran of terrorist plots against him and hostile propaganda calculated to inflame his country's Shiite majority. The eight-year war

was costly to Iraq: 300,000 dead and 900,000 wounded. Iran's casualties were even greater: 400,000 dead and 1,000,000 wounded. The casualties, considered as a percentage of the two countries' populations, were higher than in any war of the 20th century. But most egregious of all, Saddam Hussein resorted to chemical attacks against his enemy and against Iraq's own restive Kurdish minority.

Before the eight-year war ended in a virtual stalemate, Iran had some 2 million men under arms, many of them still children, while Iraq had an army of some 500,000. The financial cost has been calculated to be about $600 billion. The added folly of this marathon war—never decisive for either side—was seen when Saddam Hussein relinquished what minor territorial advantages Iraq had gained as a result of the war in an effort to garner goodwill and neutrality from Iran as he plunged into his new adventure in Kuwait. If in Desert Storm the Iraqi troops lacked spirit, it is not surprising considering the mockery this gesture of Saddam Hussein's made of their eight years of sacrifice.

Wars have plagued the volatile Middle East almost as often as the locust attacks that rise suddenly from the Saudi desert. As a crossroad of three continents, a reservoir of seemingly inexhaustible oil and the holy land for three major religions, it may be inevitable that the Middle East is, and perhaps will be for some time to come, a breeding ground for angry passions and a battlefield of sand. ☐

An Egyptian MiG-17 fighter-bomber streaks over burning Israeli vehicles in the Sinai during the Yom Kippur War of October 1973. The Egyptians used combined-arms doctrine in the defensive mode with devastating effectiveness throughout the first week of the war, until a brilliant Israeli counterstroke turned the tables.

CHAPTER TWO

THE RAPE OF KUWAIT

F. DEMULDER, SIPA-PRESS

By invading Kuwait and threatening Saudi Arabia, Saddam Hussein hoped to make Iraq a power to be reckoned with.

ON AUGUST 2, 1990, at 2 a.m. local time, more than 100,000 Iraqi troops and several hundred modern tanks swarmed into the lightly armed emirate of Kuwait. The spearhead of the invasion swept aside the slight resistance it encountered and raced down the 80-mile stretch of superhighway and into Kuwait City.

Explosions rocked the city's modern buildings. Iraqi armor thundered through the debris-lined streets. Tanks assaulted the city's central bank and the crews carried off its wealth. An air-and-ground attack made a shambles of the Dasman Palace of Emir Jaber al-Ahmad al-Sabah—but not before the Iraqis encountered a pocket of resistance. Said a relative of one of the Kuwaitis who died while defending the palace: "The Iraqis were too many. He died along with his two sons." The emir and some of his staff barely escaped with their lives, fleeing the palace by helicopter.

The last transmission of the Kuwaiti state-owned radio station was an appeal for help. Within hours, Iraq's ruler, Saddam Hussein, had the country completely in his power. The foreign population, including thousands of workers and diplomatic staffs, were detained as "guests"—hostages, in reality.

First reports of the invasion, many of them from CNN (Cable News Network), sent shock waves throughout the world. The United States was totally unprepared—a K-11 satellite and other intelligence had verified Iraqi troop movements in advance of the invasion, but this had

been written off as Saddam's posturing and saber rattling. Arab leaders, including President Hosni Mubarak of Egypt, King Hussein of Jordan and King Fahd of Saudi Arabia, expressed stunned surprise. U.S. President George Bush said, "this will not stand...this invasion of Kuwait." "He must be stopped," said British Prime Minister Margaret Thatcher, who was coincidentally on a U.S. visit at the time of the lightning-fast Iraqi attack.

The invasion was certainly not out of character with the personality of its architect, Iraqi President Saddam Hussein, as was readily apparent in the savage war with Iran and during the Kurdish uprisings, when poison gas was used.

G. PRESTON SALOOM, SIPA-PRESS

Saddam, 53, was born to an impoverished family in northern Iraq. In the mid-1950s, he was a member of the socialistic Baath Party and participated in an abortive assassination attempt against Abdul Karim Kassem, Iraqi strongman. After the Baath Party staged a successful coup in 1968, Saddam rose rapidly through party ranks, becoming Iraq's president in 1979. Although he introduced some badly needed modernization and reforms to Iraq, his bloody trail to power involved mass executions and assassinations—his own brother-in-law was among the victims.

Saddam had played a key role during some 30 years of animosity between Iraq and Kuwait.

In 1961, shortly after Kuwait was granted its independence by Britain, Iraq had threatened to invade its smaller neighbor. Now, Saddam justified the action by claiming that Kuwait was keeping the price of oil low by producing more than OPEC (Organization of Petroleum Exporting Countries) quotas. Further, he demanded that Kuwait forgive a $10 billion debt for aid given to Iraq by Kuwait during Iraq's eight-year war with Iran.

Other Iraqi demands included a lease on the islands of Warbah and Bubiyan, which blocked Iraq's access to the Persian Gulf, and reparations for oil alleged to have been stolen by Kuwait. What made this aggression different from doz-

On the morning of August 2, 1990, the citizens of Kuwait City are rudely awakened to the spectacle of Iraqi tanks rolling down the elegant boulevards of Kuwait's capital.

Apart from a lone blue automobile, the only traffic in Kuwait City is colored Iraqi desert tan. As Tamerlane did with Baghdad 590 years earlier, so the Iraqis will begin plundering Kuwait City of everything they consider to be of value—and destroy much of the rest.

ens of other so-called conflicts in the world's hot spots was Saudi Arabia. Sharing a border with Kuwait, the Saudi kingdom was vital to the fiscal health of the West—and thus to the rest of the world, due to other nations' strong dependence on the developed world for foreign aid and technology. If Saddam controlled Iraqi, Kuwaiti and Saudi oil pipelines, he could make good on his boast to be a leader not only of regional but of world standing...a force to be reckoned with.

In terms of oil alone, the stakes were enormous; of the world's 102 trillion barrels of crude-oil reserves, Saudi Arabia held 257 billion barrels, Iraq 100 billion, Kuwait 97 billion and the nearby United Arab Emirates 98 billion barrels. By annexing Kuwait, Saddam Hussein, in one breathtaking act, doubled his control over

crude-oil reserves from 10 percent of the globe's total to almost 20 percent.

Obviously, a key element in Operation Desert Storm's timing was the sheer barbarity of the seven-month-long Iraqi occupation that followed. Although it was impossible to verify every incident in the horrific campaign against ordinary Kuwaitis, the many accounts, taken in the aggregate, persuaded the intelligence community and human rights groups that they had some basis in fact.

The stories that were substantiated were, indeed, grave enough to warrant intervention on purely humane grounds—no matter what the wider strategic implications.

Sentiment in favor of winning back from Iraq its ill-gotten gain—the nation of Kuwait—rapidly mounted. Middle East Watch, a well-respected,

houses are seized, food cooperatives plundered, and food distribution volunteers detained, terrorized and in some cases executed."

These conclusions paralleled those of other groups and with data in U.S. intelligence reports released by the press during occupation. It cannot be discounted that people under occupation have a vested interest in exaggerating horror stories. In Kuwait's case, the international relief and human rights groups worked around the clock to learn the truth or falsity of claims flooding into their offices.

For example, no one would accuse Middle East Watch's sober director Andrew Whitley of holding a brief for anyone but the oppressed. He wanted all claims verified. When scant evidence emerged to support allegations of wholesale theft of incubators from Kuwait hospitals, he announced this finding.

In seven months, Iraq's occupation forces raped an estimated 250 Kuwaiti women of all ages. One, calling herself only by her first name, Rasha, was awakened along with her parents in late August to find 10 armed Iraqi soldiers in their home. The 18-year-old told reporters after Kuwait's liberation that after ransacking the house, cutting the phone lines and plundering their home's contents, the Iraqis beat and shot her ailing father. They then repeatedly raped her mother while Rasha was forced to watch.

The armed intruders next turned their attention to Rasha, a virgin. Now she is pregnant and, sobbing anonymously through a black gauze headcloth, she told a reporter, "I don't want to live any more."

Observed Dr. Khalid Shaliwi of Mubarak Hospital in Kuwait City: "Nobody estimated this problem. It's worse than the Iraqi invasion. That lasted for seven months. This is for a lifetime."

In some cases those lifetimes are liable to be painfully short. Authorities already are recording suicides—one a particularly horrible case where a young woman burned herself to death.

In months of horrifying reports, many corroborated from multiple sources or eyewitnesses, the Saddam regime never directly contradicted any of them.

After Amnesty International published its December 1990 survey, Iraq's ambassador to Britain issued a typical response. To the dozens of painstakingly documented, highly detailed cases cited, the Iraqi envoy complained instead of the unpleasant results of the allies' embargo on Iraq.

At the same time, Baghdad routinely denied any rights groups' requests to enter Kuwait to monitor conditions there. Even the International Red Cross was barred.

New York-based human rights organization, was created to fix its sights on the Mideast. It issued several separate reports during the crisis and war. The grim main points of its November 16, 1990 report: "Summary executions of scores of people have been carried out in detention centers and in public, in front of their families. Families are being terrorized by midnight searchers and arbitrary arrests of close to 5,000 people—including children. Detainees are subjected to torture...and kept in crowded and unsanitary conditions, without access to families or lawyers, and without opportunity for trial. Collective punishment is meted out in response to acts of armed resistance: houses are burned, buildings demolished, curfews imposed and families of suspects detained. Occupation authorities interfere with food distribution, ware-

An Iraqi soldier rounds up civilians from the streets of Kuwait City while, elsewhere, his commanders and comrades commence the systematic dismantling of the occupied capital.

Iraq's looting of Kuwait—unlike the frequent randomness of its soldiers' everyday thuggery toward civilians—was organized and wholesale. Entire auto and truck dealerships were emptied; medical gear of every kind was shipped back to Iraq; hospitals were requisitioned for the Iraqi military's use, with children, pregnant mothers and cancer patients dying for lack of adequate care; and Iraqi taxis returned home stuffed with loot.

Everywhere stood huge portraits of a smiling Saddam Hussein, as if anyone needed to be reminded who was responsible for all the destruction. One Iraqi explained, "This is a gift from the Kuwaiti people to the Iraqi government, congratulating them for coming to their country."

Perhaps more striking was the systematic dismantling of the country's institutions. All government property was seized, along with the furnishings of private homes and ruling-family residences. Identity papers such as passports were routinely confiscated by Iraqi officials. Among the "miscellaneous items" seized by the Iraqis were $4 billion in cash and gold from the National Treasury, computers, copy machines, typewriters, hundreds of miles of water pipe, traffic lights, buses, heavy equip-

ment, parts of dismantled factories, masses of construction equipment of all kinds, commercial kitchens, office furniture, ballpoint pens and erasers.

Exhilarated by the seemingly endless booty, Iraqi guards near the cargo trucks were often heard laughing about their newfound wealth and saying, "Ali Baba! Ali Baba!"

In addition to obliterating Kuwait's infrastructure—buildings, computer and telecommunications networks, census data—Iraqis looted Kuwait's art museums, as well.

Bands of marauding Iraqi soldiers broke into the National Museum shortly after the invasion, taking many Kuwaiti cultural treasures. In mid-October, the Sheika Hussa Sabah Al-Salem Al-Sabah, a member of the ruling family and a world authority on Islamic art, gave an emotional press conference in Washington, D.C. Before breaking down into tears, she said that among the plundered antiquities were "unique pieces that can't be replaced: a signed Mamluk jar, carpets, glass pieces."

Not even her country's liberation could reverse this cultural disaster, the sheika stressed. Many items were bound to turn up on the giant black market in stolen art, and many collectors and dealers would buy them "no questions

Victim of desultory but occasionally sharp resistance by the overwhelmed Kuwaiti armed forces, an Iraqi truck burns outside of Kuwait City.

asked." Photos of the missing items and other identification would lead police and other authorities nowhere.

Also, some of the rarities were probably badly damaged in the wholesale theft. A museum official added that, "the cases are protected by Plexiglas, so you have to use an electric drill, and by doing that you will certainly destroy the objects, no matter how careful you are."

To the grieving sheika, the loss of the artifacts amounted to "the loss of the country."

"Just total devastation! That's how I would describe it," said Richard Curtiss, a retired Foreign Service officer and the editor of the *Washington Report on Middle East Affairs,* who went into Kuwait City seven days after the occupation ended. "I couldn't help thinking: but I've seen all of this on television. I've watched the CNN reports that graphically displayed the destruction of the capital. However, you can't really feel that total destruction that is 360 degrees around you.

"If you ask the Kuwaitis about the unspeakable atrocities they endured for seven months, of course, each has a story to tell."

And tell, they did, often at events such as the "Free Kuwait Day" at Washington's American University. The September rally drew a crowd of several thousand. The pro-Kuwaits were a mixed bag: Arab faculty members, U.S. intellectuals from American University and other colleges and institutions, students, human rights activists and leftists. Several U.S. lawmakers also appeared. One rose and strode angrily to the podium to denounce Saddam's "rapacious aggression."

The crowd listened sympathetically to witnesses like Ms. Abdullah. The young woman, born in the United States of Kuwaiti parents, had transferred from American to Kuwait University, one of the Arab world's finest. She escaped Kuwait on September 15, 1990.

The scenes "were all very scary," she said in the outdoor amphitheater. "You're under their mercy. You don't know if they're going to let you out or not. It's according to whim."

Asked about people she knew who were maltreated by the Iraqi forces, the Kuwaiti-American spoke of two relatives. "They were tortured, to the point of when they returned them you couldn't recognize them—all for having a pamphlet with the word 'Kuwait' on it in their car."

The Iraqi servicemen, she reported, "badly beat them, made them walk on broken glass, turned cigarettes on their bodies. They used to hit them with clubs." At times, Ab-

"Ali Baba." Truckloads of Iraqi soldiers roll into Kuwait City. Soon, those same vehicles would be returning to Iraq, loaded down with everything those troops could loot.

JORGE FERRARI, SIPA PRESS

dullah and other Kuwaitis told the rally, Iraqi officers framed civilians by putting "incriminating" evidence in their cars and then arresting them.

Abdullah said at the American University rally, and during later dramatic testimony before the U.S. Congress: "Me being American, too—I don't want to see any bloodshed, but already blood is being shed. Kuwaitis are dying every day. And I'll tell you: We, the Kuwaitis, are going to be the first ones ready to fight as soon as we get help...It's our country. We don't mind sacrificing ourselves to free Kuwait. This is our obligation toward our country and toward our people."

Even more graphic testimony came from a teenaged Kuwaiti victimized by "extrajudicial" actions by the Iraqis. It's one of hundreds documented by respected groups like Middle East Watch, Amnesty International and other monitoring organizations:

"My brother...had been with me in Al Jahrah [a municipality] but they did not release him. He was held for 36 days, and then in mid-October they brought him back to our house.

When we saw him he was still alive. They threw him down on the doorstep and then shot him in the head with a pistol fitted with a silencer. He was handcuffed at the time."

The brother was taken to a hospital, but was dead on arrival. There, doctors in attendance found that "his feet were covered with blue bruises, and his body lined with marks caused by extensive beatings. There was a deep hole in his thigh which appeared to have been caused by some sort of drilling tool...late that afternoon we buried him in Al-Bigga Cemetery. The Iraqis had earlier made it known that public mourning for the dead would not be permitted. Nevertheless, people came to our house to offer their condolences."

The two brothers had been arrested September 9 after the Iraqis found arms in their house. The surviving brother was himself severely tortured for three days.

Animals as well as humans suffered from the invasion; Kuwait's wildlife, farm livestock and zoo populations were hit hard. The statistics were particularly grim for farm stock: of 1,500 cows alive before the invasion, only 200 re-

mained. Shamseddin Husseini, a Kuwaiti farmer and dairy manager, showed visitors a pen holding 80 starving animals. Hundreds of cows, many of them high-quality Holsteins, littered the roadsides weeks after the liberation, victims of starvation, cluster bombs and hungry Iraqis and Kuwaiti refugees.

As for the remaining animals of every kind, their welfare obviously counted for much less than the pressing needs of human beings. Still, eyewitnesses cringed at some once-prized racehorses that were found alive but showing their ribs and open wounds, and at the scrawny cats prowling among the rubble.

One of the more bizarre finds after the occupation finally ended was an amusement park that had been trashed and shot up by the Iraqis. Entertainment City had covered 220 acres about seven miles outside of Kuwait City. It was the Middle East's version of Disneyland, and hugely popular as family entertainment. What happened there, according to a spokesman for the U.S. company that developed the $80 million park, was a case of "attacking the innocent. An amusement park is innocent." An American

reporter viewing the swath of violence said, amazed, "In this battle, it is clear. Mickey Mouse never had a chance."

Thirty-eight-year-old Paul Eliopoulus, an American citizen and computer consultant, was among those seized by the Iraqis just after the invasion. Like many other kidnap victims, he spent months in Iraq, fearing for his life while helping defend Iraq's infrastructure as a "human shield"—moved with other hostages from such potential targets as nuclear sites to chemical installations and finally to Saddam Hussein's hometown, Tikrit.

When the Burke, Va., native finally returned to his Kuwait home, complete devastation greeted him. Amid the Iraqis' leavings was a bloody couch—he didn't even want to speculate how it got there.

"The Iraqis went through every single photo album," he said. "That's 14 years of my life with my family and wife. They peed and defecated on everything." The occupiers, finding the human inhabitants gone, had sliced open the blue teddy bear of Nicole Eliopoulus' 8-year-old daughter. Nearby was a singed tricycle.

"But," the American went on, "it's not the destruction, it's that they apparently were taking pleasure in doing it." Quietly, Eliopoulus assembled all the salvageable remnants of his years in Kuwait. Everything fit in a small suitcase.

That one nation could, in 1990, so thoroughly plunder a neighbor and randomly kill its people appeared utterly, breathtakingly out of synch with the times—despite the many areas suffering disorder and chaos around the globe. Nothing on so vast a scale had been experienced since World War II. Many scholars found the best comparisons in ancient history—the sacking of Carthage, the final death rattle of Rome.

The sheer viciousness of the invasion struck home in the United States, and polls showed that the American public had no problems with President Bush's description of Iraq's leader as "evil." Many Americans indicated that they wanted their country to help drive Iraq out of Kuwait—it was the right thing to do. Yet Bush, as leader of a 28-nation coalition backed by the United Nations, gave Saddam several months' "grace period" to withdraw from Kuwait (until January 15, 1991).

But it wasn't to be. War was in the air. And so, just over 24 hours after the deadline passed, a sleeping Baghdad was blasted awake by the deafening fall of missiles from allied warplanes. It was 6:30 p.m., Washington, D.C. time; 2:30 a.m. local Baghdad time. What was to become known as the stunningly brief "Microchip War" had begun. □

CHAPTER THREE

FORGING AN ALLIANCE

ROBERT F. DORR

First reaction: Members of the 82nd Airborne Division prepare to leave Fort Bragg, N.C., for Saudi Arabia in August 1990.

AT 2:30 A.M., Thursday, January 17, 1991, coalition aircraft streaked through the skies over Baghdad unleashing their awesome array of bombs and other weaponry to destroy numerous targets in and around the city. The Persian Gulf War had begun.

Since Iraq's August invasion of Kuwait, the United States and other nations, with vastly different ideologies and political outlooks, assembled to stand up to Iraqi leader Saddam Hussein's naked aggression against that small, virtually defenseless country. However, President George Bush was confronted with a myriad of problems that could splinter this already fragile alliance.

First and foremost, if Israel, a staunch ally of the United States, entered into the conflict, would the Arab nations still remain in the coalition? Second, could U.N. sanctions coerce Iraq to leave Kuwait? And how much time would be needed for the sanctions to work? A year? Eighteen months? Nobody was really sure. Lastly, could the president receive the authority from Congress to wage war, and would the support of the American people remain with him if the use of force had to be implemented to achieve final victory?

These were some of the hard questions facing President Bush in those early first weeks of the Gulf crisis. On August 2, 1990, Saddam Hussein's army had thrown Bush and nearly everyone else off balance by invading Kuwait, laying virtual siege to the U.S. Embassy and holding thousands of foreign hostages as "guests."

Saddam's "surprise" was made possible because, while U.S. intelligence knew that his ultimate goal was to control the Gulf, Americans did not anticipate any act of aggression by him so soon after Iraq's 1988 cease-fire with Iran. American diplomacy called for encouraging the Iraqi government to moderate its behavior toward the West. Even though Iraq was making strong accusations against Kuwait, experimenting with chemical weapons, attempting to develop nuclear weapons, and violating human rights constantly, the United States continued to attempt to reason with Saddam and press for peaceful solutions.

U.S. Ambassador April Glaspie, in Baghdad, was at the forefront of this policy that made "incentives" rather than "sanctions" the guiding force in dealing with the Iraqi strongman. "It

Supporters of George Bush's decision to send troops to the Gulf rally in Omaha, Neb. Opponents of American intervention also marched, but they were out of step with the majority, who stood behind the president.

is better talking to this man than isolating him," Glaspie said. She had talked to him July 25, 1990, when Saddam called her to his palace and accused Washington of plotting with Kuwait to keep oil prices down and waging economic war against Iraq. He threatened terrorism in response and even implied that warfare was possible when he stated, "Yours is a society which cannot accept 10,000 dead in one battle." The ambassador did not warn Iraq not to attack Kuwait—those were not her instructions, she contended. "I have direct instructions from President Bush to seek better relations with Iraq," she said to Saddam. Glaspie would later take considerable heat for her perception of American policy.

In late July, the White House was well aware from satellite photos that 100,000 Iraqi soldiers had amassed along the Iraqi-Kuwaiti border. Even so, almost everyone in the U.S. intelligence community failed to predict there would be an invasion. The consensus, not just in the United States but among Arab leaders as well, was that Saddam was bluffing.

Saddam had lied to everyone about his intentions, and the lie worked—it took his large army less than a day to successfully pull off the invasion of Kuwait. Saddam had clearly won the first round, but President Bush acted quickly to make sure that the "Bully of Baghdad" didn't win another round. Just hours after learning of the invasion from National Security Adviser Brent Scowcroft, the president signed an order freezing all Iraqi and Kuwaiti assets in the United States. Next, he turned his hand to organizing the industrialized democra-

After independent French efforts at reaching a settlement with Baghdad turned sour, François Mitterrand committed his armed forces to the liberation of Kuwait.

cies, most of the Arab League and the United Nations into an allied coalition that he hoped would transcend any differences and do whatever was necessary to "free" Kuwait.

On August 6, just four days after Iraq's invasion of Kuwait, the United Nations condemned the incursion and voted to place worldwide economic and military sanctions against Saddam Hussein's regime. A multinational contingent of naval warships arrived in the Persian Gulf to enforce the action. Still, the United States moved cautiously and avoided using the word "blockade" in describing the embargo. Addressing a group of reporters, Bush said, "The main thing is to stop the oil from coming out of there and that is what we're going to do."

However, whether U.S. officials liked the term blockade or not, in essence, that is what the United States did to choke off the flow of supplies into the country. With an AWACS (airborne warning and control system) radar-surveillance plane airborne 24 hours a day, the United States was able to maintain a constant vigil in the area to assure that the embargo levied on Iraq was being observed.

On August 18, U.S. frigates fired warning shots across the bow of Iraqi vessels attempting to run the blockade. The Iraqis managed to find a safe haven in Yemen, but the Yemeni government did not grant permission for the ships to be offloaded. Finally, on August 25, the United Nations granted the use of "minimal force" to prevent material from entering Iraq.

Despite the severe restrictions, some supplies did trickle into the country. One of the main points of entry was through the overland route via the port of Al Aqabah, situated in the narrow Gulf of Aqaba, in Jordan. King Hussein, ruler of Jordan, began a country-hopping venture to advocate peaceful solutions to the deepening crisis. However, because Jordan was allowing supplies to enter Iraq, the king received a cool reception from U.S. government officials. As the weeks progressed, and even with the relatively meager flow of supplies getting into Iraq from Jordan, the embargo was successfully established.

Criticized from the outset, world opinion was definitely turning against Saddam Hussein. Other Arab nations, even Syria, led by fellow Baathist Hafez al-Assad—vehemently anti-Israeli and anti-American—met with Secretary of State James Baker and censured Iraqi's occupation of Kuwait. The frail coalition that President Bush was forming seemed to be jelling into a tightknit framework against Iraq's dictator.

In spite of global condemnation, Saddam Hussein tried another political ploy in an attempt to fracture the budding alliance. He announced that he would evacuate Kuwait if the islands of Bubiyan and Warbah, located in the Persian Gulf, were ceded to him. Iraq is virtually landlocked. Travel to the one port they possess, Umm Qasr, is impeded by those two islands. He also wanted the Rumaila oil field, part of which is in Iraq as well as Kuwait. The Iraqi strongman demanded that the Kuwaitis pay him 2.5 billion in reparations from the oil that, he claimed, had been taken illegally.

But the item Saddam Hussein requested that caused the most furor in the international community was the question of a Palestinian homeland, which he said should be ceded by Israel. There is probably no current issue in the Middle East that is more controversial than that one. Saddam Hussein appeared to be establishing himself as the spokesman and savior of the Palestinians, an Arabic people without a nation of their own.

Almost immediately, Palestinians in Jordan proclaimed him their hero. Marching on the U.S. Embassy in Amman, Jordan, to protest the American presence in the region, demonstrators paraded pictures of Saddam and showered him with praise and adulation. Violence erupted in Israel, as Palestinians in the occupied territories demonstrated in support of Saddam. Rioters were killed and wounded as Israeli police and army personnel fired into the crowd. Was Saddam Hussein's sly maneuver going to work?

U.S. officials strongly objected to any linkage between the Palestinian issue and Iraq's blitzkrieg-style invasion of Kuwait. Although Saddam Hussein's ruling party, the Baath ("renaissance") Socialist Party of Iraq, was secular in nature, propaganda films depicting Saddam Hussein praying and calling for a holy war incited the Arab masses.

Finally, on September 28, 1990, the U.N. Security Council decided that the Palestinian and Kuwaiti problems were indeed two diverse issues. Consequently, the council voted to have resolutions adopted to reach an accord on each issue separately. Saddam Hussein's bid to drive a wedge between the coalition members failed.

Throughout the crisis, however, the Iraqi despot would continue trying to use the Palestinian issue as a means of splitting the fragile alliance. The Arab portion of the coalition appeared to waver when violence broke out in Israel in early October. Jewish zealots tried to march on Jerusalem's Al Aqsa Mosque on October 8; worshippers at the Wailing Wall and Israeli police were pelted by rocks. The police opened fire, killing 21 Arabs. A U.N. Security Council resolution introduced by the Bush administration admonished Israel but blamed both sides for the violence. The Palestine Liberation Organization had a resolution of its own calling for "tougher

President George Bush, accompanied by British Prime Minister Margaret Thatcher and the secretary of NATO, General Manfred Woerner, in Washington, D.C., calls for "full and total" implementation of U.N. sanctions against Iraq on August 6, 1990.

measures." Israeli Prime Minister Yitzhak Shamir said the disturbance was a plot to focus world attention off the Gulf crisis and onto Israel. Although the violence in Israel was disturbing and although many Palestinians were inspired by Hussein's rhetoric and supported him, the tenuous coalition held together.

Meanwhile, as the political stakes were rising, so were the military ones. Prior to Iraq's offensive, the kingdom of Saudi Arabia had restricted the American military presence in its country. However, with the Saudis sharing borders with Kuwait as well as Iraq, it now saw itself vulnerable to attack. And would Saddam Hussein's quest for power and money be satisfied with the conquest of Kuwait alone? Was Saudi Arabia next? Iraq's savage thrust into Kuwait left King Fahd, the Saudi ruler, "quaking with fear." Six weeks later, the Saudis were secretly asking the United States and their Arab neighbors to eject Saddam Hussein from Kuwait. The Saudis were now actively requesting U.S. forces to be based in their country.

As a result, troop deployments began in earnest. On August 7, Bush ordered U.S. military forces to Saudi Arabia. Within days, the U.S. naval presence revealed itself in the Gulf region. The aircraft carrier *Saratoga*, the battleship *Wisconsin*, and the helicopter carrier *Inchon*, with a Marine landing team, steamed toward the Persian Gulf. In an unprecedented show of support, Egyptian President Hosni Mubarak permitted the aircraft carrier USS *Eisenhower* to proceed through the Suez Canal.

On August 6, a squadron of F-111 fighter-bombers redeployed to Turkey. Turkish President Turgut Ozal, never a friend of Iraq, had severed the oil pipeline that crossed into his country from Iran, denying Hussein one-third of his exports. Anxious to become a member of the European community, Ozal allowed other U.S. aircraft to be based at Incirlik.

Other coalition squadrons began moving to the Gulf region. Quickly, they were in position and poised to strike. This huge air armada consisted of an array of aircraft: F-117 Stealth fighters, F-16 Falcons, F-15 Eagles, AV-8B Harriers, British and Italian Tornados, French Mirage F1s and 2000s, plus Saudi, Egyptian and Kuwaiti aircraft. In addition, the venerable but still potent B-52s established a base on Diego Garcia and readied themselves for combat duty.

Meanwhile, the ground element was busy transporting troops to Saudi Arabia. U.S. Army and Marine units began arriving within the first week after the invasion. Colonel Carl Fulford, commanding officer of the 7th Marine Expeditionary Brigade (MEB), said: "The 7th MEB was among the first ground elements to arrive in Saudi Arabia. I think a brigade of the 82nd Air-

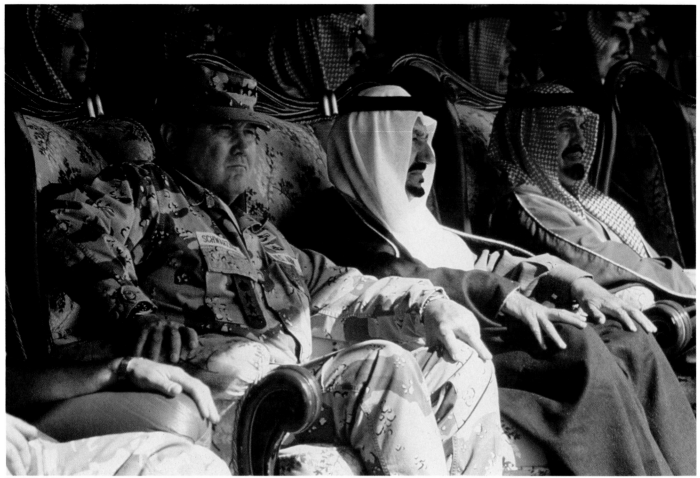

"Okay, the Americans are here now, they'll take care of everything." General H. Norman Schwarzkopf reviews the first coalition forces in Saudi Arabia with Saudi King Fahd.

borne preceded us by four days. My guys started flowing in there by August 12. By the 16th we were all in and by the 24th we were in the field. When we first went in, we obviously had a defensive mind-set. We had very little intelligence and few maps. All we knew was that Hussein's folks had taken Kuwait. Also, we knew they were on the border and certainly capable of going into Saudi Arabia and seizing that northeastern section of the country which is their breadbasket. So, in the beginning, our mission was to defend. We were the first unit on the ground with ammunition and food to do that. We remained in this defensive posture from August until about October."

Soon, other troops, especially armored units equipped with the M1 and the new M1A1 main battle tank, poured into Saudi Arabia. Captain Matt Johnson, S-3 officer for the 2nd Brigade, 24th Mechanized Infantry Division, recalled: "We were alerted on August 6. The main body deployed from August 22 to the 26th. We unloaded at the port of Ad Dammam. In the beginning, the heat was a real problem. There was a concern to run tracked vehicles during the hottest part of the day because the adhesive on the road reel would melt. Also, the M1 tanks have 'V' packs or air filters. These air filters

would clog up with sand, so they had to be blown out constantly."

The harsh weather conditions were a concern for the military planners. How would the high-tech, sophisticated weapons perform under desert conditions?

"We received the new M1A1 heavy armored tanks in January and immediately proceeded to perform gunnery exercises with them," said Lieutenant W. Ebert, executive officer, 3rd Armored Cavalry Regiment. "We also test-fired the new M3A2 and M2A2 Bradley fighting vehicles about the same time. We had no mechanical failures with the M1A1s—they ran like tops. Coming from Fort Bliss, Texas, we were used to the sand and other weather conditions which are somewhat similar to the Middle East. We would pull out the filters in the M1A1s and clean them by using a scavenger fan. It's a wand with a 25-foot hose on it that blows out air at 50 psi and at 750 degrees Fahrenheit."

Despite the pessimistic attitude of some weapons experts, most weapons systems performed admirably. However, there were the inevitable malfunctions. "There were an awful lot of failure rates because of sand getting into the equipment," remarked Captain Sal Granata of the U.S. Army Maintenance Command. "However, the amazing fact is—units

Soviet-built Syrian T-62 tanks disembark from a Saudi Arabian transport ship on November 4, 1990. Syria's censure of Iraq's invasion of Kuwait and its commitment of more than 2,500 troops and 100 tanks was a surprising testimony to the strength of the coalition against Saddam Hussein.

PAT HAMILTON, REUTERS/BETTMANN

that wanted to keep their guns running, did. There were innovations, like putting plastic covering over everything. Everybody had to adapt to the conditions."

Questions were raised about the effectiveness of the military arm of the coalition. Could language, cultural and religious differences be overcome? Could this polyglot force coordinate its combined arms and defeat a reportedly powerful Iraqi army firmly entrenched in Kuwait?

"When we first arrived in Saudi Arabia the attitude of the Saudis was: Okay, the Americans are here now, they'll take care of everything," said U.S. Marine Captain Jim Braden, 1st ANGLICO (Air and Naval Gunfire Liaison Company). "We worked exclusively with the 2nd SANG [Saudi Arabian National Guard]. They were good planners, but you had to show them everything. However, they had some very bright officers. One in particular, Captain Khalid, later distinguished himself at the Battle of Khafji. The Saudis have a different outlook on things. They're more laid back, while our attitude is one of let's get it done now. In the beginning, at the Battle of Khafji, there was a reluctance on their part to be aggressive. But when they saw they outgunned the Iraqis with their M60 tanks, their confidence swelled and there was no stopping them. In fact, when they

heard Marines were trapped inside the city, they rushed up to save them because they thought it was one of my ANGLICO teams. That really impressed me. We made some friends over there."

Also, with so many dissimilar types of aircraft in the country, could the U.S.-led coalition planners properly control the air space and integrate all of them into the air campaign successfully?

"When you look at the air war," explained Colonel Ralph Cossa, U.S. Air Force, "and the preponderance of aircraft that were involved, they all had flown together either in the context of NATO or the Bright Star [training] exercises. Even though the coalition was an ad hoc force, many of the members had operated together in bilateral and multilateral environments. Each person had his own sector and you coordinated it accordingly. It's by no means a simple task—but not an unmanageable one.

"I was very impressed by the Saudi air force," Cossa continued. "In 1982 or 1983, the Iranians were conducting some flights over the northern Persian Gulf. Well, the Saudis went out and shot down two of them. Right after this, the Iranians stopped flying tactical aircraft in the northern Gulf."

Flanked by photographs of King Hussein, Yasser Arafat and Saddam Hussein, a Jordanian waves his country's flag beside a replica of an Iraqi Scud missile targeted against Israel during a pro-Iraqi demonstration in Al Mazar, Jordan, on February 12, 1991.

In all, 28 countries sent some form of military aid to the Persian Gulf. When then Prime Minister Margaret Thatcher of Great Britain heard about Saddam's invasion of Kuwait, she told President Bush, "He must be stopped." Indeed, of all the European nations in the coalition, Britain would make by far the largest military commitment toward stopping Saddam. London, even after the change from Thatcher's administration to John Major's, shared Washington's sense of the importance of having Arab, American and European soldiers fighting side by side against a common enemy—Saddam Hussein. In supporting virtually everything President Bush said and did

during the Gulf crisis, the British seemed to concur with the American president's belief that such an unprecedented alliance would not only stop Saddam now but also make world peacekeeping easier in the future. On August 8, 1990, the multinational operation was dubbed Desert Shield.

In an impassioned appeal to the United Nations, the emir of Kuwait, Sheik Jaber al-Ahmad al-Sabah, said: "Our last attempt at a peaceful resolution of our problems with Iraq was the bilateral round of talks in Jiddah, kingdom of Saudi Arabia, in the course of which Kuwait stressed the need to resolve its outstanding problems within an Arab context.

Cheney said as many as 100,000 more troops would be sent to Saudi Arabia. U.S. Reserve and National Guard units, particularly medical, motor transport and supply outfits, were being activated and sent overseas.

"In October, we got the word we were going to liberate Kuwait," said Marine Colonel Carl Fulford. "The initial task for my Marines was to breach a fairly substantive obstacle belt that we had learned about through intelligence analysis. At that time, we were looking at ditches, berms, fire trenches and minefields. We built ourselves a training range that had simulated Iraqi defensive positions. We developed tactics and techniques that we felt would work and trained day in and day out. We added our equipment and developed our fire support plans. By the time we got ready to do it, we could breach those minefields in our sleep. It worked out very well for us."

Other units were also preparing for the inevitable assault into Kuwait. The 24th Mechanized Infantry, which would be situated on the western flank, began maneuvers. As Captain Matt Johnson explained: "We had gunner practice and conducted situational training exercises on platoon, company, battalion and brigade level, to hone our command and control capabilities. We also utilized this time to coordinate all our support arms such as our artillery, tanks and helicopters. The Apaches were super. I can't say enough about them. They were the main tank killers on the battlefield. They were operational when called upon and performed great."

While the coalition forces were training for eventual combat, Saddam Hussein was still attempting any trickery that would create a schism in the alliance. His failure to release U.S. and European hostages from Kuwait and Iraq, repeatedly calling them "guests," angered the American people. When it was reported that these "guests" were being held as human shields in the event of an attack on Iraq, President Bush was infuriated. Feeble propaganda attempts by Baghdad television, such as Hussein patting a little British boy on the head, did not convince the world that his "guests" were staying behind of their own choosing. Consequently, facing mounting world pressure, the Iraqi tyrant released all the hostages by Christmas.

When it became obvious that Iraq would not voluntarily leave Kuwait, a United Nations resolution was passed in late November by a 12-2 vote in the Security Council authorizing the U.S.-led coalition to take military action by January 15, 1991, if the sanctions proved to be futile. A deadline had been set. There would be no turning back.

As January 15 approached, a flurry of diplomatic gestures were made by several individuals

TSGT ROSE REYNOLDS, USAF

Secretary of Defense Richard Cheney and General Colin Powell are greeted by Saudi Brig. Gen. Abdul Aziz bin Khalid al-Sudairi on February 10, 1991.

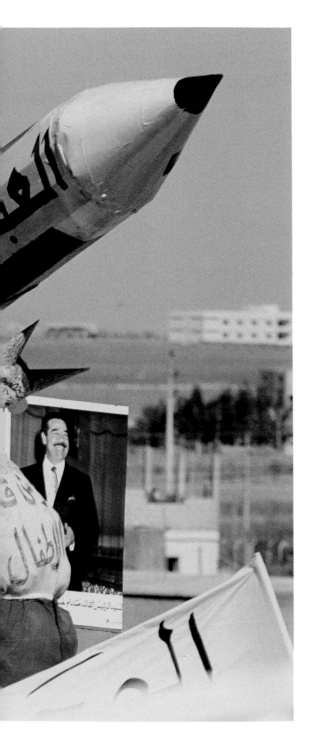

"But Iraq's plans were not anchored in any legal framework or based on any formal legal instruments. In fact, Iraq was bent on sweeping through the entire territory of Kuwait, violating its sovereignty and violating the sanctity of Kuwaiti citizens' lives and property. As a consequence, rape, destruction, terror and torture are now the rule of the day in the once peaceful and tranquil land of Kuwait...at this very moment an intense campaign of terror, torture and humiliation continues unabated in that dear land...."

By October, the defensive nature of Desert Shield was changing to an offensive one. On October 25, U.S. Secretary of Defense Dick

American Secretary of State James Baker (third from right) and Iraqi Foreign Minister Tariq Aziz (seated third from left) meet in Geneva for a last-ditch attempt at a peaceful settlement on January 9. After 6½ hours of dialogue, the talks ended in failure.

in a last attempt to avert a war. Just days prior to the deadline, Secretary of State James Baker and Iraq's Foreign Minister Tariq Aziz met in Geneva, Switzerland, for an eleventh-hour quest for peace. As the pair shook hands for the photographers over the conference table, there was a resurgence of hope. Most of the world was hoping for a breakthrough. President Bush, though, had strong doubts that anything could be accomplished—he had no confidence in Aziz. Indeed, when Aziz and Baker emerged 6½ hours later, it was revealed that the talks were fruitless and no progress had been made.

Aziz had no new offer to make Baker, and the secretary of state reiterated that there could be no link between resolving the Gulf crisis and an international conference on the Palestinian problem. Baker presented Aziz with a letter from Bush to Saddam that warned Iraq not to use chemical or biological warfare or destroy Kuwait's oil facilities, but that also said Iraq could rejoin the international community if it complied completely with U.N. resolutions. Aziz, apparently trying to please the inflexible hardliners back in Baghdad, refused to accept the letter after reading a copy of it and determining that the language was not "polite" enough.

Other last-ditch efforts to find a peaceful settlement were made by U.N. Secretary General Javier Perez de Cuellar, Soviet President Mikhail Gorbachev, French President François Mitterrand, King Hussein of Jordan, and would-be peacemakers in countries from Algeria to Zambia. All of these efforts turned sour. The mood

turned somber as hostilities appeared inescapable. To some it became apparent that Saddam wanted war because even in defeat against the hated Americans, he could emerge as a heroic, more influential leader in the Arab world. Saddam, in fact, said he was ready for "a showdown between the infidels and the true believers."

Back in the United States, there was fear of terrorism on American soil. In an apparent attempt to uncover any terrorist plots, the FBI began interviewing numbers of Arab-Americans. The U.S. Immigration and Naturalization Service established a procedure in which all foreign visitors entering the country on Iraqi or Kuwaiti passports would be both photographed and fingerprinted. On college campuses there were some reminders of the peace movement that had boiled during the Vietnam War, and antiwar organizations held demonstrations in various cities. "No blood for oil" was a popular slogan among demonstrators in Washington, D.C. However, rallies in support of Bush's Gulf policy and America's armed forces in the Gulf seemed to dwarf the anti-war protests. Doubts about national purpose and fear of war flourished, but clearly the American public was not about to slip into a Vietnam-era mind-set.

On January 10, Congress began debates on the use of military action to expel Saddam Hussein from Kuwait. The proposal, called the "Authorization for Use of Military Force Against Iraq Resolution," was supported by the president.

Members of the Iraqi National Assembly vote to defy the United Nations ultimatum on January 14, 1991, putting Baghdad on the road to war and hobbling Tariq Aziz's options for peaceful negotiation.

PATRICK DE NOIRMONT, REUTERS/BETTMANN

Republican Rep. Dante B. Fascell from Florida, one of the resolution's sponsors, said it was the "practical equivalent" of a declaration of war.

Opponents of the proposal, such as Democratic Sen. Paul D. Wellstone from Minnesota, an outspoken critic of military action, urged the president to be prudent before making the decision to go to war. "This cause is not worth fighting for right now," he insisted. "We must stay the course with economic sanctions, continue the squeeze, continue the pressure, move forward on the diplomatic front, and, Mr. President, we must not rush into war."

Congressmen and senators who backed the proposal were equally as vocal in their support of the president. On the floor of the U.S. Senate, Joseph I. Lieberman, Democratic senator from Connecticut, said this: "Sanctions are a blunt instrument which hurt civilians before the military; the weak before the strong. Is it more moral to adopt a strategy designed to inflict the most punishment on the poorest, oldest, most infirm elements of Iraq's population? If you think sanctions will work, you must think they will bring terrible destruction on the heads of the Iraqi people themselves. Consider the morality of that result before decrying the immorality of war."

After heated and, at times, emotional statements were heard from both houses of Congress, the votes were cast. In the end, the House of Representatives voted 250 to 183 and the Senate voted 52 to 47 to approve the resolution and permit President George Bush to use

military force to drive Iraq from Kuwait under the mandate of the U.N. resolutions.

The final hurdle had been scaled. The frail alliance that took U.S. officials months to build and nurture, had withstood the attempts to dismember it. All that remained was for the go-ahead to be delivered to General H. Norman Schwarzkopf, commander of U.S. forces in the Gulf, to launch the air war, or Phase I of the campaign. Bush's course was clear: Since Saddam Hussein was intent on testing the overwhelming firepower of the coalition forces, then the allies must hit the Iraqis hard and fast.

Early Wednesday morning, January 16, 1991, Secretary of State James Baker phoned King Fahd of Saudi Arabia. Using a code word, Baker informed the king that the war would begin by the end of the day. By nightfall, after nearly six long, arduous months, coalition aircraft were bombing Iraq and Kuwait. The American people girded themselves for war. "I think the president went about it the right way," remarked one citizen. "He set a deadline. He waited for the deadline. . . .The only thing that I was surprised about was, it didn't happen earlier."

As the sobering reality of war set in with all of its uncertainties, Thomas Pickering, U.S. ambassador to the United Nations, speaking in August right after Iraq's invasion of Kuwait, asserted: "We have drawn a firm line in the sand." To which, one Arab diplomat replied: "Fine. Now let us pray we can control the winds."

Desert Shield was now Desert Storm. □

CHAPTER FOUR

THE BUILDUP

ROBERT F. DORR

The pilot of a Lockheed C-5A checks out his cockpit prior to takeoff for Saudi Arabia.

WHEN SADDAM Hussein's Iraqi army swept over Kuwait on August 2, 1990, the United States had no armed forces in the region. Six months later, 425,000 Americans were in the Persian Gulf, with 1,200 main battle tanks, seven carrier battle groups, a dozen fighter wings, and a supply line of arms and ammunition that stretched halfway around the world.

It was the most spectacular buildup of military force in history. But when it began, there was no assurance it would work. The men who planned it at the beginning feared that the first Americans to reach the desert would be "chewed up and spat out," as one general put it, while they were still vastly outnumbered.

When President George Bush made a decision to respond to the Iraqi invasion of Kuwait, he dispatched Defense Secretary Dick Cheney to Riyadh (it was August 5 in Washington) to consult with Saudi Arabia's King Fahd. The following day, hidden away at Camp David in Maryland's Catoctin Mountains, Bush ordered the deployment of U.S. forces to the Middle East in Operation Desert Shield.

There was no contingency plan to cover this. Although thousands of staff officers had spent thousands of hours creating war fighting plans for every piece of geography on the planet, no one had been able to foresee *this*. The closest thing, quickly dusted off, was Warfighting Plan 1002-88 to move 2⅓ ground divisions to the Middle East in 30 days—a real challenge to the nation's air and sea transport capacity. But Sad-

dam Hussein, poised to overrun oil fields in eastern Saudi Arabia, might not allow a few days, let alone 30. At that juncture, no one foresaw that Bush would eventually send ten times as many troops or that they would be transported far faster than any plan had called for.

In launching Desert Shield, Bush set four goals: 1) Deter and, if necessary, repel further Iraqi aggression; 2) Effect the withdrawal of all Iraqi forces from Kuwait; 3) Restore the legitimate government of Kuwait; 4) Protect the lives of American citizens.

But Saudi Arabia had a mere 68,000 troops, hardly a match for Iraq's half-million. Ameri-

can military operations in the Middle East were the responsibility of U.S. Central Command (Centcom), headed by General H. Norman Schwarzkopf—but Centcom was headquartered at MacDill Air Force Base, Fla., half a world away. To be sure, units earmarked for Centcom had *practiced* deploying to the Middle East, but *this* buildup was anything but practice. Wouldn't the first Americans to reach Saudi Arabia simply be overrun by the more numerous Iraqis?

The aircraft carrier USS *Independence* (CV-62) battle group made steam from the Indian Ocean. Also tabbed for rapid deployment was the 1st Tactical Fighter Wing at Langley Air Force Base, Va., under Colonel John M. "Boomer" McBroom, whose instructions were "to lean forward and green up" for action. Along with troop-laden Starlifters, McBroom's F-15C Eagles launched within 18 hours of receiving the Desert Shield execute order.

F-15C Eagle pilots like Dan Booker, Lou Defidelto and Bill Wignall, bred to defeat MiGs in close-quarters dogfights, found themselves hurtling aloft not to outfight an enemy but to endure the longest fighter deployment in history. They were to fly nonstop from Langley Field to Dhahran, with six air refuelings en

A venerable Lockheed C-130 Hercules (foreground) joins the C-141 Starlifters and C-5 Galaxies at Rhein-Main Air Base, Germany, in support of the airlift during Operation Desert Shield.

An F-15E Strike Eagle of the 4th Tactical Fighter Wing moves in for refueling from a KC-135 Stratotanker during Operation Desert Shield. The first 48 F-15Cs sent to Dhahran from Langley Air Force Base had to refuel six times in the course of a grueling 14- to 17-hour nonstop flight.

TSGT HANS DEFFNER, USAF

SSGT F. LEE CORKRAN, USAF

A Lockheed C-5A prepares to unload trucks airlifted from Germany to the U.S. Army's VII Corps in Saudi Arabia, December 23, 1990.

route. When they arrived, they would be alone—facing Iraq's forces.

The ordeal of the Langley pilots began with a 14- to 17-hour solo crossing in their jet fighters. A fighter pilot, strapped in his cockpit, is bound like a trussed pig—lashed to his seat by two Koch fastener buckles at his chest, two more at his hips; by seat belt, oxygen cord and interphone line; by the round tube from the air blower for his G-suit. All this time, a helmet bears down over his head, a visor hangs in front of his eyes, an oxygen mask is strapped fast across his face—chafing, itching. Even a *one-hour* flight in a fast jet can become unspeakable torture if one small glitch arises with any of this gear—if, for example, the HGU-55P helmet is slightly out of fit, producing a "hot spot" on the skull that begins as an ache and grows to excruciating pain. Even with no glitch, a *long* flight in a fighter is an ordeal. These F-15C Eagle pilots were undertaking the longest such flights, ever.

The 48 F-15Cs were the first Desert Shield forces to land in Saudi Arabia. At the time, there was a real fear they might have to shoot their way in. Their arrival was timed for dusk, in the belief—later proved—that Iraqi pilots didn't like to fly at night. Even then, the tem-

perature was 120 degrees. "Welcome to Saudi Arabia," crew chief M.P. Curphey said to several of the fighter pilots. "You're going to be hostages in three hours." No one laughed.

Along with the Langley F-15Cs, the 2,300-man "ready brigade" of the 82nd Airborne Division at Fort Bragg, N.C., was alerted on August 6. Paratroopers, attired in desert garb, boarded C-141B Starlifters for the 15-hour journey to the Saudi summer. The brigade was armed with light anti-tank weapons and M-551 Sheridan light tanks, the latter no match for Saddam Hussein's Soviet-built T-55, T-62 and T-72 main battle tanks. U.S. plans had always called for the 82nd to stand and die in order to buy time for reinforcements to arrive, but the paratroopers never felt more alone than when they began fanning across the unfamiliar desert on August 7.

From their first day, the Langley F-15Cs began combat air patrols. A story in the *Washington Times* that two Iraqi MiG-23s fired at them with missiles and cannons apparently was in error, but there was little to prevent the Iraqi air force from "coming across" any time it chose.

In those early days, General Schwarzkopf and other key planners agonized over the vulnerability of a bare few Americans who stood against Saddam's million-man army, which had eight years' combat experience against Iran. Their fears grew when a new CIA analysis showed that Iraq had 2,000 more tanks and 250 more combat aircraft than previously known. While struggling to get enough forces in place quickly, Schwarzkopf and others also went through a massive reappraisal of how much was enough. From Bush on down, it was becoming clear that Desert Shield would involve far more aircraft and troops than had been envisioned at the start.

On August 26, Schwarzkopf moved his Centcom headquarters from Florida to Saudi Arabia. On the heels of the Langley F-15Cs, other fast jets began the long deployment—F-117A Stealth fighters from Tonopah, Nev.; F-15E Strike Eagle bombers from Seymour Johnson Air Force Base, N.C.; F-16 Fighting Falcons from Shaw Air Force Base in South Carolina. Eight-engine B-52 bombers were positioned on the Indian Ocean island of Diego Garcia, the Saudi government agreeing to permit them on its soil only if shooting actually started. More Navy carrier battle groups were also dispatched, beginning with USS *Dwight D. Eisenhower* (CVN-68), which passed through the Suez Canal en route to the Gulf on August 7.

In Riyadh, Schwarzkopf's deputy, Lt. Gen. Charles ("Chuck") Horner, took the reins as the coalition's supreme air commander. He directed Brig. Gen. Buster C. Glosson to set up shop at Saudi air force headquarters near Riyadh. Glosson built small offices in an underground maze that became known as the "Black Hole," and put key officers to work orchestrating the arrival of new forces and scoping out ways to survive while the U.S. buildup of ground forces gained momentum.

Early to mid-August was a time of hard work, innovation, and some serious worrying on the part of the leaders who orchestrated the Desert Shield buildup. To this day, no one is fully certain why the early arriving troops were not attacked. Hard-charging fighter and bomber pilots, like the 82nd Airborne's paratroops, arrived to "kick some ass and launch a counterinvasion," as one of them put it, and instead they found themselves combating boredom. They had expected to be heroes. Instead, the heroes of Desert Shield were the men and women who flew the greatest airlift of all time.

Even now, looking back at the way fast-thinking generals cobbled together an air bridge to move people and equipment around the world, it's difficult to appreciate how extensive the effort was—a C-5 or C-141 landing at Dhahran every seven minutes, around the clock; the tonnage of the 1948 Berlin airlift ex-

ceeded in the first 22 days and doubled a week later; 200,000 troops and much of their equipment moved to the Saudi sands by October. The crews of giant transport aircraft, many of them reservists who flew on a voluntary basis before being called to active duty on August 29, kept their aerial supply line moving, moving, moving, around the clock—pushing themselves beyond weariness, beyond exhaustion.

General H.T. Johnson, chief of the Military Airlift Command, threw nearly all of his 265 C-141B Starlifters and 85 C-5 Galaxies into the massive effort to move people and weapons to the Persian Gulf. Maintenance people began coaxing extra capabilities out of the aircraft. Crews staged out of familiar bases in Europe—Torrejon, Zaragoza, Rhein-Main and Ramstein. At Spain's Torrejon, where transport crews rested after the eight-hour haul from the American East Coast and before the nine-hour trip downrange to Saudi Arabia, the transient quarters were so full that men and women slept in hallways and bathrooms. The flight line was so packed with C-141s and C-5s that a pilot had to be given a map to find his plane.

A typical airlift job, for example, could be to haul equipment for the 82nd Airborne from Fort Bragg. A crew would be assigned to fly the first leg—for example, from Fort Bragg (actually adjacent Pope Air Force Base) to Torrejon. There, another crew in a revolving pool would pick up the mission and the aircraft and continue downrange. The "eastbound stage," they called it, evoking memories of the stagecoaches that, although moving in the opposite direction, had opened up the American West. Downrange, there was no place to stop for rest, so the crew members would have to bring their C-141 or C-5 *back* to Torrejon before they could sleep.

It was a time of enormous tension. On some crews, nerves were frayed and tempers flared. Nor was the job as simple as moving people and cargo from Point A to Point B. To quote General Johnson, "You don't just fly a lot of airplanes to different places, ask people to fill them up, and take off again to carry them overseas." Plans had to be made on how to move a unit, how to meet priorities.

If, for example, you were transporting the Air Force's F-16-equipped 363rd Tactical Fighter Wing out of Shaw Air Force Base, S.C., to a new home in the Persian Gulf—where an airfield was to be carved out of nowhere—how did you do it? Did you first move the people who would provide security, or those who would provide food? Did your huge transport planes take off first with portable buildings and furniture for creature comfort, or with supplies and ammu-

Lieutenant General Charles Horner, supreme air commander of the coalition forces, goes over his preflight checklist in the cockpit of an F-16 at Al Ain Air Base.

Members of the 101st Airborne wait for C-130s to transport them and their M-551 Sheridan air-transportable light tanks to forward locations along the Saudi-Kuwaiti border.

nition to be carried by the 363rd's F-16s? An F-16, with air refueling, could be moved to the Gulf quickly—Shaw's pilots in mid-August did a re-run of the marathon deployment made earlier by Langley's—but did you want the fighter to arrive before its support people and equipment could get there?

General Johnson relied heavily on Airlift Control Elements (ALCEs), teams of experts who set up shop at both ends of the air bridge, optimizing loading techniques, departures and arrivals. These "nerve centers" were populated with Air Force people laboring around the clock to ease the job of moving an army around the planet.

Still, there were horror stories. One C-5 Galaxy pilot had to struggle with ground personnel who tried to load too much cargo and with command post personnel confused about his destination, and then undertake a three-hour quest for any empty bed at the end of his 30-hour "workday." Another spent a day of

equal length hauling supplies from Torrejon downrange, then returning, while struggling with a nose wheel that wouldn't come down (until lowered manually), an altimeter on the blink, and a latrine in the aircraft that hadn't been cleaned. Shortcuts *had* to be taken in maintaining aircraft, and especially in cleaning them—one C-141 was needed so badly it was pulled out of the paint shop and flown to Saudi Arabia in its natural metal, colorless—to keep troops and materiel moving. To those who participated in the C-5 and C-141 missions that went on, on, on, around the clock, and tested people and equipment beyond any limits ever imagined...it would forever be like a badge of honor to be able to say, as one bumper sticker now proclaimed: I FLEW THE EAST-BOUND STAGE.

The use of air power to build up the force and draw a line in the sand would have been futile, of course, without the contribution of the air re-

fueling tankers operated by Strategic Air Command (SAC) and its reserve crews. KC-135 Stratotankers and KC-10 Extenders flew up to 300 missions per day at the peak of the buildup. No large-scale military operation had ever been carried out at such distances before, and although air refueling had become routine, the number of tankers and the ability to use all of them, all the time, had never been stretched so much.

KC-135R Stratotankers from the 41st Air Refueling Squadron at Griffiss Air Force Base, N.Y., made the 17-hour-plus journey that terminated downrange, and set up shop at another of those air bases that arose out of empty desert in tiny nation-states ringing Saudi Arabia (Pentagon rules still prohibit naming most of them). SAC tanker crews began working out of tents, trailers and hastily fabricated wooden buildings, with nothing to occupy them but work, an occasional newspaper, lizard races,

and a diet of MREs, those plastic-sealed rations known as "meals, ready to eat." Although MRE rations can be tasty, troops proclaimed that the acronym meant "meals rejected by Ethiopia."

Transports, tankers, fighters...By October 17, 2½ months after the Iraqi invasion of Kuwait, Defense Secretary Cheney said that 200,000 Americans were in the Persian Gulf. The equivalent of seven fighter wings were now arrayed on the desert, including a second squadron of F-15E Strike Eagles that arrived without target-designator pods and had to be rigged with "dumb" munitions rather than the "smart" bombs they were designed for. The original plan for a buildup—the 200,000 figure was larger than had ever been announced—was near completion. People began to talk not of Desert Shield but of Desert Sword—the term everyone knew would be used if a defense of Saudia Arabia became an attack to dislodge Saddam from Iraq.

The early days were over. The threat of being overrun by Iraqi forces was over. But just as aircraft are lost in peacetime operations, so, too, were they lost in Desert Shield. The otherwise flawless airlift was marred by the August 29 crash of a C-5A Galaxy at Rhein-Main in Germany, killing 13 and blamed, finally, not on the ever-present problem of crew exhaustion but on a faulty engine thrust reverser. An F-15E Strike Eagle was lost on September 30, an RF-4C Phantom on October 8, an F-111F Aardvark on October 10—two crewmen killed in each instance.

With help from the British (Tornados, Jaguars), the French (Jaguars), exiled Kuwaitis (Skyhawks, Mirages) and Saudis, the Americans had put together an air armada with the destructive power of the force that had been fielded against the Third Reich on D-day.

But Iraq had been busy, too. Saddam Hussein's forces had had long weeks to dig in. Although some of the reports were later to prove inaccurate, General Schwarzkopf was being told that the number of Iraqi troops in and around Kuwait had gone up from 250,000 to 500,000. By late October, Schwarzkopf was telling his leaders—among them, General Colin Powell, chairman of the Joint Chiefs of Staff, who visited him on October 21—that an "enhanced option" would be to *double* the size of forces in the Desert Shield buildup. To the original plan were now added three more aircraft carrier battle groups, a second battleship, and two additional Marine expeditionary brigades, as well as additional armor from Europe.

The "enhanced option" was kept quiet until November 8, when President Bush announced an increase that would result in the deployment of more than 200,000 more troops, raising the total eventually to 425,000. In the face of Iraq's

While the airlifted American elements "hold the fort" in Saudi Arabia, M1 Abrams tanks wait to be loaded aboard the rapid response vehicle cargo ship USNS Algol (T-AKR-287) at Savannah, Ga., on August 17, 1990. In order to bring the American forces to full strength, it became essential to supplement the Navy's efforts with civilian volunteers from the U.S. merchant marine.

apparent bolstering of its own strength, this new level of strength would meet the Pentagon's long-held principle that when force was deployed, it should be overwhelming.

The air buildup that preceded the actual Desert Storm fighting on January 17 was very much a combination of low tech and high tech: the F-117A Nighthawk Stealth fighter, operating from a mountainous Saudi base, was to rule the skies over Baghdad, but the F-15E Strike Eagle, even without its laser-bomb technology, was to prove highly effective dropping old-fashioned bombs. Iraq's defense radars were often shut down to deceive the "black boxes" aboard RC-135 reconnaissance aircraft, or jammed and disrupted by Air Force EF-111As and Navy EA-6Bs. Yet there were a half-dozen other weapons that were now long in the tooth,

among them the A-10 Warthog tank-killer and the Navy's A-6 Intruder, which employed fairly ancient technology—and worked.

Centcom's Horner, who directed the war from the "Black Hole" near Riyadh, later said that the coalition's success in the air was due, in great measure, not to weapons but to people. Speaking only of the great airlift that brought people and machines to the desert, ALCE Captain Christopher Mardis expressed a similar view when he spoke of his pride in his nation, in his buddies, and in the airlift that made it happen. "We have achieved something unique," Mardis said as a C-5B Galaxy taxied past. "These men and women made it happen. A lesser group could not have done it."

Although the U.S. displayed an extensive airlift capability whose speed was as impressive as it was vital, it would not have been sufficient by itself to serve the needs of the immense coalition building up in the Gulf. One armored division, for example, required 500 tons of ammunition daily. And General Schwarzkopf wanted 60 days of supplies and ammunition on hand before the ground campaign began. That meant millions of tons of ammunition, not to mention the tons of other necessary supplies.

The service that the merchant marine provided, therefore, cannot be underestimated. Between the Navy's Marine Sealift Command and the private shipping companies, a total of 215 ships—including antiquated freighters, modern Ro-Ro (roll-on, roll-off) vessels and two hospital ships—were pressed into service. Manned by volunteer civilian crews, they emptied entire bases in Europe, Korea, Okinawa, the Philippines and elsewhere, and transported their personnel and equipment to the Gulf.

"We never, in our wildest dreams, could have visualized the tremendous amount of ammunition and other dangerous cargo we would be moving into Saudi Arabia," commented Rear Adm. Vance Fry, commander of the Navy's Cargo Handling Force. "Remember, they were flying, on the average, 2,000 sorties a day. And this lasted for over a month. We pushed a lot of ammunition as fast as we could."

Fry directed the Navy's 12 reserve and two active duty "Combat Stevedore" battalions in the Persian Gulf. "We had a couple of our reserve battalions with the Marine expeditionary force that was poised to land near Kuwait City," he said. "In a four-ship squadron, we can carry enough water, food, ammunition, fuel, you name it, to support an 18,000-man force for the first 30 days of a war anywhere in the world. This is amazing, especially when you're on board one of these massive vessels and you walk down to the eighth deck and every level is wall-to-wall equipment. It's just awesome.

The U.S. Navy ocean minesweeper Impervious *and other vessels are positioned on the deck of the Dutch heavy lift ship* Super Servant 3 *prior to offloading near Bahrain in October 1990.*

The squadron from Diego Garcia was the first to arrive in Saudi Arabia, even before the Army thought about getting any equipment there."

Second Mate Robert Guttman, a merchant marine officer with previous sea time in the Middle East who served during the Gulf crisis aboard the ammunition ship SS *Rover*, wrote home describing the war as seen through the eyes of a civilian volunteer:

Jiddah, January 25, 1991: "Greetings from the Front! Actually, we're out of Scud-range here, which is fine with us. We were on our merry way to the Gulf when we got the word to divert to the Red Sea. That was fine with us. The next day, the war began.

"So we sit here for two days and nobody even knows we're here....On the third day, they built a perimeter around the berth—'Fort Apache' we call it, naturally—and they began discharging into trucks. When they load about 15 trucks, they 'head 'em up and move 'em out'....Building the fort was simple, by the way, they just stacked two tiers of containers all the way around, sort of like the ration boxes and mealy bags at Rorke's Drift.

"We have a couple of World War II veterans on board, both merchant marine vets. One able bodied seaman is 76 years old. After dodging U-boats and kamikazes, they both find this trip a bit of a yawner, except for the heat."

Dammam, Saudi Arabia, February 8, 1991: "Here's another bit of 'Good Patriotic Stuff'. The 24th Transportation Battalion, late of Fort Eustace, Va., is the longshore battalion we have been working with both times we have been here, and they have been in Saudi longer than any other unit except for the 82nd Airborne, having arrived August 24. They work 12 hours a day, seven days a week, unloading ships here, and they blew up a Scud right over their barracks with a Patriot missile before we arrived."

The SS *Rover* was about to hoist a fresh shipment of ammunition aboard at Guam when word arrived that it would not be necessary—the war was won. *Rover* was laid up for an overdue refit and 2nd Mate Guttman returned Stateside on March 1.

In all, merchant ships moved 88 percent of the supplies used by the American forces, at 30 percent less cost than the 12 percent that was airlifted. Without their contribution, it was estimated that an American ground offensive would not have been able to sustain itself for three days. Without the airlift, however—and if Saddam Hussein had chosen to take the offensive into Saudi Arabia in August or September 1990 while coalition forces were still relatively small—there may not have been protection for port facilities on which the ships could have unloaded. □

LIFTING THE FOG OF WAR

DEWAYNE B. SMITH, U.S. NAVY

An intelligence specialist passes the word at a control and reporting center.

AS IN THE EARLY days of any battle, the fog of war is present. But having been in the outset of several battles myself...I would tell you that we probably have a more accurate picture of what's going on in Operation Desert Storm than I have ever had before in the early hours of battle," said General Norman Schwarzkopf during his first press briefing on Operation Desert Storm.

The "picture" that Schwarzkopf spoke of was actually a mosaic, a jigsaw puzzle of bits of information that combined to form a work of art. Even in Desert Storm, though, the picture was not perfect: the number of Iraqi troops may have been considerably less than the estimated 540,000, and there were more Scud missile sites than first realized. On balance, though, the intelligence was far better than in any other modern conflict—certainly better than Iraq's intelligence mosaic.

Before the first F-117 Stealth fighter-bomber took off with its load of "smart" bombs or the first Tomahawk missile was launched into the night on January 16, 1991, each pilot had been briefed and each system programmed on exactly where to find the target. And before the first tank crossed the Iraqi border or the first Marine breached the Kuwaiti minefields on G-day, everyone knew exactly where they were to go to defeat Saddam Hussein's plan for the "mother of all battles." Every asset available to a high-tech nation had been utilized.

It began five months earlier, shortly before August 2, when an American spy satellite noted a buildup of tanks, armored personnel carriers and more than 100,000 Iraqi troops on the Iraqi-Kuwaiti border. Behind them were convoys of trucks, supplies and other equipment. The satellite relayed this information to Washington, but the intelligence analysts, in a classic case of making the intelligence fit a theory instead of just the opposite, labeled the activity "intimidation" on Saddam's part. That theory was dispelled at 2 a.m. on August 2 when the T-72s of the Republican Guards Division charged across the border toward Kuwait City.

The United States and the United Nations, though caught completely by surprise by this transgression, quickly reacted and began deploying military forces to the Gulf. But from the outset Schwarzkopf faced the same questions encountered by every military commander in history: what was the other guy up to, where was he, and how strong was he?

No military operation can be successful without intelligence, and Operations Desert Shield and Desert Storm were no exception. Centcom's (Central Command) first objective was to keep the Iraqi army out of Saudi Arabia long enough to build up sufficient forces, then, when enough information was gathered, formulate a plan to force Iraq to leave Kuwait.

Certain facts had to be ascertained and questions answered before any plan could be made. Enemy troop movements, strength and deployments had to be determined. Troop displacements, defensive positions, SAM and communications sites, artillery emplacements,

bunkers, fuel and ammunition storage areas had to be located and plotted. Command and control networks had to be found and traced and, finally, weak spots in Saddam's defenses had to be identified for future use. Any plan developed would revolve around the gathering of intelligence.

This information would come from four sources: PHOTINT, the photographic and image-gathering capabilities of satellites, spy planes and tactical reconnaissance jets; COMINT, the communications interception intelligence; ELINT, electronic emissions intelligence; and finally HUMINT, or human intelligence. These four sources would provide the total "picture" for General Schwarzkopf—and possibly, a plan.

High above the desert sands orbited three of the most advanced satellites in history. Flying in polar orbits, from which every country on earth can be watched as needed, are two KH-11 "Keyhole" photoreconnaissance satellites and an even more advanced "Lacrosse" spy satellite. Each, by use of on-board maneuvering rockets, was maneuvered into orbital positions so that Iraq and Kuwait were under almost constant surveillance.

The KH-11s, originally placed into orbit by the space shuttle, carried the cutting edge of camera, video and electronic imagery equipment. Part of the system included what is known as a charge coupled device, or CCD. Similar to the light sensors used in home video cameras, the CCD provides the KH-11 with an extremely ef-

ficient light-sensitive video system. By utilizing semiconductor technology, CCDs are constructed by covering a flat surface with rows of light-sensitive elements in a grid pattern. Each element senses light and generates an electrical charge that is sent to an individual picture element known as a pixel. A postage stamp array of 800 by 800 CCDs can generate a picture of 640,000 picture elements. Hundreds of such chips can be clustered together to form a massive "lens" that transmits pictures by radio link to a tracking station or through a relay satellite to Washington, D.C. The resolution on a KH-11 allows the equipment to recognize objects 100 miles below that are only a few feet in length. Although it can't read the numbers on a license tag, as the fable goes, it can tell the difference between the types of tanks or artillery pieces it sees. But the KH-11 has a downside: it can't see through clouds or smoke. Because of this, it was joined over the Gulf by a newer bird—the Lacrosse.

Carried aloft in December of 1988 aboard the space shuttle *Atlantis,* the Lacrosse was placed into polar orbit carrying a new system that would address the weakness of the KH-11. Known as SAR (synthetic aperture radar), this system permits the Lacrosse to "see" through clouds, smoke and haze. By utilizing a 48-feet-by-12-feet rectangular transmitting and receiving antenna, the Lacrosse radar signals can receive imagery either in an aimed "snapshot" or by sweeping signals over the rows upon rows of transmitter/receiver elements in a phased-array

Supplementing satellite intelligence for the Americans was the TR-1, a more advanced version of Lockheed's 36-year-old U-2. Basically a jet-powered sailplane, this slow but efficient spy aircraft could photograph objects 50 miles away.

A Boeing E-3 Sentry airborne warning and control system (AWACS) on duty over northern Saudi Arabia on February 3, 1991. With its ability to ''see'' hundreds of miles and ''loiter'' for hours over the battlefield, the E-3 directed the air campaign and made it almost impossible for an Iraqi aircraft to take off without being detected.

pattern. Ground terrain can be painted, and objects as small as three feet can be identified.

Each of these "birds" began watching large swaths of Iraq and Kuwait, sending down constant data that provided Washington and Centcom with exact Iraqi unit deployments, defensive positions, active airfields and logistical locations, updated twice each day.

Below the satellites flew an airplane that owed its heritage to a design developed by Lockheed's premier designer, Clarence L. "Kelly" Johnson, and his famous "Skunk Works" 36 years before. The U-2R and its latest derivative, the TR-1, soared along the borders of Iraq and Kuwait, scanning and photographing well inside the enemy-occupied territory with oblique-mounted cameras capable of taking photos of objects 50 miles away.

And when the air war began, RF-4C Phantom II reconnaissance planes—stripped down versions of the famous Mach 2+ F-4 Phantom fighter-bomber—blasted in to take both prestrike and poststrike photos. Each RF-4C carried up to four cameras: one forward oblique, two side oblique (right and left) and one vertical—either panoramic or large-frame still camera. The oblique and vertical cameras are "framing" cameras, capable of taking either 4.5-inch-by-4.5-inch or 9-by-9 negatives. The panoramic camera, by using a rotating prism to bend light rays, can take a wide swath photo directly below the aircraft that, depending on altitude, can run from horizon to horizon. With the aid of infrared film, photos can be taken at night. But because the RF-4Cs flew over heavily defended enemy territory, and at a much lower level than the U-2R and TR-1, the job was quite a bit more hazardous. At 20,000 feet, which was normal mission altitude for RF-4C photography, SA-6 SAMs and anti-aircraft artillery could prove deadly.

"We were up along the Iraqi-Kuwaiti border," relates one RF-4C pilot, "when all of a sudden

I felt a *whump*—a major concussion—on the left side of my head. It was like someone had set off dynamite right outside the cockpit. I looked to my left and there was this huge puff of black smoke. Triple A. Immediately a couple of more blossomed around me, and I knew it was time to get out of there."

Despite allied efforts at SAM suppression, there were still a few that remained operational. One "Wizzo" (weapons systems operator) flying back seat in another Phantom said: "We were flying a two-ship mission about 30 miles south of the Iraqi airfield at Jalibah when I got RWR (radar warning tone). Within seconds they had launched five SA-6s. It was a matter of break-turns, ECM and flares to decoy them away that saved us. You just had to watch out on every sortie. Relax too much and you had a long walk home."

But the recce pilots, both those of the U.S. Air Force, Navy and Marines and those of the Royal Air Force (RAF) flying specially fitted Panavia GR1 Tornados, managed to bring back the imagery that provided Centcom with rapid intelligence on targets and bomb-damage assessment available by no other means. Other players entered the picture when the jets returned: camera crews downloaded the film packs from the nose bays and rushed them to technicians who processed the negatives within minutes. Photo interpreters then analyzed the imagery and passed the negatives on to more technicians who then made hard prints. Before the Phantom's engine even had time to cool, the imagery was rushed to either Riyadh or the requesting commander in the field.

Imagery sent to Riyadh was in turn studied and, if needed, dispatched out for target assignment. Using Learjets, Centcom could rush target photos to the fighter squadrons quickly and sorties could be launched. Afterward, the recce jets would return to the target areas to get imagery for bomb-damage assessment. If necessary, the targets would be hammered again.

During Desert Shield, special COMINT (communications intelligence) aircraft patrolled the border gathering information that would later prove devastating to the Iraqis' ability to communicate. Four-engine EC-130H "Compass Call" derivatives of the Hercules transport monitored Iraqi communications, recording frequencies and locations of transmitters. After pinpointing the exact location of each emission, they were all programmed for later mass jamming—a capability also of the Compass Call—and eventual destruction by fighter-bombers.

Monitoring Iraqi air traffic was handled by the E-3 AWACS (airborne warning and control system) aircraft. These converted Boeing KC-135s—military versions of the venerable 707—sporting huge revolving saucer-shaped radomes on stilts mounted over the fuselage, kept track of shifts in enemy air force units. Because Iraq had more military airstrips than it did squadrons, most were left empty but serviceable to serve as auxiliary strips should others become unusable. Whenever so much as a single MiG or Mirage took to the air, it immediately came up on the AWACS radar and was tracked. This information was recorded and constantly updated for later airstrikes.

Radar sites, identified through various ELINT methods, were first jammed by such aircraft as the EF-111A Raven, the radar jamming version of the F-111A fighter-bomber, and the Navy's EA-6B Prowler, the electronics version of the A-6 Intruder. SAM radar was of primary concern, as surface-to-air missiles are controlled by ground radar. Because of the intelligence gathered on the locations and frequency spectrums of these radars, they proved of little value to the Iraqis when the air war started.

But airplanes and satellites can only do so much. It still takes a human presence to find out what goes on close-up. This on-scene human intelligence (HUMINT) was provided by three resources: indigenous personnel, such as Kurdish agents who infiltrated various towns and villages inside Iraq; agents of the Kuwaiti Free Resistance in Kuwait City; and allied coalition special operations units and scouts.

From Kuwait City, messages and updated intelligence from the resistance was sent by voice over the telephone, utilizing cellular systems after the land lines to Saudi Arabia were cut. Written messages, which included hand-drawn maps, were sent by Fax machine. Troop strengths, status of water supply, food and medicine, construction of defenses and other valuable pieces of information were smuggled out, often by Bedouin tribesmen who "wandered" the desert.

In the desert, Special Forces and scout units did their part. Central Command sent MH-53 "Pave Low" helicopters equipped with night-vision equipment into Iraq and Kuwait during darkness to deposit or drop Special Forces surveillance teams to search out and identify fire-control and early-warning systems. On one such mission, commandos parachuted deep inside Iraq before dawn to find a missile launcher that had eluded the airborne reconnaissance missions. Wearing night-vision goggles and riding lightweight camouflaged motorcycles equipped with silenced mufflers, the commandos efficiently eluded Iraqi patrols and checkpoints as they made their way over the rocks and sand in search of their target.

After finding the missile site, the commandos fixed its location by bouncing signals off a

U.S. NAVY

communications satellite with hand-held transmitters. The data was relayed back to headquarters, and within minutes F-15s swooped in and obliterated the target.

Other scouts, provided by the various allied divisions, spent weeks inside southern Iraq—the area Saddam's convoys had to cross to get to Kuwait. By digging in and camouflaging their positions near roadways, real-time intelligence of enemy movements was transmitted on a continuous basis.

Captain Frank Moreno, who commanded six six-man long-range surveillance teams from the 24th Infantry Division, explained the value of the LRSTs: "This is real-time intelligence. It can't be matched by a satellite that takes three or four hours to get information to a commander. An enemy tank column of 100 tanks can pass by and be eating dinner in Baghdad by then. Our information can be in the commander's hand in half an hour, max."

By means of intelligence, the Iraqi army's eyes and ears were located, and then systematically eliminated. Once Schwarzkopf knew Saddam was blind, he shifted his high-speed armored and air assault forces west—past the last static defenses in Kuwait. Then, in a blitzkrieg move reminiscent of the German end run around the Maginot Line, he performed what he described as his "Hail Mary" play. The rest is history.

Because of the allied coalition's ability to use intelligence and the Iraqi military's inability to do the same, Saddam Hussein suffered from a dilemma aptly described more than 140 years earlier by none other than Arthur Wellesley, the Duke of Wellington, when he said, "I have spent all my life in trying to guess what lay on the other side of the hill."

General Norman "Bear" Schwarzkopf did not have to guess—he knew. Because of his intelligence assets, the fog of war had been lifted. □

ROCKWELL INTERNATIONAL

TOP: The U.S. Navy used an electronic variant on their Grumman A-6 Intruder, the EA-6B Prowler, to jam Iraqi radar. In the first two days, high priority was given to the elimination of radar at surface-to-air missile sites, with an effectiveness that paid off in the weeks that followed. ABOVE: Weighing less than 17 pounds, the Collins GPS manpack helped to improve the efficient and timely transmittal of vital information at troop level.

CHAPTER FIVE

DESERT SHIELD

ROBERT F. DORR

Specialist Chris Fadness of the 3rd Battalion, 73rd Armored Brigade, 82nd Airborne Division, points to bullet dents on an M-551 Sheridan from Operation Just Cause in Panama. Both he and the tank were veterans of that December 1989 operation.

THE M-551 SHERIDAN tank strained and sputtered. A mechanical problem—that damned *sand* again. Specialist Chris Fadness was driving the light tank up the ramp to go aboard a truck trailer bed when the Sheridan abruptly bucked, spun its treads in place for a split second, coughed black smoke, and tipped over. Somebody cried out. Fadness groaned. His Sheridan came to an abrupt halt on its side in the gritty sand of the Saudi desert.

It was on the eve of Operation Desert Storm. Chris Fadness and his buddies in the 3/73 Armor, 82nd Airborne Division, were at the cutting edge of the coalition force. They'd arrived in Saudi Arabia 10 days after the August 2 invasion of Kuwait by Iraqi forces. Fadness, a native of Hood River, Ore., was just past his 20th birthday and just promoted to specialist (E-4). He was a veteran of Operation Just Cause in Panama, where hostile bullets had punched dents into the front of another Sheridan in his charge.

Dating from 1959, more than a decade before Fadness was born, the Sheridan was a 20-foot, 8-inch, 34,898-pound, diesel-powered light battle tank with a 152mm gun. It was also, in the words of another 82nd soldier, "a confounding gadget with a lot of age on it." The Sheridans certainly seemed too flimsy for any conflict against Saddam Hussein's 5,500 main battle tanks—most of which weighed three times as much and were more heavily armed and armored. But the Sheridan was the only

tank that could be airdropped, and so it was the tank of choice for the 82nd. Yet, it had not been made for the desert. Fadness: "Believe me, the desert is unforgiving." Fadness and his Sheridan tank. A soldier and his weapon.

As Operation Desert Shield unfolded in late 1990, American readiness to fight on the desert was a top item in headlines and on cable TV news. Because the news came instantly by satellite, warriors and weapons were exposed as never before to merciless public scrutiny. Both men and machines were at the heart of the question being asked by Americans about possible war in the desert: Are we ready?

Almost everybody began raising questions about the weapons. "Humvee" Army utility vehicles arrived in 110-degree Saudi heat with

their tires inflated to full pressure, and soldiers watched in frustration while tires exploded. Night-vision goggles worked well most of the time but, in a pinch, could fail to define contours on unchanging expanses of landscape. In the heat, batteries in portable radios blew up, or sputtered and coagulated into a bubbling, frothing version of Silly Putty.

Above all, there was the sand. The sand was wearing down helicopter blades, confusing the seeker heads of infrared missiles, and clogging the air filters on tanks. So troublesome was the Saudi sand that Army scientists shipped 500 pounds of it back to U.S. laboratories to find out how it differed from sand in California, where American soldiers were undergoing desert training. They found it coarser, grittier, more abrasive.

Americans in uniform during Desert Storm were a new breed. Compared to the draftees of the U.S. "citizen army" of 1940-1975, they were more black, more Hispanic, more female, more married. Compared to total U.S. population, they were fitter, better educated, and nearly free of crime and drugs.

As a people, Americans had made a decision that they didn't want their sons drafted. They had turned to a force made up of volunteers and had gotten professionals—people who saw military service as a job. "Till now it never occurred to me that I'd be in a war," said five-year veteran Sergeant Michael Curphey, loadmaster on a C-5 Galaxy. In U.S. history, by and large, not many Americans in uniform have ever come up lacking on the battlefield, but in late 1990 the ques-

Watching and waiting: a member of the 436th Security Police Squadron from Dover Air Force Base keeps an eye out for trouble in the Arabian desert.

Newly arrived M-551 Sheridan light tanks of the 82nd Airborne Division. As was the case in Panama, the M-551 was the only tank capable of being airlifted quickly to the trouble spot, but it would have been no match for a serious Iraqi armored assault. The airborne troops could only grit their teeth and hold on until the heavier reinforcements could arrive.

tion had to be asked—could the people of this new, volunteer army *fight?* Fight and win on the desert? This question would be asked again and again, at least until the ground war quickly unfolded in late February 1991.

The cause of Fadness' tank's breakdown is not on record, but other Sheridan drivers reported a persistent problem with sand clogging a cooling grille, causing the engine to overheat and the vehicle to buck, abruptly, like a spooked pony. And, so, the question persisted.

Are we ready? *Really* ready?

In November 1990, when Operation Desert Shield was 3 months old, 240,000 Americans had been deployed to the Persian Gulf, and a massive second wave of 200,000 more had been announced; experts were saying that if war could only be delayed *another* three months, the military balance and the season would strongly favor American forces. By February 1991, they

said, the buildup of troops and weaponry would be complete. The temperature on the desert would be at its coolest. The nights would be crisp and clear. Americans, the experts said, were better trained than Iraqis to strike and kill on the desert at night.

At least, there was time to prepare—a luxury Pentagon war-gamers of future conflict had never relied upon. The taxpayer was perhaps entitled to feel that, with six months to get everything into place, the high-cost, high-tech American arsenal doggone well *ought* to be ready for war.

But Iraq had been granted time, too—to solidify its hold and bolster its forces in Kuwait. Americans, supported by troops from half a dozen other countries, had now committed nearly all of the troops they possessed, leaving almost no reserve for contingencies elsewhere in the world, and were still outnumbered.

The Road to Kuwait City: The perennial Bob Hope adds his quips to the USO Christmas Tour at Bahrain.

To dislodge Saddam Hussein from Kuwait and deal a knockout blow to the Iraqi leader's future ambitions, the United States would have to mount a massive air campaign to clear the skies of opposing warplanes and to strike Iraq's military installations, supply lines and massed armored forces on the desert. To this end, the first U.S. aircraft deployed to Saudi Arabia were F-15C Eagle fighters, followed by an armada of more than 600 warplanes, ranging from F-117A Nighthawk Stealth fighter-bombers to F-111s, F-16s, F-15E Strike Eagles and A-10s. B-52s went to the island bastion at Diego Garcia. These warplanes used radar, infrared and other technologies to fight at night, and all held up remarkably well in the harsh desert climate.

A canard soon to gain attention was that American planes would be unable to cope against American-made Hawk surface-to-air missiles captured by Iraqi forces in Kuwait. In fact, within 72 hours of arrival, all Air Force combat aircraft had their missile jammers upgraded to counter the Hawks.

There would be strong reliance on air power, but no one—not even the Air Force chief of staff, General Michael J. Dugan, who was sacked for talking about it—thought that bloodshed on the ground could be averted. The popular thinking at the time was that there would have to be amphibious landings in the northwest Persian Gulf to dislodge Iraqi troops and, ultimately, to liberate Kuwait. And there would still be armored battles in the desert, where advancing tanks were sending columns of dust high into the sky, a telltale warning to the other side. "This will not be a walk in the park for you," Iraqi Foreign Minister Tariq Aziz had warned. "It will not be Grenada or Panama." Said Saddam Hussein himself, "There will be a line-up of dead bodies with a beginning but with no end."

Practitioners of war know that once the shooting starts, smug conclusions held during peacetime can be chucked out the window. In war, everything goes wrong. A kind of Murphy's Law takes hold—if something can get screwed up, it will.

"Once you push off and begin jockeying for position, all of your finely ordered plans become chaos," said Lt. Col. Fred Newman, a battalion commander with the 1st Cavalry Division. "One guy doesn't come up on the radio when he's supposed to. You find that somebody forgot to fuel his vehicles or to load ammo. You get one platoon wandering off in the wrong direction. That's *before* you make contact with the opposing force and discover that he's infiltrated *his* people *behind* you. Then all hell breaks loose."

It's called the fog of war. In training, soldiers are drilled to expect it and to improvise. But very few beyond the top U.S. echelon had the sustained combat experience of a Vietnam veteran like Newman. Unlike the Iraqis, few Americans sent to the Gulf had been in combat before. Those who had, generally gained their experience in limited conflicts in Grenada and Panama.

Of course, before any Americans could fight on the deserts of the Middle East, they needed to get there. At first, the key was airlift, which meant transport planes hauling people and equipment. The Military Airlift Command (MAC), during the first two months of Desert Shield, logged 145,000 hours of flying time. Not everything came by air, though. The merchant marine sealifted food, ammunition, weapons and other supplies by the hundreds of thousands of tons. The air-and-sea lift was a superhuman effort, and it succeeded. American forces reached the Middle Eastern deserts.

U.S. Marines conduct a landing exercise. Although the Iraqis were expected to be ready to defend Kuwait's beaches, the option of a Marine landing was kept open, either as a serious invasion or as a diversion.

Members of 1st Battalion, 10th Marines, take part in a mass casualty decontamination drill. The coalition forces' readiness to defend themselves against chemical attack was a deterrent in itself.

What is a desert? The ancients took the name from words meaning "a place where connections are severed"—a reminder to a superpower that had to keep up an air bridge and seagoing supply line over thousands of miles merely to reach the scene.

Deserts cover one-fifth of the earth's surface. Among the least hospitable on this planet is the hot desert of the Arabian Peninsula, which includes parts of Kuwait and Iraq. The myth persists that the desert is flat—but peaks, ravines, and shifting dunes blown by the constant wind combine with heat and aridity to make the barren Saudi expanse a challenge to mapmakers, Bedouin nomads and M1 Abrams tank drivers. At least Iraq's soldiers knew the climate. Aziz, again: "We live here."

Nothing hampered U.S. operations more than the difficulty of navigating an austere sea of shifting sands where a road could be obliterated that was visible two days earlier, where the horizon was not where it seemed, and where there were few landmarks to guide troop movements. Early in Desert Shield, almost every American soldier in the foreign land had the experience of being lost on the desert.

After decades of preparing to fight in Europe or Korea, the armed forces turned toward the Middle East in a serious way during the Carter years, 1977-81, with the building of a Rapid Deployment Force. The RDF, as Pentagon experts saw it then, was intended to quickly move into the Persian Gulf to blunt a Soviet armored assault on Iran. On January 1, 1983, the RDF was absorbed by U.S. Central Command (Centcom in Pentagon jargon), in the latter's responsibility for all operations in the Middle East—headed up, in 1990-91, by General Norman Schwarzkopf.

To prepare to fight on the desert, the U.S. Army in 1984 created the world's biggest classroom on the brownish-red desert near Barstow, Calif.—the National Training Center (NTC) at Fort Irwin. The Army cycled battalions through Fort Irwin on 9-to-22-day maneuvers in the desert. Twenty-eight heavy battalions, including National Guard combat battalions, trained annually at the NTC. Every battalion commander in the United States trained there during his command tenure.

Soldiers at NTC waged real battles against an elite Opfor (opposition force) run by the 177th Armored Brigade, which simulated Soviet tactics and used Soviet equipment. In place of real bullets, M-16 riflemen, Dragon anti-tank crews, and M1 tank gunners fired lasers using the center's MILES (multiple integrated laser engagement system), which scored "hits" and "kills," and even produced a computer readout of how a battle unfolded.

At the NTC, soldiers learned that fighting on the desert means movement. Taking out an enemy security post using light, fast M2 Bradley fighting vehicles or maneuvering a battalion to outsmart enemy armor, officers and NCOs (non-commissioned officers) stressed mobility, fluid action, and constant reassessment of the situation under pressure. The troops might grumble about sand and heat, but they did not have to fret about standing still.

To bolster the NTC experience, more realistic training exercises, called Bright Star, were held in Egypt—but they were costly and infrequent.

Critics argued that the lessons of Fort Irwin did not always reach anyone below the battalion commander or lieutenant colonel level. The lessons, according to this argument, produced more reading for Pentagon staff officers than insights for young soldiers who bleed and die in a real conflict. A 20-year-old M1 Abrams tank driver could go through 22 days of training at Fort Irwin without being told how the battle unfolded, what went wrong, or why. This was bad business in an army where an enlisted person might have a college degree and hold goals for the future. In this new, questioning army, soldiers wanted to know what was happening and why.

Officers and NCOs, it was argued, were under career pressure to pick up graduate degrees in management or to serve in staff jobs, and did not

TOP: An F-16C of the 388th Tactical Fighter Wing from Hill Air Force Base, Utah, overflies the Saudi-Kuwaiti border. LEFT: Members of the 82nd Airborne Division train in the desert. BELOW: Battling boredom during the months of buildup and uncertainty, U.S. military personnel indulge in a game of football.

Enter the big guns: an M1 main battle tank adds some serious punch to the allied buildup.

spend enough time leading troops. Rotation of sergeants and officers happened so frequently that units often lacked personality, integrity or shared experience. Recommendations to improve equipment or tactics, based on hard nights in the desert, could become buried in a military bureaucracy that at times paid more attention to the format of a staff paper than to what it said.

The Navy had its own special problems. Just as the Arabian desert is hostile, so, too, was the Persian Gulf. "Reflagging" operations in the Gulf in 1988 were successful, but pointed to flaws in the Reagan-era "maritime strategy," which relied on forward-deployed carrier battle groups to strike Soviet bases with nuclear bombs.

In those 1988 actions, when U.S. warships escorted vessels carrying oil from Kuwait—the ad-

versary then being Iran—the United States had no nearby minesweepers or fast patrol boats and had to rely instead on larger, ultramodern ships. This resulted in a series of disasters—the crippling of the tanker *Bridgeton* by a mine, the attack on the frigate USS *Stark* (FFG-31) by Iraqi aircraft carrying Exocet missiles, and the shooting down of an Iranian airliner by the Aegis cruiser USS *Vincennes* (CG-49), which misidentified the airbus as a hostile fighter.

The emphasis on high tech dealt a telling blow to the Navy's main weapon, the carrier battle group. In perhaps the worst procurement decision for a decade, the Navy in 1988 canceled the A-6F Intruder—a re-engined version of its proven A-6—in favor of its ultra high-tech A-12 Avenger. The "Stealth" A-12 Avenger had to be canceled, too—on the eve of Desert Storm—be-

cause it was overcost and overweight. The lower-technology A-6F Intruders could have been on carrier decks in the Persian Gulf in 1990-91, along with the aging A-6E Intruders that eventually had to carry the brunt of the fighting.

Some of the problems facing a seaborne force in the Persian Gulf received cable-news prominence on November 17-18, 1990, when the United States launched Operation Imminent Thunder, a landing of Marines on Saudi soil that was supposed to cow Saddam Hussein. Helicopter-borne forces landed on the Saudi coast in a mock assault from U.S. Navy ships hidden over the horizon, supported by 1,100 U.S. carrier-based and allied aircraft in one of the biggest "joint" maneuvers ever. But high seas blew the wind out of Imminent Thunder: 10-foot waves postponed the Marines' mock

storming of beaches on November 17 and 18 by causing their high-tech LCACs (landing craft, air cushioned) to founder. When war finally came, no amphibious landing was made, and it remained questionable whether the United States had ever been ready for one.

What, then, about the most alarming threat to Americans on Middle Eastern deserts, summed up by that Pentagon acronym NBC— for nuclear, biological and chemical warfare? In the Persian Gulf, officers and NCOs readied troops to throw on NBC gear on sudden notice.

Saddam Hussein didn't have atomic bombs, but Iraq could make biological war. Iraq's research had focused on anthrax, an infectious cattle disease that can be transmitted to humans, symptomatized by malignant, pus-filled blisters. In the chemical warfare arena, the Iraqis possessed nerve agents such as sarin. Invisible, tasteless and odorless, sarin breaks down the bridge between nerve synapses—throwing the nervous system out of whack and causing muscle spasms that lead to convulsions, respiratory and heart failure and death. Iraq also had mustard gas—actually a thick liquid, either colorless or dark brown, that can blister the skin or damage the eyes.

Why were these horrors not used during Desert Storm? From the beginning, U.S. officers had felt they would not be very effective. All were delivered only by bombs or artillery shells, which presumably could be hit before launch by U.S. airstrikes. On the desert, biological and blister agents dissipated rapidly and nerve gas would be dispersed by the wind. General Schwarzkopf's troops were geared up for highly mobile desert warfare, not for sitting still.

Soldiers and Marines in Saudi Arabia kept at hand full NBC garb, which enclosed them against the outside world. The suit was heavy, bulky, hot. Soldiers could not tell each other apart—degrading the leadership of NCOs and officers. An M1A1 Abrams tank crew, at least, could fight in a chemical environment without its crew wearing protection.

It scarcely mattered. In the end, Iraq achieved little more than to force the United States to provide its armed forces with protective garb. That was an enormous diversion of effort and resources, but the very existence of the protection took the edge out of Iraq's resorting to chemical weapons and proved to be a deterrent in itself.

When war finally came and was won with ease—somewhat misleading because many Iraqis did not want to fight—were the U.S. armed forces truly ready? Clearly, Americans might have done better with an A-6F Intruder on carrier decks, with more training, and with more emphasis on the benefit of training to lower ranks. But Desert Storm had not caught America unaware. □

CHAPTER SIX

WAR AT SEA

U.S. NAVY

A Tomahawk cruise missile emerges from the water of the Gulf— fired by an American submarine—before sprouting small wings and leveling off to strike at an Iraqi target. OPPOSITE: The World War II veteran battleship Wisconsin *contributes the awesome firepower of her nine 16-inch guns to the rain of steel falling on Kuwait and Iraq.*

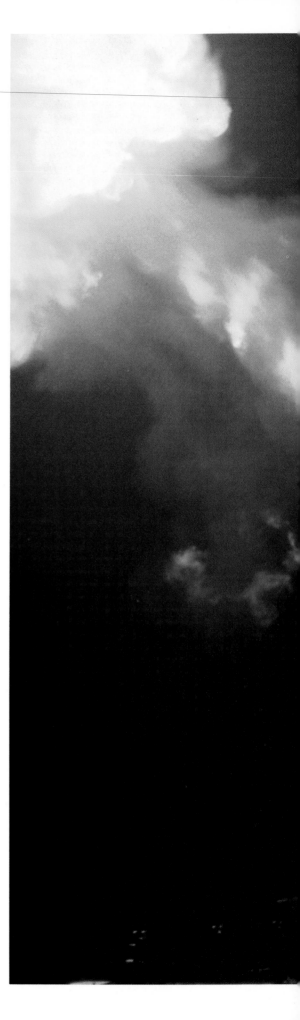

ATOMAHAWK cruise missile erupted from the surface of the Red Sea and raced toward a predetermined target deep in embattled Iraq. It had come from beneath the waves from the U.S. *Los Angeles*-class attack submarine *Louisville.* And now the missile's booster engine drove the cylindrical projectile upward while wings emerged from the sides of the pilotless craft. As the Tomahawk neared the coast, its inboard computer rapidly sifted through data from spy satellites and other sources. Once landfall was reached, a terrain contour matching system made the necessary course corrections. As the Tomahawk neared its Iraqi objective, a small video camera "read" the target, fine-tuning the final approach to impact. It was January 19, 1991, and with the warhead's detonation, a new era of sea warfare was launched.

The launch was revealed at a coalition military briefing in Riyadh, Saudi Arabia. Submarine actions are almost never publicized—one of the reasons it's called "the silent service"— but Air Force Lt. Col. Mike Scott made an exception during the briefing "to document a significant event in naval history." It was the first combat launch of a cruise missile from a submarine. Commented one Pentagon official: "A lack of fanfare is the measure of submariners' success. The only time you would know it is there is when the Tomahawk breaks the water." Later, there were reports of other missiles fired from other attack submarines among the eight rumored to be operating in the Kuwaiti theater at any given time.

66

That first historic missile constituted only a tiny fraction of the torrent of high-tech and conventional firepower unleashed by the U.S. Navy during the opening salvos of Operation Desert Storm. Lashing out toward the Kuwaiti coast and targets deep inside Iraq, cruise missiles from the World War II-vintage battleships *Missouri* and *Wisconsin* joined others fired from cruisers and submarines to usher in the most critical phase of the involvement of American sea power in the Gulf War.

Months earlier, however, the Navy, which maintains a continuous presence in the Middle East, became the initial instrument of U.N. and American resolve to remove Iraqi troops from Kuwait. With the assistance of warships from 18 other coalition countries, American naval vessels enforced U.N. sanctions with a blockade that denied Iraq the materiel necessary to sustain and replenish its war machine.

On August 2, the very day of the invasion of Kuwait, the aircraft carrier USS *Independence* had been ordered into the Arabian Sea to bolster other ships already operating there. By August 7, the Egyptian government granted the carrier USS *Eisenhower* passage through the Suez Canal into the Red Sea, while the carrier *Saratoga*, the *Wisconsin*, and the helicopter assault carrier USS *Inchon*, with a battalion of combat-ready Marines aboard, weighed anchor for the Gulf region as the first tangible show of force arrayed against Iraq. As the buildup of allied ground forces in the area began, the role of the Navy widened to include not only blockade patrolling but also protection of the shipping routes for the largest sealift effort since the Vietnam War.

Aircraft carriers traditionally have proved to be a most effective means of rapidly moving aircraft into a potential combat zone. When Desert Storm commenced, six flattops were positioned in the Persian Gulf region. The 93,300-ton *Nimitz*-class *Theodore Roosevelt*, nuclear powered and one of the largest ships ever built, joined the battle groups of the *America*, *John F. Kennedy* and *Saratoga* in the Red Sea, while the venerable *Midway*, 65,000 tons and commissioned in 1945, operated alongside the *Ranger* in the Persian Gulf. A total of 276 aircraft were deployed with the six carriers, along with a dazzling flotilla of warships and auxiliary vessels. Aggregate U.S. naval strength in the Kuwaiti theater of operations peaked at 120 ships, more than 80 of them warships and 15 powered by nuclear reactors. Along with the Navy's massive missile capability and the tremendous power of seaborne shellfire, the aircraft gave American and coalition vessels the ability to mount effective operations against Iraqi naval units offshore and to provide nearly 40 percent of the overall combat sorties flown during more than a month of hostilities.

With naval air power contributing heavily to the round-the-clock bombardment of enemy positions in Iraq and Kuwait, cruisers, destroyers and frigates screened the carriers against possible attack and began the hunt in earnest for elements of the Iraqi navy. At least half a dozen Aegis-class cruisers, armed with more than 200 Tomahawk cruise missiles and the latest air defense systems, roamed the waters of the Red Sea while escort vessels in the Persian Gulf neutralized Iraqi anti-aircraft fire from converted oil platforms and blasted enemy minelayers and patrol craft that threatened the coalition forces with their French-made Exocet missiles.

Dismissed by skeptics as maritime anachronisms, the twin *Iowa*-class battleships *Wisconsin* and *Missouri* demonstrated their worth in modern combat. Commissioned in 1944, both vessels saw action in the closing days of World War II. It was on the deck of the *Missouri* that the Japanese signed the instrument of surrender formally ending the greatest conflict mankind has ever known. Neither ship had fired its 16-inch main batteries in anger since the Korean War.

In the early 1980s, plans were put forth to resurrect these giants to provide the U.S. Navy with long-range gunfire capability. In addition, their armaments were upgraded with modern state-of-the-art weaponry.

Equipped with eight cruise missile launchers, each carrying four missiles, and four anti-ship Harpoon missile launchers, the *Iowa*-class battleships retain six of their twin 5-inch turrets along with their nine large-caliber guns for added firepower. The Vulcan-Phalanx weapons system, four 20mm Gatling guns capable of firing 3,000 rounds per minute, gives the battleships defensive capability against incoming anti-ship missiles. All this, combined with a variety of electronic countermeasure systems, improved radar and communications, makes the *Iowa*-class battleship one of the most potentially devastating weapons in the world. In addition, the stern of the vessel is modified to accommodate three helicopters for forward observation and anti-submarine warfare.

With all of their newfound versatility, the battleships' original purpose of providing supporting fire for ground forces is still a primary responsibility. Their performance as effective gun platforms is unequaled. The main batteries can fire a shell weighing the same as a compact car a distance of 25 miles on a trajectory of 50,000 feet with incredible accuracy. Following the tragic explosion of a magazine on the USS *Iowa* in 1989, there had been a ban on the firing of battleship guns, but during the Gulf War, the 16-inchers spoke again.

OPPOSITE: F/A-18 Hornets of Strike Fighter Squadron 83 (VFA-83) swarm alongside SH-3H Sea King helicopters of Helicopter Anti-submarine Squadron 3 (HS-3) and A-6E Intruder aircraft on the deck of the carrier Saratoga in the Red Sea on November 28, 1990.

ED BAILEY, U.S. NAVY

Caught south of the Khauer al Kafka oil terminal, an Iraqi tanker burns after being hit by allied fire on February 6, 1991. Surviving crewmen were rescued by the guided missile frigate Curts.

ROBERT CLARE, U.S. NAVY

When the peril of Iraqi mines and naval vessels was diminished, the *Missouri* and the *Wisconsin* swept close to the Kuwaiti coast to pound enemy targets. The *Missouri* lobbed seven 2,000-pound shells into a concrete-reinforced Iraqi command and control center. "Enemy are scurrying about out there," remarked Lt. Col. Jan Huly, a 2nd Marine Division spokesman who was watching from the shore. Three days later, the *Wisconsin* silenced an artillery position that had been harassing coalition ground forces.

The ships used unmanned drones to help improve their fire. Launched from the battleships, the drones hovered close to the target to direct the shelling, and then photographed the area for a later assessment of the damage. The UAVs (unmanned aerial vehicles), resembling model airplanes, were then recovered aboard ship with a net. "The Navy is fighting for the life of the last two battleships to show [they] still have a role to play in the modern era," said military analyst David Sorenson. In an ironic twist, while the *Missouri* and the *Wisconsin* gained recognition in the Gulf, the 58,000-ton USS *New Jersey,*

the Navy's most-decorated battleship, was being quietly decommissioned at Long Beach, Calif.

Certainly, one of the Gulf War's lasting images is the streak of flame following a cruise missile into the night sky from the deck of the *Wisconsin*. Heralding the onset of combat, this spectacular display combined technology used by previous generations with that of the Space Age. The Tomahawk cruise missile is, in itself, a technological marvel. "It cost a lot of money," said Sen. Sam Nunn of Georgia. "But when you look at the precious savings of lives, I think the dollars are well invested." At $1.35 million each, more than 300 cruise missiles were fired during the conflict. Launched in leapfrogging patterns with manned air attacks, they were directed against high-priority installations considered too heavily defended for conventional air missions, including biological and chemical warfare facilities, storage tanks for petroleum, oil and lubricants, and command and control centers.

Developed to carry either conventional or nuclear warheads, the Tomahawk can deliver a 1,000-pound payload at a range of 1,500 miles.

Using three separate navigational systems, it strikes its target with incredible accuracy. Usually, the missile is accurate within 10 feet. "We feel we could launch a Tomahawk from Boston Harbor aimed at RFK Stadium [in Washington, D.C.] and put it through the goal posts," remarked Bob Holsapple of the Navy's cruise missile project. Numerous Western journalists reported breathtaking firsthand accounts of the missile's virtually unerring accuracy. One recalled seeing a Tomahawk roar past his balcony at the fashionable Al-Rashid Hotel in downtown Baghdad and explode on impact with the nearby Iraqi Defense Ministry.

The first naval personnel to carry the war to the Iraqis were the pilots of carrier-based aircraft. Three weeks into the war, the Navy had flown more than 44,000 combat missions into hostile territory. "This is really and truly an Air Force effort," remarked Rear Adm. Douglas J. Katz. "But we're trying to add to it as best we can."

In supporting the six-week-long air campaign, Navy F/A-18 fighter bombers and A-6E Intruder attack aircraft struck repeatedly at Iraqi airfields, aircraft shelters, artillery emplacements, Scud missile sites and other key installations. Using laser and television-guided "smart" bombs with a nearly zero percent probable-error factor, the planes were able to consistently deliver their ordnance to within three feet of the target.

One of the most versatile aircraft in the Gulf War, the F/A-18 pulled double duty in air-to-air combat as well as on bombing missions. Rapidly replacing the older A-7E Corsair, the F/A-18 carries advanced targeting systems and air-to-ground radar, a 20mm Gatling gun, AIM-7M Sparrow radar-guided missiles, and heat-seeking AIM-9M Sidewinders. Fully loaded, the A-6E can deliver a payload of nine tons of bombs. This subsonic heavy attack jet is equipped with ground-mapping radar for night attacks and the infrared TRAM (target recognition and attack multisensor) system. The EA-6B Prowler and the KA-6D, both modified versions of the A-6E, complement the carrier air arm. The Prowler is a sophisticated electronic warfare aircraft, and the KA-6D is an air refueling tanker.

The Navy's front-line carrier-based fighter is the F-14 Tomcat. Capable of speeds in excess of Mach 2, the Tomcat can track up to 24 aircraft simultaneously at a range of 115 miles with its AWG-9 radar. Armed with a combination of Sparrow, Sidewinder and AIM-54C Phoenix air-to-air missiles, the Tomcats went virtually unchallenged by Iraqi fighters for control of the air. Other naval aircraft involved in Operation Desert Storm included the E-2C Hawkeye early-warning aircraft, the S-3A Viking anti-submarine aircraft, the SH-3H Sea King and CH-53 Sea Stallion anti-submarine helicopters, and the CH-46 Sea Knight transport helicopter.

Despite their successes, naval aviators provided the American public with several poignant moments during the Gulf War. Lieutenant Scott Speicher became the war's first American casualty when his F/A-18 was hit by an Iraqi

A Kuwaiti island reclaimed by allied forces after its mortar and anti-aircraft installations were destroyed and troops were landed from the American guided-missile frigate Nicholas.

A weary member of the Tomahawk missile battery aboard the battleship USS Wisconsin *takes a breather.*

surface-to-air missile on the first night of Desert Storm. Next, the battered face of captured Intruder pilot Lieutenant Jeffrey Zaun sparked outrage among Americans as he was paraded in front of Iraqi television cameras and coerced into saying, "I think our leaders and our people have wrongly attacked the peaceful people of Iraq." Zaun and his fellow prisoners of war were released after several weeks in captivity. Once freed, he explained, "I had enough faith in Americans to know that anybody who saw this was going to say, 'This is ridiculous.'" Speicher is still officially listed as missing in action. Both pilots flew from the deck of the *Saratoga*.

Aboard the command and control ship USS *Blue Ridge*, meanwhile, the choreographer of Desert Storm naval operations, Vice Adm. Stanley Arthur, himself a former naval aviator, performed the minor miracle of coordinating bombing sorties against strategic targets, providing tactical support for ground troops, preparing for a possible amphibious invasion of Kuwait, keeping the waters of the Gulf free of Iraqi mines, and subduing the Iraqi navy. At Arthur's disposal was the most powerful armada of warships ever assembled. Of the coalition nations, France and Great Britain sent the largest naval contingents of those partners outside the Gulf. France dispatched 14 ships, while Great Britain contributed 13. The Soviet Union sent the destroyer *Admiral Tributs* and an anti-submarine ship.

Armed to the proverbial teeth, the guided-missile cruiser USS *Ticonderoga* was representative of the American naval commitment to Desert Storm. Equipped with the advanced Aegis air defense system, the *Ticonderoga* brandished eight Harpoon missiles in two quadruple launchers, the Phalanx anti-missile defense system, a pair of 5-inch guns, the ASROC (anti-submarine rocket), SM-2 surface-to-air missiles, torpedoes and the Tomahawk cruise missile. The *Ticonderoga*'s nuclear-powered cousins of the *Virginia*-class were also on station in the Gulf, as were the *Kidd*-class guided-missile destroyers, arguably the finest warships of their kind in the world. The still smaller frigates of the *Oliver Hazard Perry*-class and the *Knox*-class performed admirably during the brief war on picket duty as well as in offensive operations.

A host of specialized vessels, including minesweepers, ammunition ships, fleet oilers and tenders of all types, accompanied the warships to the Gulf. Prepared for a flood of casualties that never materialized, the hospital ships USNS *Comfort* and USNS *Mercy* provided 2,000 beds and 24 operating rooms between them. In addition, U.S. Coast Guard personnel were available to serve as prize crews for any Iraqi ships seized during the conflict. Navy SEAL

(sea, air and land) units were deployed with their versatile Sea Fox infiltration boats to perform reconnaissance missions, serve as boarding parties, clear mines and obstacles from Kuwaiti beaches, and disrupt enemy communications. Because of the clandestine nature of the SEALs' varied missions, little has been released as to their actual participation in the Gulf War.

Against the coalition fleet, the Iraqi navy could muster four guided-missile frigates, six corvettes, 21 patrol boats, eight minesweepers, and numerous smaller craft used in gathering intelligence or sowing mines in Kuwaiti coastal waters. Most of the Iraqi vessels were capable of firing the potentially deadly AM39 Exocet anti-ship missile. These weapons originally gained notoriety when the Argentines employed them with remarkable success against the British Royal Navy during the Falklands War. It was two Iraqi Exocets, allegedly fired by mistake from two French-made Mirage F-1 fighter-bombers during a sweep against Iranian tankers in the Gulf, that nearly sank the frigate USS *Stark* during the Iran-Iraq War, killing 37 American sailors. Largely ineffective against overwhelming odds, the Iraqi navy ceased to exist as an effective fighting force by the third week of the Gulf War. More than 60 of its vessels, some of which were commandeered from the Kuwaitis, were destroyed or damaged.

No hits were scored by Exocet missiles launched either from the Iraqi ships or from the Mirage F-1 fighter-bombers, which were considered a much greater threat. As large numbers of Iraqi aircraft began to flee to sanctuary in Iran, sailors kept a close watch for surprise attacks. "It's sort of like being in a woodpile with a copperhead snake," mused Admiral Arthur. "They give you no warning. You can play around in the woodpile a long time, and you can still get a nasty bite." Iraqi planes hugging the Gulf coast might come within 40 miles of the coalition surface fleet before showing up on radar screens. With the attacking planes coming on at the speed of sound, a window of only four minutes would be available to ward off the Exocets.

Although coalition aircraft had made the destruction of any Iraqi missile launchers a priority, Iraqi gunners managed to fire two Chinese-made Silkworm missiles at the coalition fleet. The apparent target of these Silkworms was the USS *Missouri*, which was firing its 16-inch guns in support of the ground offensive. One of the missiles ditched far from its mark, and the other was intercepted by Sea Dart anti-missile missiles from the British destroyer HMS *Gloucester*, which was "riding shotgun." "Undoubtedly there are some relieved sailors aboard another coalition vessel due to the quick action

A catapult officer gives the signal to launch an A-6E Intruder of Attack Squadron 196 (VA-196) from the carrier USS Independence in the Gulf.

Its variable-geometry wings and arrestor hook extended, a Grumman F-14 Tomcat comes in for a landing aboard a U.S. Navy aircraft carrier in the Gulf.

U.S. NAVY

On guard against Saddam Hussein's promised terrorist campaign (which never materialized), a U.S. Coast Guard port-security boat conducts a patrol near the Marine amphibious assault ship Iwo Jima.

of a radar operator aboard HMS *Gloucester,''* reported Commander John Tighe, a Royal Navy spokesman.

On January 18, the frigate USS *Nicholas,* joined by a pair of U.S. Army helicopters and a patrol boat belonging to the Kuwaiti government in exile, attacked nine Iraqi-held oil platforms in the northern Persian Gulf. The occupying Iraqis had been harassing allied aircraft with small arms and shoulder-fired missiles. The *Nicholas* blasted one Iraqi patrol boat out of the water and crippled two more before closing to engage the oil platforms. The frigate's gunners dueled with the Iraqi troops, who fired rifles and machine guns for three hours before several of their platforms were set ablaze. A dozen Iraqi soldiers, five of them wounded, surrendered to the detachment of Marines aboard the *Nicholas.*

The first Iraqis captured in combat, these 12 were fed, treated for their wounds and interrogated before eventually being turned over to the Saudis. The Iraqis had subsisted by dropping hand grenades into the water to bring up fish. Maroon berets among their effects indicated that at least some of the 12 were members of the elite Republican Guards. The Marine guards were careful not to give their prisoners MREs (meals ready to eat) containing pork, for fear of offending their Islamic religious beliefs.

Numerous prisoners expressed surprise at their good treatment in American hands. Rumors had circulated among them that non-Christians would be tortured and even killed if taken alive. To their great relief, the Iraqis were even allowed to perform their daily prayer ritual while in captivity. One tried to kiss a captor in gratitude—but was firmly rebuffed.

The U.S. Navy also earned the distinction of liberating the first piece of Kuwaiti soil, the tiny island of Qaruh (sometimes called Kura). That action took place on Thursday, January 24. It began shortly before noon when the guided-missile frigate USS *Curts* cautiously maneuvered into the area. Though the island was only 400 yards wide and was partially submerged at high tide, it had been identified as an intelligence-gathering post from which Iraqis could radio details of allied air and sea activities.

The *Curts'* crew was at general quarters with all weapon systems manned, while observers stationed in the bow warily scanned the water for surface mines—a constant threat in the Gulf. "The first gut-wrenching experience came about 20 minutes after we went to general quarters," said Commander Glenn Montgomery at a later briefing. "We got the first report of aircraft inbound...three Iraqi aircraft over the land mass, headed in our direction." The frigate's crew readied missiles and began evasive maneuvering. After nearly 15 tense minutes, the contact faded. "I don't know what the enemy did, but honest-to-goodness at that point I really didn't care what he did, as long as he didn't keep coming in at me," said Montgomery.

SEALs and Marine units quickly secured the spit of land, and the *Curts* sent a boarding party to take over an Iraqi minelayer that had been strafed by A-6s from the *Theodore Roosevelt*. "These people were hurting and thinking about abandoning ship when we showed up," continued Montgomery. "We tried to help them expedite their decision." A total of 51 Iraqis were taken prisoner—22 from the minelayer and 29 from the island. The Iraqi post had been equipped with night-vision goggles, radios and a variety of weapons, ranging from shoulder-fired surface-to-air missiles and heavy machine guns to sidearms. "The flag of free Kuwait flies again over a piece of Kuwait territory," Montgomery announced after Qaruh was secured.

Radio Baghdad vehemently denied that its troops had been forcibly evicted from Qaruh, saying the island had been evacuated for military reasons and not due to "any alleged victory by those deprived of victory." Further, it boasted that Americans had made up the entire episode. "In a reckless attempt, the infidel, occupying aggressor Americans are trying to cover up the miscalculations which led them to perpetrate the crime of unsuccessful aggression and killing."

On the evening of January 24, the Saudi guided-missile patrol craft *Faisal* located a blip on its radar screen and dispatched a helicopter to determine its identity. When the vessel was confirmed as an Iraqi minelayer operating in Saudi territorial waters, the *Faisal* loosed a single Harpoon missile at a distance of 22 nautical miles and left its target a blazing hulk. Scores of Iraqi ships that ventured into the open were destroyed or disabled with little word as to the fate of crew members.

In several encounters with U.S. naval vessels, planes and helicopters, the Iraqi navy was systematically decimated. On January 29-30, coordinated attacks by U.S. A-6Es and F/A-18s and Royal Navy Westland Lynx helicopters destroyed most of a group of 17 Iraqi vessels operating near the Kuwaiti coast. The Lynx's superb Sea Skua missiles often scored against enemy patrol craft.

While the danger of attacks by Iraqi naval and air units diminished as Desert Storm proceeded, the constant threat posed by mines remained. That threat became all too real in the early morning hours of February 18. Within 10 miles and 2½ hours of one another, the 18,000-ton helicopter assault carrier USS *Tripoli*

BURGE, U.S. NAVY

ITALIAN EMBASSY

ABOVE: One of the four ships of the American Mine Countermeasures Group—USS Leader, Avenger, Adroit *and* Impervious—*keeps a vigilant watch for mines in the Gulf. The threat was real: Mines damaged the helicopter assault carrier* Tripoli *and the Aegis missile cruiser* Princeton.
LEFT: Elements of the Italian naval contingent on patrol in support of the U.N. embargo prior to hostilities: The guided-missile frigate Libeccio *escorts the supply ship* Stromboli.

and the Aegis missile cruiser USS *Princeton* were damaged by two of what was thought to be hundreds of mines sown in the waters of the northern Persian Gulf.

Serving as the flagship for the coalition mine-hunting effort, the *Tripoli* was rocked at 4:35 a.m. by a floating contact mine. "The first thing I thought of was getting into my general quarters gear, grabbing my gas mask...ran up here, got my flash gear and my rubber duckie and just hoped for the best," said one breathless crewman. Another commented, "I heard the explosion before anything else, and I thought, this is it, we're going down." A third recalled, "I felt the ship start to rock and I heard a large blast and I saw water spray over the bow."

The blast tore a 20-foot-by-20-foot gash in the hull of the *Tripoli*, which was carrying 1,300 Marines. The explosion had been near the bow, and flooding in a forward compartment was controlled with temporary repairs, but not before the ship sank three feet lower in the water.

Lieutenant Commander Steve Senk, the *Tripoli*'s chief engineer, and Chief Warrant Officer Van Cavin took immediate action in the assault carrier's moment of peril. The force of the explosion ruptured tanks full of helicopter fuel and ripped open a paint locker, quickly filling the ship's lower decks with the toxic fumes of paint thinner. Senk rushed below and assessed the damaged area without an oxygen mask. He discovered the flooding, which was nearly 30 feet deep in some areas. Cavin then joined Senk in leading an emergency crew of 60 men to rescue shipmates overcome by the fumes. For their gallantry in action, both Senk and Cavin were nominated for the Silver Star.

"When we don't have people in the brig, my partner or I slept there sometimes," said a smiling 30-year-old Navy master of arms named Edwin Alvarez. "I was asleep and thrown out of my rack. I remember wondering if I was dead. At first I thought a plane had hit the side of the ship. Then I realized I was cut up and covered by something. It was just paint." Alvarez also said he would be sleeping above deck for the foreseeable future.

Unlike the *Tripoli*, the 9,460-ton *Princeton* was believed to have been damaged by an influence mine. "Surprisingly, there is no hole," exclaimed Marine Brig. Gen. Richard Neal when briefing reporters in Riyadh. The influence mine is intended to lie on the sea floor and can be set off by the magnetic signature, sound or water pressure of a ship passing overhead.

The most noticeable evidence of the *Princeton*'s encounter was its wrinkled hull. However, the mine, which exploded near the ship's stern, jammed its port rudder and started leaks around its port propeller shaft seal, causing one of its

turbine engines to be shut down. The explosion lifted the *Princeton* partially out of the water and caused serious cracks in its superstructure.

The *Princeton* was ordered into port hours after the incident, while the *Tripoli* was pronounced "fully mission capable" after damage assessment. Still, the assault carrier was ordered to the Asry Shipyard in Bahrain, where dry-dock facilities were available for repairs. Three *Princeton* crewmen, one in serious condition, were transferred to a nearby British vessel for treatment, while four members of the *Tripoli* crew were treated for injuries on board the ship.

In the seven months of increased naval activity in the Gulf, more than 160 contact mines were detected. Close encounters of the "mine" kind were commonplace. HMS *Gloucester* missed one by a scant 15 feet. "Several days ago we saw this thing, black, round, with a spike sticking up," remarked Captain James Burke of the guided-missile destroyer USS *Turner*. "In the binoculars, it looked like a mine. It turned out to be a tied-up Hefty bag. You just can't take any chances."

In 1988, U.S. officials estimated that as many as 200 mines left over from the eight-year Iran-Iraq War might still be floating in the Gulf. More recent Iraqi efforts only compounded the threat. American ships operating in the area posted mine spotters in their bows at all times. However, spotting a floating mine in rough water is often a nearly impossible task.

While the floating contact mines, tethered to anchor cables, are a constant menace, the influence mines are extremely difficult to detect. These "smart" mines can be tuned to the frequency of a particular type of ship through programming a self-contained microprocessor and strike virtually without warning. Their presence in the Persian Gulf dramatically increased the danger to coalition warships.

To counter the perilous mines in the shallow waters of the Gulf, the U.S. Navy utilized "the world's most-sophisticated mine countermeasure gear," according to spokesperson Lieutenant Dana La Joye. The state-of-the-art American minesweepers *Avenger*, *Impervious*, *Leader* and *Adroit* patrolled the area around the clock with SQQ-32, the latest in sonar detection equip-

ment. The SQQ-32 is particularly effective in locating mines laid on the sea floor or tethered just below the water's surface. Also available in the fight were remote-control platforms that carry television cameras, sonar and explosives to blow up any mines located. Several Sea Stallion helicopters dragged minesweeping sleds and sonar gear through the water. Warships that discovered mines marked them for disposal, and divers were deployed from helicopters to attach explosive charges and detonate them at a safe distance. Smaller minesweeping ships made primarily of wood or plastic to minimize the attraction of magnetic mines dashed close to the beaches in preparation for a possible Marine amphibious landing on the Kuwaiti coast.

Saddam Hussein likewise anticipated and prepared for an amphibious assault, the card that the overall allied commander, General Norman Schwarzkopf, held but never played. Motivated by the presence of 17,000 Marines and 31 ships offshore in the northern Gulf, the Iraqi dictator declared war on the fragile Gulf ecosphere in an attempt to protect himself. Ten miles off the Kuwaiti coast, Saddam's soldiers

A CH-53E Super Stallion helicopter lifts an external load from the flight deck of an Iwo Jima-class amphibious assault ship in support of Operation Desert Shield on October 15, 1990. The threat posed by a 17,000-man Marine landing force off the Kuwaiti coast diverted much Iraqi attention from the massive allied land offensive.

A Westland Lynx (foreground) and a Sea King IV of the Royal Navy fly across the desolate Kuwaiti landscape. Armed with Sea Skua missiles, Lynx helicopters from the destroyers HMS Manchester and Cardiff and from the guided-missile frigate HMS Brazen took a heavy toll of Iraqi patrol craft.

turned on the pumps at Sea Island Terminal, the small, oil-rich nation's main loading facility for supertankers. Capable of discharging up to 2.4 million barrels of crude per day, the pumps combined with 3 million gallons of oil the Iraqis emptied from five Kuwaiti tankers to create the largest slick the world has ever seen.

According to Schwarzkopf, American military planners were not the least bit surprised by the Iraqi tactics. "It's not something that's going to impede the progress of the campaign," he remarked at the time. Rear Admiral Dave Frost called the spill an "act of desperation," but added, "We do not have a lot of experience operating ships in oily waters." Interestingly, the allied plan of attack for the ground war, which made use of only the *threat* of an amphibious operation, was adopted more than two months before the Iraqis released the oil.

The largest amphibious assault force assembled since the 1950 Inchon landing during the Korean War flexed its muscle with intense training exercises, supported operations on land and sea with sorties by Harrier jump jets and helicopters, and approached within striking distance of the Kuwaiti coast, but never went ashore en masse, because the threat alone achieved the strategic purpose of diverting Saddam's forces. From the brass to the rank and file, it was accepted that a successful landing through mined waters and beaches in the face of concentrated Iraqi fire would probably be the most costly element of the ground offensive. "Most of the people realize they will have heavy casualties, but no one likes to talk about it much," said Marine Corps Lance Cpl. Rod Sturkie aboard the helicopter assault carrier USS *Okinawa*.

As the deadline for the ground war approached, pre-invasion activity intensified. SEAL units began "small-boat operations" against mines, beach obstacles and communications links; the air bombardment increased; and the

Casualty of war: A cormorant lies dead on the beach at Manifah Bay, a victim of the massive oil slick unleashed in the Gulf by the Iraqis. The dire ecological consequences of this bizarre strategem could last for decades.

battleships drew close to shore to soften up possible invasion corridors. With the prospect of house-to-house and street-to-street fighting, reminiscent of the battle for Hue in the Vietnam War, looming ahead of them, many Marines were convinced their job would be to liberate Kuwait City. "The cities are more dangerous," stated Lance Cpl. Thomas Fix. "You never know where anyone is in there. You've got to go in and find them."

Ultimately, Schwarzkopf stuck by his decision to keep the Marines aboard their ships. He denied the request of Lt. Gen. Walter Boomer, the Marine overall commander, that the troops be allowed to storm ashore.

The possibility of an amphibious landing alone was enough to tie down Iraqi divisions in occupied Kuwait. Had those Iraqi troops moved west to contest the main allied thrust, the attack on the shores of Kuwait would probably have been set in motion. But the clever deception succeeded beyond anyone's wildest expectations.

Early news on the ground war included reports of a landing on Faylakah Island, at the mouth of Kuwait Bay about 20 miles east of Kuwait City. U.S. officials denied the story, and indeed Faylakah was occupied a week later, with 1,045 Iraqi prisoners taken—one of them a brigadier general. The Iraqis gave up when U.S. Navy helicopters blared surrender messages in Arabic.

Even after the main Schwarzkopf offensive was underway, the amphibious force commander, Marine Maj. Gen. Harry Jenkins, insisted that a landing was still possible. From the deck of the helicopter carrier USS *Nassau*, Jenkins hinted at the role of his troops. "As long as they [the Iraqis] are watching the coast, they are not engaging our troops in Kuwait and farther west." The ground war would be won in just 100 hours. In retrospect, contributing to the coalition's success on the ground, Jenkins' Marines were probably just as effective aboard ship as they would have been on the beaches under fire—and with a much lower price tag.

While it cannot be said that the U.S. Navy would have so dominated the sea war against a more capable enemy, American naval units in the Kuwaiti theater of operations did once again demonstrate their bravery and devotion to duty in bringing about final victory. In chasing Iraqi vessels, enforcing the U.N.-sponsored blockade, actively participating in the air war, hunting mines, menacing the shores of Kuwait, or combating environmental sabotage, the U.S. Navy and its U.S. Marine Corps, Coast Guard and merchant marine companion forces were equal to the task. Rapid deployment and supply capabilities have been noted as areas where performance could have been improved, and a number of costly ship-borne defense systems remain untried. However, assessment of overall naval performance is continuing, and the top commanders point with pride to the phenomenal success of sea-launched smart weaponry and the several significant "firsts" recorded in the campaign. □

CHAPTER SEVEN

SMART WEAPONS

McDONNELL DOUGLAS

Integrating man and machine, the pilot of an AH-64 Apache helicopter prepares to go into battle with an awesome array of weaponry that is partially controlled by the helmet that he wears.

ON THE NIGHT of January 17, 1991, the world changed. The euphoria of the previous night's air operations had turned to grim horror and anticipation when the word of the first Iraqi Scud missile attacks on Israel came over the wire services. There were reports of death and injury, and possibly even chemical weapons being used. For a few hours, it looked as though Israel would attack Iraq, the allied coalition would break up, and efforts to expel the forces of Iraq from Kuwait would fail. After all of the incredible efforts and preparations over six long months, the allied effort was going to be undone by a few poorly aimed, 1950s vintage ballistic missiles fired by a madman.

Then, later in the evening, from the depths of despair came a sudden surge of hope to those watching the live coverage on television. Standing on a balcony overlooking the air base in Dhahran, Saudi Arabia, a news commentator was discussing the implications of the Scud attacks on Israel with the network anchorman when suddenly, from behind the newsman, a streak of light rose like a fiery arrow from the far side of the base. It flew into the low cloud base, and a few seconds later a red flash of light was seen and a dull explosion heard. For a few seconds, the commentator and the network anchor said nothing. Then they realized what had happened.

For the first time in history, a ballistic missile had been shot down by *another missile*. A U.S.-made Patriot (MIM-104) surface-to-air missile

(SAM) had shot down an Iraqi surface-to-surface missile (SSM) over the air base. In just a few hours, the Iraqi force of Scud-based SSMs had gone from a weapon that could checkmate the allied effort to liberate Kuwait, to an also-ran. And what had done it was a high-tech missile system that seemingly came from nowhere to become the shield of the U.S. forces. And just as quickly, it was realized that perhaps the Patriot system could shield Israel as well, possibly convincing Israel not to hit back.

Among the defenders of the airfield at Dhahran was Bravo Battery of the 11th Air Defense Artillery Brigade, out of Fort Bliss, Texas. The battery had arrived on August 13, 1990, less than two weeks after Iraq's invasion of Kuwait. Much of the crew's time was spent keeping sand out of the equipment, which consisted mainly of a radar set—engagement control system (ECS), where the screens are monitored; the electric power plant (EPP); the antenna mass group (AMG); and the launchers themselves. "Of course, a complicated system such as the Patriot will suffer part breakdowns from time to time," said Spc.4 Angela Rooney. "But, on the whole, everything operated pretty well and it stood up against the abrasive sand and other harsh weather conditions we experienced. There was a lot of fog at times, but the Patriots performed great even then."

"At that point, we all hoped to go home without knowing if the Patriot system would ever work, if the crisis was resolved peacefully," said Captain Joseph DeAntona. "But if there was a

Advances in the electronic state of the art resulted in the metamorphosis of the MIM-104 Patriot from an overpriced anti-aircraft missile to an effective anti-missile missile. In January 1991, Saddam Hussein's Scud missile attacks on Israel transformed the Patriot from a tactical weapon to a vital instrument of diplomacy.

An explosives disposal team assigned to the 4409th Combat Support Group recovers the remains of an Iraqi Scud missile found 39 kilometers northwest of Riyadh.

war, we wanted to demonstrate that it could work. Not to ourselves, because we have faith in it, but to the disbelievers. Finally, on January 20, we had a chance to prove what we said we could do."

That was the night Bravo Battery was credited with its first kill. Lieutenant William Barrentine was on duty as tactical control officer (TCO), assisted by Pfc Jeffrey Gilley. "We work in teams, side by side in the van," said Barrentine. "You feel quite a bit of anxiety. It's hard to sit back and analyze everything in detail, things are happening so fast." When the Scud alert was sounded, Gilley adjusted the equipment. "We started tracking the inbound Scuds and the system quickly analyzed them and fired the Patriots to destroy them," Gilley said. With a rumble that shook the control center, the Patriot left the tube. "We have what we call a symbology on our scope that shows our missile going upward to engage the incoming Scud," Barrentine said. Tensely, the crew watched the missile's track as it extended upward to intercept the path of the incoming Scud. The screen showed a clear kill.

Barrentine's only regret was: "I'm sorry we didn't get a chance to test it against the Iraqi air force. If you think our performance against Scud missiles was good—you should see what we can do against enemy planes! Just like

General Schwarzkopf said: 'You ain't seen nothing yet.'"

On the night of February 25, 1991, however, a Scud dealt coalition forces a devastating blow by demolishing a barracks housing the 475th Quartermaster Group from Farrell, Pa., at Al Khubar, a few miles from Dhahran. Although the Scud broke up in midair, the warhead remained intact, punching through the structure, a converted warehouse made of corrugated metal. An observer reported an explosion about 400 feet in the air, followed by a rain of glowing metal that quickly spread fire throughout the building. For hours, stunned survivors and other personnel sifted through the wreckage while ambulances and other vehicles carried victims to medical facilities. The final toll was 28 dead, including two women GIs, and more than 100 persons injured.

Ironically, just a few short years before the Gulf War, the Patriot system had come very close to being canceled. Like many of the high-technology systems being developed for the world's military forces in the 1980s, it had a number of teething problems. But, it survived the technical gremlins and the criticisms of those politicians and analysts who wanted "simple and cheap weapons that would work." The Patriot, and a number of other so-called smart weapons and sensors, did survive their long gestation periods to become the star performers of Operation Desert Storm. Their story is the story of technology that has matured—not only the "gee-whiz" gadgetry shown in the daily press briefings at the Pentagon and Riyadh, but systems that have changed some of the basic assumptions about just how wars will be fought in the future.

Before a single bomb or missile was fired in Operation Desert Storm, however, the targets had to be found—for if the forces of the allied coalition were to hit any of the targets that would have to be destroyed, those targets would not only have to be found but monitored. In addition, after the targets were struck, the damage inflicted upon them would have to be assessed. In this way, it would be known if they would have to be attacked again, or if other eligible targets could then be struck.

That was the job of the many sensor and support systems that were used by the allied forces in the Persian Gulf. Those ranged from strategic satellite systems to portable night-vision goggles. A single critical objective was sought in their use—to achieve a tactical advantage that would translate into more rapid victory and fewer casualties for the allied coalition.

The sensor systems were a mix of emerging and mature technologies blended into the most sophisticated network of "eyes and ears" the world has ever seen. Using this network, the allies were rarely surprised, and never really fooled, as to the intentions of the Iraqi forces that opposed them. And though the sensor network had holes, it was more than good enough to get the job done.

At the top of the sensor chain were the numerous satellite systems deployed by the United States. These systems, which range from intelligence gathering spacecraft to navigational satellites, are the direct descendants of systems in use as early as 1960. What makes the systems of today different are their greatly expanded capabilities and the wide diversity of their users.

Certainly the most glamorous of these systems is the new series of photoreconnaissance satellites. This new system, the follow-on to the famous KH-11 Kennan, is a vast improvement over the film-based systems of the 1960s and 1970s. The new system, tentatively called the KH-12, apparently uses charged coupled devices (CCDs) as the photographic elements. These CCDs, which are similar to the elements in home video camcorders, are capable of "seeing" a much broader range of the light spectrum (from infrared and visible light, to the ultraviolet part of the spectrum), with added boost from the new family of lens systems that has recently come into use.

While the photo satellites seemed to have performed their missions as specified, serious shortcomings in their use were revealed. The problem was that each photo satellite (there were probably two in orbit at the time) could only make one pass at the Iraqi-Kuwaiti theater of operations each day. That clearly limited the opportunities and coverage that the satellites could provide. While it was adequate for prewar target identification and mission planning, it appears to have been less than effective during the actual bombing campaign. What was required then was rapid assessment of damage to targets that had been struck. With only two photo-satellite passes available each day, this meant that the mission of collecting the poststrike bomb damage assessment (BDA) photos fell on a limited number of tactical photoreconnaissance aircraft.

TOP: Firefighters hose down burning cars in Tel Aviv following the fifth Scud attack against Israel on January 25, 1991. Israel's decision not to retaliate against him was a diplomatic and strategic defeat for Saddam Hussein. ABOVE: Rescue crews search for bodies under the U.S. military barracks at Al Khubar after its destruction by a Scud on February 25. The Iraqi missile fell on the barracks after being intercepted by a Patriot.

87

The battleship USS Missouri *launches a BGM-109 Tomahawk missile in January 1991. With a range of up to 1,000 miles, the independently controlled cruise missile extended the destructive capability of all ships on which it was installed— including submarines.*

If the photoreconnaissance satellites fell short of expectations, it is very likely that the satellites designed for electronic and communications (ESM/ELINT) surveillance performed perfectly. The new series of these satellites, code-named Magnum, is designed to collect a variety of electronic signals, from television to radar. They appear to have been extremely successful. Another category of sensor satellites are the Lacrosse radar reconnaissance satellites. The first of these, designed to detect vehicles on the ground, appears to have been operational during Desert Storm. Their utility, though, must have been limited because they, like their photographic counterparts, could only make a single pass over the theater. In addition to the other sensor satellites, the allies also had ready access to the Defense Support Program (DSP) satellites, which normally are used to detect missile launches from the Soviet Union. With their sensors aimed into Iraq, the DSP satellites were used to provide early launch warning and targeting on the Iraqi Scud missiles that were fired into Israel and Saudi Arabia.

Satellites were also used in a number of supporting roles. As in the rest of the world, the daily weather forecast was derived primarily from orbiting satellites. In addition, commercial satellite photographs could be used to help develop maps for ground and air forces, as well

as mission planning for Tomahawk cruise missiles and SLAMs (standoff land attack missiles). This material could be generated by the U.S. LANDSAT and French SPOT satellite systems.

But certainly the most exciting and innovative use of satellites in Desert Storm came from the first combat use of the new NAVSTAR global positioning system (GPS) satellites. GPS is a system of earth-orbiting satellites that form a constellation of electronic navigation beacons. What makes GPS different is both the accuracy and the availability of the system. Currently, with the satellite constellation only partially completed, GPS can provide three-dimensional navigational positions with an accuracy error of less than five meters (approximately 15 feet). When completed, GPS will be able to provide accuracy to within three meters (about nine feet). That makes GPS a suitable navigation system for almost anything from aircraft and ground vehicles to guided missiles such as the new SLAM cruise missile.

But even more important than its accuracy, is the low cost and ease with which GPS can be used by a large variety of users. The reasons for this are the small size (about the size of a car stereo) and low cost (less than $1,000 in quantity) of a GPS receiver (also called a global positioning device). Thousands were issued to troops in the allied forces, and appear to have completely solved the traditional problem of navigation in the desert. Some of the receivers, in fact, were bought by family members and friends and sent to individual personnel in the Gulf.

"It was extremely difficult to figure out where you were in the desert," said U.S. Army Captain Sal Granata, who directed maintenance of high-tech hardware at a facility near the port of Dammam. "Entire grid squares were nothing but yellow on the maps. So if you had to navigate around a minefield, it could be very hard to get your bearings. That's where the global positioning device came into play. In some ways, it replaced the map and compass. With the GPD, you just punched in a few numbers on a transmission box. This would be relayed to a number of satellites in the sky. It would tell you exactly where you were on the ground. You punched in where you wanted to go and it would transmit grid coordinates, bearings, distances, and how to get there. It was ideal for artillery and armor units—especially artillery. And all this stuff was basic technology just brought off the shelf."

GPS was also used for rough guidance in the new SLAM cruise missile, as well as aircraft navigational systems. Clearly this first use of GPS in a combat situation must be considered a spectacular success. And with the cost of GPS receivers dropping—as well as the many civilian applications being developed for GPS—it appears that this may become one of the most enduring results of Desert Storm.

In addition to the satellite systems that were used by the allies, a number of airborne sensor and support systems were used. While they had many of the same missions and capabilities as their satellite counterparts, what made them different in this particular case was who controlled them. The satellite systems are controlled by a variety of government agencies based in the United States. In the case of the airborne systems, though, they were controlled by the allied commanders in Riyadh. In addition, the photoreconnaissance aircraft could be used to collect information whenever needed, as opposed to the photographic and radar reconnaissance satellites that are tied to their fixed orbits.

Certainly the most visible and well-known of those airborne systems were the various airborne warning and control (AWACS) aircraft used to monitor and control the airspace over and around Saudi Arabia, Kuwait and Iraq. Two different models were used by the allied forces—the carrier-based Grumman E-2C Hawkeye, and the Boeing E-3 Sentry. These two aircraft were the most important sensor platforms for controlling the air battles that paved

the way for the ground offensive that liberated Kuwait. Both systems are based upon transport aircraft and packed with sensitive radar and listening equipment. The E-2 was used mainly to provide radar surveillance for the ships of the allied fleet. The larger E-3, with its longer-range sensors, larger crew and greater loitering ability, was used over the Arabian land mass to direct the actual air campaign. With an ability to "see" several hundred miles into enemy airspace, the E-3 was the primary reason that no Iraqi aircraft could get off the ground without one or more allied fighters being vectored toward it.

For all of the power of the AWACS radar systems, AWACS aircraft could not tell the allied commanders what was happening on the ground. That was not a new problem, and several responsive programs had been devised by the U.S. Department of Defense and private industry. The first to reach service was called the joint strike and reconnaissance system (JSTARS) program. JSTARS is composed of several different parts, the most visible of which is a converted Boeing 707 transport aircraft, called the E-8, equipped with a side-looking airborne radar (SLAR) and a data processing center. The SLAR can spot vehicles as small as a jeep to several hundred miles into enemy territory. When the SLAR locates a concentration of vehicles, the data link aboard the E-8 can immediately relay the information to artillery units on the ground or specially equipped aircraft such as the F-15E Strike Eagle. It is also likely that some of the new F-16C Fighting Falcon and F-117A Stealth fighters were equipped to receive and use information from the JSTARS aircraft.

When the Persian Gulf crisis broke in the summer of 1990, the first of the E-8 aircraft were deep in their operational test cycle in the United States. Despite the fact that they had not even finished their testing, and not all of the system's equipment had been installed, the first two E-8 aircraft and their crews were dispatched to Saudi Arabia to assist in what was already recognized as the single worst problem the allied commanders had—being able to get fast, accurate data on the location of ground targets for the coming air campaign. Each E-8 aircraft was assigned to fly an eight-hour mission each day. Those missions became truly vital, though, when the Iraqis began to launch their Scud missiles into Israel and Saudi Arabia. With their ability to see patterns of vehicles on the ground, the E-8s became the primary means of targeting the mobile Scud launchers and were a major factor in the declining number of Scuds that were launched later in Desert Storm. Without a doubt, the E-8/JSTARS system was one of the big winners of Desert Storm.

A Pioneer I remotely piloted vehicle (RPV) makes a rocket-assisted takeoff from an American battleship. Capable of operating 10 miles from the ship for up to eight hours, the RPV uses a stabilized television camera and laser designator for over-the-horizon targeting and reconnaissance.

In addition to the radar-carrying E-2, E-3 and E-8 aircraft, the allied forces deployed a range of electronic intelligence-gathering aircraft, including RC-135s, EP-3Bs and EC-130s. Much like their ESM/ELINT counterparts in orbit, these aircraft were designed to "hear" radar, television and voice signals over a wide range of frequencies. They were apparently successful.

If there was a failure on the allied side during Desert Storm, it was the lack of necessary tactical photoreconnaissance aircraft and related equipage for use by the allied forces. The simple fact is that both the U.S. Air Force and Navy had allowed their tactical reconnaissance capabilities to decline. Part of the reason was the growing dependence upon satellite reconnaissance. But much of it had to do with the fact that the new advanced tactical reconnaissance system (ATARS) being developed for use by the Air Force, Navy and Marine Corps was behind schedule due to budget cutbacks. As a result, the allied forces in the Persian Gulf probably had fewer than 75 tactical reconnaissance aircraft available for service when Desert Storm began. That force probably included approximately 24 F-14As equipped with TARPS (tactical advanced recon pallet system) reconnaissance pods, 48 RF-4Cs, and a few modified Mirage F1s. While the aircraft that the allies had were fairly well-equipped from a sensor standpoint, they were clearly lacking in numbers. With more than 1,000 strike sorties being flown every day during Desert Storm, there just were not enough reconnaissance aircraft to go around. This is why the job of bomb damage assessment, or BDA, bogged down during the middle part of Desert Storm.

Ironically, the United States threw away a system in the 1970s which might have provided enough photographic coverage to meet the BDA needs of the allied coalition. This was the Teledyne-Ryan Model 147 reconnaissance drone program that had been so effective during the Vietnam War. Currently, the only surviving remnant of this impressive capability in the U.S. forces is the AAI Pioneer remotely piloted vehicle (RPV) operated by the U.S. Marine Corps. These small aircraft, which resemble oversized model airplanes, are equipped with television cameras that are used to target and spot artillery rounds. Four detachments of Pioneer RPVs were used during Desert Storm by the Marines.

The Pioneer quickly won the praise of Marine Colonel Carl Fulford, commander of Task Force Ripper, part of the frontal attack force that punched across the Kuwaiti border at the outset of the ground war. "Utilizing an RPV, we called in naval gunfire from the battleships *Wisconsin* and *Missouri*, both of whom were on station, and close air support, to eliminate the

enemy's armor," Fulford said. "We then moved to block any enemy forces from trying to retreat from Kuwait City."

A Pioneer RPV was involved in one of the more bizarre incidents of the war when a number of Iraqi soldiers from a coastal bunker "surrendered" to a Pioneer orbiting overhead. In all, these highly successful craft logged more than 500 missions and 1,500 flight hours during operations in the Persian Gulf.

The sophisticated sensor systems that were used in Desert Storm were not limited to systems in satellites or aircraft. On the contrary, a number of the most important systems were employed by the ground forces. These included a number of systems that would get their first trials during Desert Storm.

Among the first major systems that arrived during the Desert Shield buildup was a network of ground-based air search radars. Composed

U.S. NAVY

mainly of Hughes-General Motors TPS-43 radar, this system helped form a network for the control of the thousands of allied combat sorties, as well as backing up the E-3 AWACS aircraft in defending Saudi airspace. The crews of these radars received none of the glory of the Patriot crews, but their work was vital to the smooth operation of Desert Storm.

Another type of ground radar was the Firefinder radar built by Martin-Marietta. This radar is designed to detect enemy artillery shells while still in flight and plot the exact location of the guns that had just fired them. The system apparently worked so well that the standard for Firefinder crews was to have the coordinates for enemy guns plotted before the first enemy shell even hit the ground! The information was then fed to allied artillery units for rapid counterbattery fire, usually a unit of multiple rocket launcher system (MRLS) vehicles. The elimination of an entire battalion of Iraqi heavy guns during a border skirmish just before the start of the ground war was a testimony to the effectiveness of the Firefinder and MRLS systems.

Desert Storm also provided a unique demonstration of a war that was run round-the-clock. The ability to run the war day and night was based on a simple premise: being able to see in the dark. That capability of night vision was provided by two families of sensor systems: night-vision goggles (NVGs) and forward-looking infrared (FLIR) systems. NVGs are electronic amplifiers of faint light from sources such as stars and the moon. Used by personnel ranging from fighter and helicopter pilots to infantry commanders, the NVGs were successful in the desert in allowing users to see a low-resolution version of what they would have seen in daylight.

Carrier-borne AWACS: a Grumman E-2C Hawkeye prepares to take off from the USS Saratoga. Packed with sensitive radar and listening equipment, the Hawkeye's job was primarily to provide radar surveillance for the ships of the allied fleet.

Iraqi radar was neutralized by
specialized electronic radar-jamming
aircraft such as these two EF-111A Ravens.

U.S. NAVY

The American soldier in Saudi Arabia was backed up by the most technologically sophisticated hardware in military history. Even the artillery fired "smart" shells that could be guided to their targets, while MLRS missiles did their World War II forebears one better with their ability to be independently targeted.

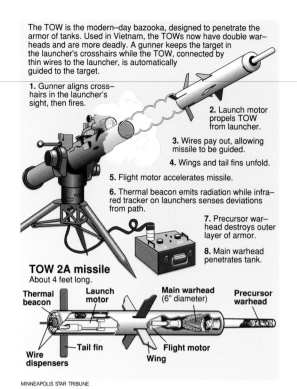

The TOW is the modern–day bazooka, designed to penetrate the armor of tanks. Used in Vietnam, the TOWs now have double war-heads and are more deadly. A gunner keeps the target in the launcher's crosshairs while the TOW, connected by thin wires to the launcher, is automatically guided to the target.

1. Gunner aligns cross–hairs in the launcher's sight, then fires.

2. Launch motor propels TOW from launcher.

3. Wires pay out, allowing missile to be guided.

4. Wings and tail fins unfold.

5. Flight motor accelerates missile.

6. Thermal beacon emits radiation while infra-red tracker on launchers senses deviations from path.

7. Precursor war-head destroys outer layer of armor.

8. Main warhead penetrates tank.

TOW 2A missile
About 4 feet long.

Thermal beacon
Launch motor
Main warhead (6" diameter)
Precursor warhead
Wire dispensers
Tail fin
Flight motor
Wing

MINNEAPOLIS STAR TRIBUNE

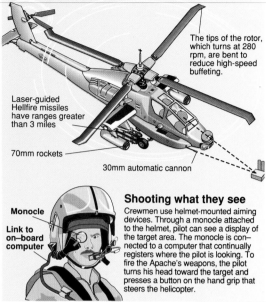

Armed with rockets, Hellfire missiles, an armor–piercing 30mm cannon and state–of–the–art tracking systems, the Army's Apache helicopter is one of the deadliest weapons in the Mideast. It is designed to destroy tanks and will see extensive use in a ground war. The helicopter, with a crew of two, is fast and maneuverable but requires high maintenance.

The tips of the rotor, which turns at 280 rpm, are bent to reduce high-speed buffeting.

Laser-guided Hellfire missiles have ranges greater than 3 miles

70mm rockets

30mm automatic cannon

Shooting what they see

Monocle
Link to on–board computer

Crewmen use helmet-mounted aiming devices. Through a monocle attached to the helmet, pilot can see a display of the target area. The monocle is con–nected to a computer that continually registers where the pilot is looking. To fire the Apache's weapons, the pilot turns his head toward the target and presses a button on the hand grip that steers the helicopter.

MINNEAPOLIS STAR TRIBUNE

Even better penetration of darkness was provided by the variety of FLIR systems on allied vehicles and aircraft. FLIR systems "see" by sensing the heat given off by certain objects and mapping it into a video picture for video display. "Hot" objects, such as a tank or truck with its engine running, would stand out from the relatively "cold" background of the desert. In addition, because infrared energy can travel through a wide variety of atmospheric conditions, FLIRs can appear to "see" through smoke or dust. A number of allied coalition aircraft, including the F-117A, F-111E, F-15E, F-16C, OV-10D, A-6E, F-18A/C, AH-1W and AH-64A, were equipped with FLIR systems. In addition, a number of ground vehicles were equipped with FLIR "thermal sights." These allowed vehicles like the M1A1 Abrams main battle tank and the M2/M3 Bradley fighting vehicles to operate and "see" in virtually every type of weather, day or night.

On February 27, the edge given by night vision was readily apparent when elements of the 1st Infantry Division engaged a Republican Guard armored unit after breaching the Iraqi lines. "I can't tell how long the battle lasted—you lose track of time," said Sgt. 1st Class Mike Bachand. "We didn't lose any tanks or Bradleys in the fighting. We used the thermal sights and could see them before they could see us. And we had the range on 'em, too, with our 120mm main guns. They had T-55s and T-72s. It was a 'hands down, see you later jack' victory. We blew the hell out of 'em!"

When one looks at the Desert Storm operations, it seems logical to ask just what kind of

sensor capabilities the Iraqi forces had when the war started. The fact is that they initially possessed a wide variety of ground and airborne sensor systems. These ranged from an impressive array of Soviet- and French-built ground radars for air surveillance to several primitive AWACS aircraft built from Soviet-made Il-76 Candid transport aircraft. The Iraqi troops were also equipped with a variety of night-vision systems for their troops. Yet, within a matter of hours from the opening of Desert Storm, the allied air forces had attacked most of the ground radars and the communications network that was needed to support it. The allied forces had put out the "eyes" of the Iraqi military.

If the sensors were the "magic eyes" of Desert Storm, then the so-called smart weapons were the "silver bullets." There is a popular misconception that guided weapons are a relatively new development. Nothing could be further from the truth. In fact, the first combat use of guided weapons took place in 1943 when German bombers sank the Italian battleship *Roma* with Fritz-X guided glider bombs. Several of the most widely used guided weapons, such as the TOW (tube-launched, optically-sighted, wire-guided) and Maverick anti-tank missiles, and laser-guided bombs (LGBs), had their combat debuts almost 20 years ago in Vietnam and the Middle East.

What made the guided weapons used in Desert Storm different was their maturity. Where such weapons might have been considered "black magic" in Vietnam, they were a part of the day-to-day operations of allied forces in 1991. The intervening 20 years of experience

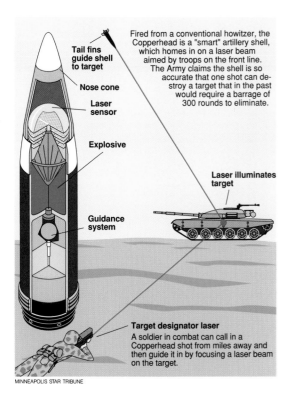

Tail fins guide shell to target

Nose cone

Laser sensor

Explosive

Guidance system

Fired from a conventional howitzer, the Copperhead is a "smart" artillery shell, which homes in on a laser beam aimed by troops on the front line. The Army claims the shell is so accurate that one shot can destroy a target that in the past would require a barrage of 300 rounds to eliminate.

Laser illuminates target

Target designator laser
A soldier in combat can call in a Copperhead shot from miles away and then guide it in by focusing a laser beam on the target.

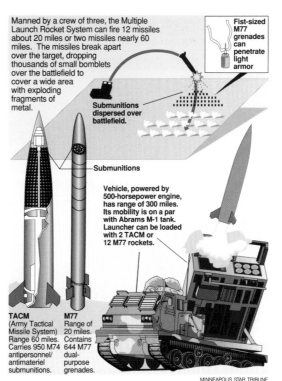

Manned by a crew of three, the Multiple Launch Rocket System can fire 12 missiles about 20 miles or two missiles nearly 60 miles. The missiles break apart over the target, dropping thousands of small bomblets over the battlefield to cover a wide area with exploding fragments of metal.

Fist-sized M77 grenades can penetrate light armor

Submunitions dispersed over battlefield.

Submunitions

Vehicle, powered by 500-horsepower engine, has range of 300 miles. Its mobility is on a par with Abrams M-1 tank. Launcher can be loaded with 2 TACM or 12 M77 rockets.

TACM
(Army Tactical Missile System). Range 60 miles. Carries 950 M74 antipersonnel/ antimateriel submunitions.

M77
Range of 20 miles. Contains 644 M77 dual-purpose grenades.

with guided weapons had allowed them to become more reliable as well as more effective. In fact, the extremely high reliability rates and hit probabilities of today's guided weapons is testimony to the hard work and persistence of the military and contractor personnel who spent years perfecting them.

The various families of guided bombs and missiles that tore up the framework of the Iraqi military machine employed a variety of guidance systems and payloads. Certainly the most common type of guided munition is the laser-guided bomb (LGB). First used in Vietnam, this weapon works on the principle of homing in on a dot of laser light aimed from a spotting aircraft. Sometimes the spotting aircraft is also the launching aircraft. Other times, the spotter aircraft lets other "carrier" aircraft deliver the weapons. Examples of aircraft equipped with laser-dot trackers during the Gulf War included the F-117A, the F-111E, the F-15E, the OV-10D, and the A-6E. LGBs were usually composed of conventional "slick" aircraft bombs (such as a guided 2,000-pound Mk-84), fitted with a guidance kit and fins.

Thousands of these bombs were assembled and dropped by allied aircraft during Desert Storm, and the effects were devastating. Used in their various forms (GBU-29, Skipper II, etc.), the LGBs were employed to destroy everything from point targets in downtown Baghdad to hardened aircraft shelters at airfields. LGBs were so versatile that, when some bunkers and shelters proved to be difficult to destroy, special hardened bomb cases were hurriedly produced in the United States and shipped to Saudi

Arabia just days after they were ordered. LGBs have been an important part of the U.S. arsenal for more than two decades, and will clearly continue to be so for many years to come. In addition, the AS-30 produced by Aerospatiale and the Hughes-GM AGM-65D Maverick air-to-surface missiles (ASM) use laser guidance to find their targets.

Another type of seeker weapon used by the allies was based upon electro-optical guidance. In this type of system, a television camera assembly is fitted to the nose of the weapon. What the seeker homes in on is the line of contrast between, for example, a dark object (such as a tank), and a light background (like the desert). The United States has a number of weapons that make use of this type of guidance, including the Rockwell GBU-15 and AGM-130, as well as the Hughes-GM AGM-65A version of the Maverick missile. The advantage of such weapons is that they can be "flown" by the launching aircraft via a television data link that allows the crew of the launching aircraft to "look" through the nose of the bomb and see what *it* sees. This was the source of many of the "greatest hits" videos shown during the allied press briefings. It should be noted, though, that laser and electro-optical guidance has been used for more than 20 years on bombs and missiles.

The one kind of guidance system that was truly new in Desert Storm was the imaging infrared (IIR) seeker. Instead of tracking a dot of laser light, or trying to home in on the edge of a shadow, IIR seekers "look" for the heat signature of vehicles and naval vessels. But instead

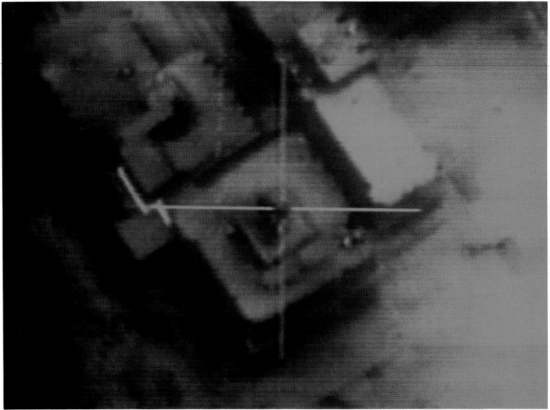

Dead center: Photographed from an F-117 Stealth fighter-bomber on January 19, 1991, a laser-guided bomb plunges through the roof of the main communications building in Baghdad, destroying it.

REUTERS/BETTMANN

of using only a single detection element, the IIR seeker uses an array of seeker elements, allowing users to see a televisionlike picture from the seeker head. It also has the advantage of being "launch-and-leave"—it requires no additional target designation once it is launched. Several allied weapons were equipped with this new type of "eye."

The first of them were the AGM-65F and AGM-65G versions of the Maverick ASM, produced by Hughes-GM and Raytheon. Used by the U.S. Air Force, Navy and Marine Corps, they were responsible for the destruction of the bulk of the Iraqi tanks and other high-priority vehicle targets. And since they could be used under any lighting or weather conditions, Maverick missiles quickly became the weapon of choice for hitting targets during the battlefield preparation phase of Desert Storm.

The other missile that utilized the IIR seeker was the amazing AGM-84E SLAM missile produced by McDonnell Douglas. Developed from that firm's highly successful A/RGM-84 Harpoon missile, the SLAM is equipped with an IIR seeker head, a GPS receiver, a 500-pound warhead, and a data link to allow it to be launched and flown to targets up to 60 miles away. The combat debut of the SLAM may have been the most spectacular "hit" of the entire war. An A-6E Intruder from the USS *John F. Kennedy* launched a pair of SLAMs several minutes apart. Controlled from an escorting A-7E Corsair II attack bomber, the first missile

was guided to blow a hole in the side of an Iraqi hydroelectric powerhouse. Several minutes later, the second SLAM flew *through* the hole blown by the first SLAM, to hit the hydroelectric turbines inside. The second SLAM sent back pictures of the turbines, as seen through the hole made by the first missile—then the picture disappeared as the generators were blown apart.

This truly was precision perfected, a dramatic demonstration of the capabilities of the new generation of "smarter" weapons that were just coming on line when Desert Storm broke out.

Another weapon that uses several types of guidance systems is the BGM-109 Tomahawk cruise missile built by General Dynamics and McDonnell Douglas. This long-range missile can be launched from ships or submarines, flies without any outside control to a target up to a 1,000 miles away, and can "bull's-eye" a target like a bunker or a radar. More than 100 of these weapons were launched from battleships, cruisers and destroyers on the first night of Desert Storm.

Each missile is equipped with a guidance system that maps the terrain it flies over and matches it with a database of terrain information stored on board. When the missile gets to the target area, an electro-optical seeker guides it to a direct hit, usually within six feet of its aim point. While hundreds of these missiles were fired during the Gulf War with great success, they still had a few problems. Mission planning took huge amounts of time and preparation. In addition, the missile had to be fired under exactly the right lighting conditions for its electro-optical seeker to "see" the targets. Even so, the Tomahawk apparently enjoyed a success rate of more than 80 percent and will be an important part of the U.S. Navy's arsenal for decades to come.

Ground-based missile systems also played an important part in Desert Storm's strikes against Iraqi targets. This meant that, for the first time, U.S. Army units could significantly add to the aerial strikes, deep behind enemy lines. One example of this newfound firepower is the ATACMS (advanced tactical missile system). The LTV (Ling Temco Vought) ATACMS missile was used in great number, to hit targets more than 100 miles from its launch point. Fired from a tracked mobile launcher, and using a precision guidance system, it lays a carpet of submunitions over an area a quarter of a mile in diameter.

In addition, the allied forces fired more than 6,000 small anti-tank missiles at Iraqi targets. These included the U.S. TOW and Hellfire, French HOT, and British Swingfire missiles. Most of these were wire guided, but the Hellfire, produced by Rockwell, is laser guided. Whenever the Iraqi ground forces showed themselves, they were met by a deluge of these weapons. Colonel Carl Fulford said the TOWS were "just phenomenal," going through the armor of the Iraqi T-72 tanks "like butter on the first shot."

A number of other guided weapons continued their distinguished combat careers in the Persian Gulf. Missiles like the British Aerospace Sea Dart (SAM) and the Sea Skua (ASM) were used with particular effect against Iraqi anti-ship missiles and naval vessels. In addition, air-to-air missiles like the Loral/Raytheon AIM-9M Sidewinder, the Raytheon AIM-7M Sparrow and the Hughes-GM AIM-54 Phoenix were used with devastating effect whenever the Iraqis provided the opportunity.

The use of smart weaponry during Desert Storm was a technical *tour de force,* but it should not be considered the norm quite yet. For the simple fact is that, while thousands of guided weapons were fired by allied forces during Desert Storm, tens of thousands of "dumb" bombs and artillery shells were also fired—frequently with the same effect and accuracy. What made that possible was the advent of "smart" launch vehicles—aircraft and ground vehicles that use their own "smart" systems to aim unguided projectiles and bombs with near-guided accuracy and effect. That was made possible by fire-control systems able to calculate the launching vehicle's or aircraft's own motion relative to the target, as well as to sample the surrounding en-

vironmental conditions (air density, temperature, humidity, target range, wind speed and direction, etc.). The fire-control system then launches the bombs or projectiles on what is a nearly perfect ballistic course to their target. Examples of smart aircraft that are capable of such feats include the LTV A-7E Corsair II, the General Dynamics F-16 A/C Fighting Falcon, the McDonnell Douglas F/A-18 Hornet and AV-8B Harrier II, and the Panavia Tornado GR1. In addition, the new generation of main battle tanks, like the General Dynamics M1A1 Abrams and the Royal Ordinance Challenger, have proven able to hit moving targets at ranges exceeding one mile while moving at high speed themselves. These aircraft and vehicles proved capable of incredible weapons accuracy using "dumb" ordinance and provided a significant cost advantage over guided weapons alone during Desert Storm.

Like their allied opponents, the Iraqi forces had stocked up on a variety of guided weapons during the years leading to the Persian Gulf War, but unlike their coalition counterparts, the Iraqi weapons were almost totally ineffective. The reason for this lack of effectiveness is simple: the complete destruction of the Iraqi command and control network, as well as the supporting sensor systems, made it impossible to effectively employ that nation's guided weapons. And whenever an Iraqi unit managed to get off a shot, whether it was a Scud missile launcher or a SAM battery, it was quickly located, hunted down and destroyed by allied forces. In fact, in the later stages of Desert Storm, the very act of "lighting off" a radar or firing a weapon was tantamount to asking to be killed by the nearest allied unit. Because of Iraq's failure to protect its sensor network and its lines of communications, the fourth-largest military machine in the world would end up being routed in just 100 hours of light ground fighting.

"The way of the future is how smart you are in employing your weapons systems," cautions U.S. Air Force Colonel Ralph Cossa of the National Defense University. "I don't think you can say smart weapons won the war, per se. However, in many key areas, they certainly made the difference. The combined weaponry—air, ground and sea—is obviously going to change the way we pursue the traditional elements of warfare. We did not fight the Vietnam War again. We developed a strategy that maximized the abilities of the systems that were in the theater of operations."

Perhaps the real wonder of it all is that the Kuwaiti people were liberated by the most incredible military force in history—a force that rode in swinging the sword of technology. □

TELLING THE STORY

ED BAILEY, U.S. NAVY

Veteran AP photographer and naval reservist Ed Bailey was called to active duty during the war. He worried about protecting his camera and film in the desert battlefield.
FAR RIGHT: CNN's Peter Arnett stirred controversy and raised questions about journalistic priorities with his reports from Baghdad—all done under the supervision of the Iraqi government.

HALF A MILE downstream there were two eruptions and then a third, close together. The first two looked like some giant had thrown a huge basket of flaming golden oranges high in the air. The third was just a balloon of fire enclosed in black smoke above the housetops." A quote from Cable Network News' Peter Arnett with another scoop from Baghdad? No.

That was Edward R. Murrow reporting the bombing of London on October 10, 1940. Murrow represented the first wave of the electronic media in wartime, and despite similarities between his style and Arnett's, the Gulf War represented a dramatic change in direction for war news coverage—in print as well as in the electronic media.

During Desert Storm, "pool" coverage was the operative word. The pool, an arrangement set up by the military and agreed to in advance by a number of American media executives, appeared to be a compromise between the liberal access granted the media in Vietnam and the total news blackout of the Granada invasion of 1983. The pool was designed to improve news coverage, strengthen the security of military operations, and protect reporters (in March 1990 an Iranian journalist for the British media, Farzad Bazoft, was hanged for being found too near an Iraqi military facility). Under the new system, the media in Saudi Arabia were restricted to pool coverage under the watchful eyes of military "escorts." The escorts controlled the movements of their charges and—on some occa-

COPYRIGHT, 1991, CNN, INC.

sions—told them who to interview and what questions to ask.

Most of the 700-plus media people registered with the U.S. military's Joint Information Bureau in Dhahran, Saudi Arabia, followed the pool's structure. These included seasoned war correspondents like *U.S. News & World Report*'s Joe Galloway, who a quarter-century earlier had covered the first major battle of the Vietnam War; the *Washington Post*'s Rick Atkinson and Molly Moore; and the *Los Angeles Times*' John Broder and Melissa Healy. There were also a goodly number of neophytes who knew little or nothing about the military. The newcomers' ignorance was embarrassingly obvious in the questions they asked at pool press briefings.

"Pool-busters," as maverick reporters came to be known, risked arrest or worse in pursuit of their stories. One, Elizabeth O. Colton, a special correspondent for Mutual Broadcasting/NBC Radio News, was near the Kuwaiti border on February 26, 1991, when 11 Iraqi soldiers stepped out from their cover, laid down their weapons and surrendered to her. Before long, close to 90 others did the same. Colton, who carried only a pocket camera, tape recorder and canteen, directed the group to a nearby staging area for prisoners of war.

Another pool-buster, ABC's Forrest Sawyer, covered some of the first desertions by Iraqi troops and obtained some rare combat pictures. Still another was CBS reporter Bob Simon. Simon and his crew were captured by Iraqis near the Kuwaiti border and spent six weeks in captivity before Soviet mediators negotiated their release.

When CNN's Peter Arnett and Bernard Shaw began their live coverage of the bombs falling on Baghdad on January 16, 1991, the event came to be called "The night the networks died." The reason CNN stayed on the air long after ABC, CBS and NBC were cut off was that, long before, CNN had laid the groundwork with information officials in dozens of countries. At the Al Rashid Hotel in Baghdad, other networks relied on house phone lines, while CNN used a much less vulnerable, specially installed line with satellite hookup.

Arnett was allowed by the Iraqis to stay on in Baghdad, and even to interview Saddam Hussein. Although he maintained that he limited his coverage to what he could "see, hear or smell," some of his harshest critics branded him as traitorous, especially when he reported on the bombing of a suspected poison gas factory that the Iraqis claimed was actually a baby food plant, and when he reported on the destruction of an alleged civilian air-raid shelter in what was thought to be an Iraqi command center.

Despite the controversy over CNN's presence in Baghdad, both the Iraqi and allied commands relied on it for war updates. Lt. Gen. Charles Horner, the coalition's supreme air commander, told one reporter: "You know, some people are mad at CNN. I used it. Did the attack go on time? Did it hit the target? Things like that."

At war's end, the question of whether or not a journalist can, or should, remain neutral and objective during a war was hardly any closer to being definitively answered. "Commendable dispassion should not be confused with neutrality," commented *Newsweek*'s Jonathan Alter. "In a war like this one, full 'objectivity' is not only impossible, it's dishonest. No reporter can be expected to resolve whether he is a journalist first or an American. He (or she) is some combination of the two." □

U.S. NAVY

U.S. NAVY

ABOVE: Tom Brokaw interviews General H. Norman Schwarzkopf. Much of the American press reported events through ''pool'' coverage, supervised and controlled by the military. LEFT: Dan Rather joins the troops. Less familiar names among the press often got more interesting stories—albeit at no small risk to themselves—when they wandered farther afield and into harm's way.

CHAPTER EIGHT

AERIAL AVALANCHE

LAURENT REBOURS, AP/LASERCOLOR

Saudi Royal Air Force F-15 pilot Captain Ayedh al-Shamrani meets the press after downing two Iraqi Mirage F1s on January 24, 1991.

I T LOOKS LIKE a Fourth of July display at the Washington Monument. The sky is just brightly lighted with all these tracer rounds. Some are red. Some are white. We can see explosions. You know, air-burst explosions from these weapons...Uh-oh! Oop! Now there's a huge fire that we've just seen that is due west of our position. And we just heard...Whoa! Holy Cow! That was a large air burst that we saw. It was filling the sky."

Those words were heard by many Americans as they watched Cable News Network's John Holliman, looking out a window of the Al-Rashid Hotel in downtown Baghdad, report the first coalition attack early on the morning of January 17. Tomahawk missiles and aircraft ranging from Stealth fighters to British Tornados struck the Iraqi capital, blasting vital communications links and other military targets.

In Washington, D.C., half a world away, it was 7:06 on the night of January 16 when President George Bush entered the White House press briefing room and announced: "The liberation of Kuwait has begun."

The United Nations-sanctioned war to come would be the first in history to be won in such large measure by air power. During the first day of the conflict, the allies dropped more than 2,200 tons of high explosives and flew more than 1,000 missions. In the days that followed, the average number of missions would rise to 2,000-3,000. So much ordnance was expended that coalition supply lines would be strained to keep up.

The methodology of the destructive air campaign was the work of Air Force Lt. Gen. Charles Horner, a onetime Vietnam fighter pilot who had been placed in command of all air operations during Desert Shield. Horner's plan for the initial attacks called for coordinated strikes by a variety of aircraft from all three U.S. military air arms, along with air forces of other members of the coalition arrayed against Iraq. Even though final victory would come only after a lightning-fast 100-hour ground war, the Iraqi ground forces were quickly brought to their knees by the intensity of coalition air assaults.

According to the Pentagon, the first shots actually fired in Desert Storm were missiles launched by the AH-64 helicopter gunships of Task Force Normandy, a U.S. Army special operations mission aimed at destroying a defense early-warning radar site "deep in western Iraq." The Normandy force attacked at 2:58 a.m. local time, on the 17th. Within minutes, the fixed-wing attack force of Desert Storm poured through the gap in the defenses left open by the raid and headed for targets throughout Iraq.

First across the border were some 30 Stealth fighter-bombers. These U.S. Air Force F-117 Nighthawk attack aircraft, designed to be invisible to radar, were sent in to strike Iraqi communications centers and command headquarters in and around Baghdad in the immediate wake of Tomahawk cruise missile attacks. Stealth technology proved so effective that the F-117s were hitting their targets before the Iraqis even knew they were in their airspace. The Stealth

The crew of an F-15E Strike Eagle of the 4th Tactical Fighter Wing from Beale AFB prepare to refuel from a KC-135 over the Saudi Arabian desert.

HANS DEFFNER, USAF

Baghdad residents inspect the damage to their building after an allied air raid in February 1991. The purpose of precision bombing was to minimize damage to non-strategic targets—and to minimize Saddam Hussein's ability to exploit it for propaganda purposes—but some civilian casualties were inevitable.

fighter-bombers from the 37th Tactical Fighter Wing reportedly flew 95 percent of all Desert Storm missions against the Iraqi capital, each time hitting their targets with unprecedented accuracy. F-117 crews were able to put their bombs into *individual rooms* in the targeted buildings. As Colonel Alton Whitely put it: "You pick precisely which target you want...the men's room or the ladies' room."

One of the first targets hit by the Stealth fighter-bombers was the AT&T facility in downtown Baghdad, a key element in the Iraqi communications network. Other F-117 targets included buildings known to be used by Saddam Hussein; one video of an F-117 attack showed a laser-guided bomb flying right through the skylight of a building, then destroying the structure that sometimes served to house the Iraqi strongman. Reinforced structures such as aircraft hangars and command centers were subjected to multiple F-117 attacks, with successive bombs aimed at the same point to penetrate the reinforced concrete and steel that served to render such buildings resistant to conventional attack.

Behind the F-117s came F-15C Eagles, perhaps the best all-around air-superiority fighters now in operation, to clear the skies of any enemy interceptors. Vietnam-era F-4Gs in the "Wild Weasel" configuration attacked surface-to-air missile (SAM) sites throughout the country.

Next came an array of ground-attack aircraft flown by Americans and their partners in the air offensive—Saudi Arabia, Great Britain, France, Italy, Canada, and Kuwaiti exiles. The principal participating aircraft were U.S. Air Force F-111s, F-16s and two-man F-15E Strike Eagles; U.S. Navy A-6s, A-7s and F/A-18s (also flown by U.S. Marines and the Canadian armed forces); U.S. Marine AV-8Bs (the versatile verti-

cal takeoff [VTO] aircraft also flown by British pilots); and the British Tornados, with their special mission of airfield attack. Some of the Tornados were operated by Italian and Saudi Arabian pilots. (The Italians assembled a unit of 10 Tornados.) In addition to these ground-attack planes, six Italian RF-104Gs flew high-speed reconnaissance missions along the northern Iraqi border with Turkey, and Italian C-130s flew 135 supply missions for the coalition forces. Other coalition aircraft included French Mirages, British Jaguars, and F-5 "Freedom Fighters" flown by Bahraini and Kuwaiti pilots.

This international lineup of aircraft potentially could have led to confusion, with planes jamming or shooting one another. During the five months of waiting for the air offensive to begin, however, the commanders had enough

time to plan and practice. This preparation no doubt contributed to the immediate success of the air raids, as did the good weather. The air war began on a night that was clear and dark—the right conditions for the night-vision equipment used on coalition fighter-bombers and for cruise missiles. When the weather turned cloudy after the first 36 hours, some coalition planes—despite being loaded with "all weather" devices—were forced to return to base without dropping their bombs. But the setback was only minor; little else went wrong for the allied air forces.

"The first week of the war, called Phase I, involved softening up defensive sites, bridges, airfields, some road systems, and power plants," said Captain Mark A. Melin, a Marine A-6E Intruder pilot. "These were up north. For the first few days of the air war, we dealt primarily with Baghdad and Basra—and all the area in between. We were based out of Bahrain, so it takes 20 minutes till you go 'feet dry' to the land, right on up to the target area. We were under heavy triple-A [anti-aircraft artillery] for 20 minutes. Everywhere you looked there was fire coming up at you. Once you released your bombs and left the target area, it seemed like an eternity before you returned to base. In addition, there were numerous SAMS."

The jobs of Captain Melin and the other bomber pilots were made easier by the work done by the U.S. Navy's EA-6B Prowlers, electronic countermeasures (ECM) aircraft that used electronic systems to locate and jam Iraqi air defense radars.

Iraqi anti-aircraft fire and tracers lace the night sky over downtown Baghdad on January 17 as the air campaign begins.

103

A U.S. Navy F-14 from the carrier Saratoga extends its
wings to refuel from a United States Air Force KC-135
during a Desert Storm mission.

CHRIS PUTMAN, USAF

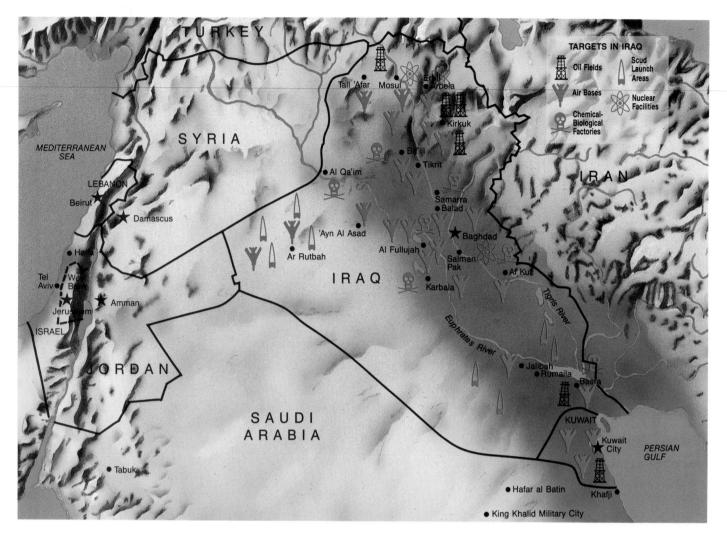

The legend reads:

TARGETS IN IRAQ

- Oil Fields
- Air Bases
- Chemical-Biological Factories
- Scud Launch Areas
- Nuclear Facilities

The first wave of allied air attacks eliminated Iraqi aerial opposition—more by the psychological crippling of its air force personnel than by the destruction of their air bases. Thus, given a freer hand, the coalition's bombers went after other strategic targets, with high priority given to seeking out and taking out Iraq's elusive mobile Scud missile launchers.

"I attribute our minimal losses to our EA-6Bs," Melin said. "They were a valuable asset. Their jamming capabilities completely shut down enemy radar. The Iraqis had to rely on visual sighting to fire, and in many cases they didn't have the time."

The strike aircraft were also defended by U.S. Air Force ECM aircraft, EF-111 Ravens and EC-130s, whose job was to confuse enemy radar operators with electrical noise. At least one such ECM plane, however, did even more than that. An EF-111A Raven piloted by Air Force Captain Jim Denton managed to record one of the first "kills" of the Gulf War even though the plane carries no weapons. It happened over an airfield in western Iraq—an Iraqi Mirage F1 launched an air-to-air missile at Denton's Raven. By using chaff and flares to confuse the missile's heat-seeking guidance system and then throwing his plane into a dive and hard turn, Denton avoided the missile. While trying to line up a second shot, the Iraqi pilot apparently lost control of his Mirage and crashed.

One type of strike aircraft, the aging but still mighty B-52, carries its own ECM equipment. That the huge eight-engine bombers were used in the initial air attacks at all was testimony

to the confidence of the allied planners in the effectiveness of ECM operations. Command and control, along with aircraft early warning, was provided by Air Force E-3 and Navy E-2C AWACS (airborne warning and control system), whose contribution to Desert Storm is considered to have been crucial. No aircraft were reported lost on the first missions. During the first 48 hours of the air war, there were 3,100 combat sorties, yet only eight allied aircraft were lost and only one pilot was reported killed in action.

"The Iraqis possessed quite a bit of AA [anti-aircraft] capability," said U.S. Air Force Colonel Ralph Cossa of the National Defense University. "They had a large number of SAMs, but the SAMs rely on radar. Both the Wild Weasels and the jamming made the SAMs ineffective. This puts you into the AAA [anti-aircraft artillery] category. It's my understanding that the Iraqis put up a wall of flak hoping one of our aircraft would fly into it. Their early-warning systems were so depleted that they didn't know aircraft were approaching. And not only with the F-117 Stealth bombers, but other planes as well. The first thing you would hear was bombs dropping, the second thing was the air raid siren, and the third thing was the AAA fire. By that time, the only thing AAA is going to do is fall back down on the ground and injure passers-by."

With Iraq's air defenses befuddled, bombs and air-launched missiles slammed into target after target—airfields and command centers of the Iraqi air force, anti-aircraft defenses, Scud missile launch sites, munitions plants (especially those suspected of making chemical weapons), storage centers and lines of communication such as railroads, highways and bridges. Reports at war's end indicated that Iraq was "bombed back to the pre-industrial age," with no bridges left standing, all electrical power stations out of service and every factory, oil refinery and other means of production destroyed or heavily damaged. The coalition air forces made the most of their technological advantages, but laser-guided "smart" bombs that hit targets with unprecedented accuracy only worked because the crews performed well—delivering the bombs and then remaining in the vicinity while directing beams of laser energy on the targets until the targets were hit.

The fighter pilots of all the coalition nations readily donned the mystique that has typically surrounded such men since World War I. For example, television viewers early in the air war saw the U.S. Air Force pilot, strolling toward his airplane, who drawled, "I thank God that I was born in a free country, that I have a good woman at home and that He made me an American fighter pilot."

Another one of the primary targets during the allied air offensive was the Iraqi air force. The first allied pilot to shoot down an Iraqi aircraft, U.S. Air Force Captain Steve Tate, was leading a flight of four F-15s escorting strike aircraft against targets near Baghdad when he picked up what he at first thought was a SAM. "My Number Three had just turned south and I was headed northeast. I don't know if the bogey was after him. I locked him up, confirmed he was hostile and fired a missile. . . .When the airplane exploded, the whole sky lit up. It burned all the way to the ground, then blew up."

On two occasions U.S. Air Force F-15 crews rolled up multiple victories against Iraqi aircraft. One pair of F-15s downed three MiG-23s and a Mirage F1. In another engagement, two F-15s shot down two MiG-21s and two Su-25s. Along with American aircraft and crews, air crews from allied air forces scored some remarkable victories. One F-15 pilot with the Royal Saudi Air Force, Captain Ayedh al-Shamrani, was credited with shooting down two Iraqi Mirage F1s while flying as one of a four-plane patrol near the Kuwaiti border. Upon returning to his base in Dhahran, Shamrani received a hero's welcome. Modestly, the victorious pilot commented, "It was my day."

ITALIAN AIR FORCE

CROWN COPYRIGHT, MINISTRY OF DEFENSE

U.S. AIR FORCE

TOP: *Two of 10 Panavia Tornados fielded by the Italian air force set out on a strike. The Italians flew 226 combat missions and lost only one airplane, whose two-man crew was captured and later returned by the Iraqis.*
ABOVE: *A Royal Air Force Jaguar prepares for a tactical ground attack mission into Iraqi territory.*
LEFT: *The U.S. Army's tactical tankbuster: An AH-64 Apache helicopter attached to XVIII Corps.*

Specialist Eugene Browne drags a refueling hose to a thirsty A-10.

PREVIOUS PAGE: An inside look at the busy cockpit of a KC-135 of the 1705th Air Refueling Squadron as 1st Lt. Orlando Nunez lines up with an F-16 on the second day of the air offensive.

It was certainly more than a matter of it being his "day." Eager to apply years of buildup, modernization and training, the Royal Saudi Air Force flew a total of more than 12,000 sorties in the weeks that followed Shamrani's success. Only the U.S. pilots flew more sorties; the Saudis flew double the number flown by the British.

International teamwork often came into play, as noted by Brig. Gen. Turki bin Nasser, air base commander at Dhahran: "We found that all of them worked together—Saudi and British fighter-bombers, escorted by Saudi and American F-15s, supported by American F-111s or British Tornados for radar suppression—it worked perfectly, no glitches." Just two losses were reported in the course of those Saudi sorties: a Northrop F-5 went down over Iraq and a Tornado suffered mechanical problems but still managed to make a soft crash-landing in the sand without incurring major damage.

"I was very impressed by the [Royal] Saudi Air Force," said American Colonel Ralph Cossa. "Flying an air force fighter in Saudi society is a very prestigious thing. A pilot would be of the elite, probably a member of the royal family. For example, Prince Bandar, ambassador to the U.S., was trained here [in the United States]."

British Tornado pilots earned accolades for their low-altitude attacks on the Iraqi airfields to deliver their special JP-233 cluster bombs, powerful weapons especially designed for use against such airfields. To deliver the weapons, the Royal Air Force pilots had to come in low, facing antiaircraft fire the pilots referred to as "curtains of death." Conversely, most American crews attacked from altitudes above the range of small-arms fire and smaller caliber anti-aircraft fire.

While 14 French Mirage 2000 fighters flew more than 600 sorties as part of Saudi Arabia's air defense or to escort the ground attack aircraft, Jaguars carried out low-level attacks against targets in Kuwait. Ironically, one French target was a munitions depot near Kuwait City where intelligence sources believed the Iraqis had stashed French-made Exocet missiles. French pilots flew Jaguars, along with six Mirage F1CRs, on more than 850 missions into Iraq against elements of the Republican Guard. One French pilot was wounded and four aircraft damaged by enemy AAA fire during these missions.

Italian pilots flew 226 missions against Iraqi targets, losing one Tornado to AAA on January 18—its pilot, *Maggiore* Bellini, and its navigator, *Capitano* Cocciolone, ejected, were taken prisoner, and released after the war. Kuwait's air

ROSE REYNOLDS, USAF

force-in-exile lost one plane during a ground attack mission. The pilot reportedly was rescued by Kuwaiti freedom fighters.

While the coalition fighter pilots constantly looked for a fight once the air war began, in most instances the Iraqi pilots either refused to or were ordered not to fight. When Iraqi fighters did decide to engage, they were usually disposed of in short order. A total of 36 Iraqi aircraft were shot down before large numbers fled the combat zone for safe havens in "neutral" Iran. Coalition totals for the conflict were 42 Iraqi aircraft shot down and 81 destroyed on the ground. American losses, all from ground fire, were 27 fixed-wing aircraft and five helicopters; other allied losses were nine fixed-wing aircraft.

The casualty rate among coalition airmen was surprisingly low, but the danger was always there—some airmen did die, some were taken into captivity. Iraqi television broadcast footage of 10 captured allied airmen—two British, one Italian, one Kuwaiti and six Americans.

"When Saddam Hussein paraded our pilots on TV it was on the third or fourth day of the war," said Captain Steve Olds, an F-15C pilot with the 27th Tactical Fighter Squadron, 1st Tactical Fighter Wing. "That's when reality set in for me. You think to yourself: My God, this could be me. It was then I knew it wasn't going to be over in two or three days."

Another typical response came from Captain Roger Vincent, also an F-15C pilot with the same unit: "If Saddam Hussein thought displaying our POWs like that was going to break our will, he was dead wrong. If anything, it

The Iraqi tankers' worst nightmare: An A-10 Thunderbolt II bores in on a target during Operation Desert Storm.

ROBERT A. ELLIOTT, U.S. ARMY

Surgical amputation: A bridge in An Nasiriyah, Iraq, destroyed by air attack. The most decisive tactical results of the bombing campaign were to effectively sever supply and communication lines to Iraqi forces in Kuwait.

made our resolve even greater. We were angry and flew with more determination."

The initial air attacks of Desert Storm were so successful that many Americans thought the war would be over in less than a week, that Saddam Hussein would order his troops out of Kuwait. This ideal scenario did not materialize because Saddam apparently was of the opinion that he could wait out the airstrikes and then inflict heavy casualties against coalition ground forces. With Saddam holding out for the "mother of all battles" and with Iraq's air force and command and control apparatus neutralized, the air war entered Phase II.

"Our standard load for Phase I was laser-guided bombs and the 2,000-pound iron bombs," said the A-6E Intruder pilot Captain Melin. "Phases II and III were the softening up ones, and Phase IV was the ground war. So, we switched to Mk-82 iron bombs and Mk-20 Rockeye [a 500-pound cluster bomb used against tanks], carrying between 12 to 16 each. And we always carried at least one laser-guided bomb. If we found a decent target, and needed pinpoint accuracy, we had it on hand.

"The Rockeye was a great area weapon to drop on trenches, artillery positions, revetted tanks, and vehicles on the road. It worked out better than we expected. It does a lot of damage which we found out about later in talking to prisoners and intelligence people.

"The AAA diminished somewhat during Phases II and III because they were running low on ammo. We were hitting their ammunition sites, and their logistical support was extremely limited because we controlled the access roads. So, they became much more disciplined as a result of these limitations. They didn't fire randomly, but rather waited for select targets. In the KTO [Kuwaiti theater of operations], cer-

tain areas had heavy concentration of AAA fire, so we planned our tactics to stay out of the envelope."

In the middle phases of Desert Storm, General Horner's airmen turned their attention toward the Iraqi ground forces inside Kuwait and in southern Iraq. Estimates of Iraqi losses place the number at about 100,000, and the vast majority of these were killed by airstrikes. Airstrikes against ground forces dated from the opening hours of Desert Storm when an assortment of coalition aircraft began hitting enemy positions in occupied Kuwait and just inside Iraq, even as others were striking targets farther north. As the air war intensified, and as the numbers of targets in Iraq dwindled, more and more missions were flown against Iraqi ground forces.

Strike aircraft from all the services and coalition air forces were directed against Iraqi positions in Kuwait and southern Iraq, but the one

aircraft most effective in the ground attack role was the U.S. Air Force's A-10 Thunderbolt II, more commonly known as the "Warthog." Conceived late in the Vietnam War era for the mission of killing tanks in a protracted European conventional war with Communist-bloc forces, the A-10 had seen much controversy in its decade and a half of service. Within the Air Force, the A-10 was considered by many to lack adequate survivability in a high-threat environment, primarily because of its relatively slow speeds (which are still far in excess of those of the speediest helicopter).

Desert Storm, however, did not turn out to be a "high-threat" theater of war because Iraqi aircraft were put out of commission swiftly or else left the field entirely, flying to Iran. Without air opposition, A-10 crews were able to operate against Iraqi tanks and other armored vehicles and very quickly established for them-

selves a highly visible role in the air war. Although slow compared to high-performance fighters, the A-10 is highly maneuverable, with a very short turning radius that allows its pilots to remain in the immediate vicinity of its target while positioning for subsequent attacks. An internally mounted 30mm cannon firing uranium-encased shells (up to 70 rounds a second) is the Warthog's primary weapon against tanks. The heavy rounds penetrate the tank's armor before detonating, usually killing the occupants and destroying the inner workings of the vehicle in the process. A-10s also carry the Maverick, a TV- or infrared-guided missile designed for use against tanks and other armored vehicles.

The A-10 was one of the coalition aircraft that proved its worth operating during the night. Even before the conflict began, night missions were recognized as crucial to the success of the

An F-117 Nighthawk of the 32nd Tactical Fighter Wing. F-117s brought their stealth capabilities into play during the crucial first day's strikes.

Venerable veteran of the Cold War and Vietnam—and still devastatingly effective—a United States Air Force B-52 assigned to the 1708th Bomb Wing departs on a daytime bombing mission.

CHRIS PUTNAM, USAF

air campaign. F-117 missions operated mostly at night, while a variety of aircraft flew both night and day missions. The 355th Tactical Fighter Squadron, an A-10 unit, was assigned exclusively to night-attack missions and performed admirably against Iraqi armored forces. Flying two and three sorties each night, the A-10 crews directed their attention primarily against the Russian-made T-72 tanks that were the backbone of the Republican Guard. One evening's work accounted for a column of 24 tanks put out of commission. Army AH-64 Apache helicopters were also used in night attacks and would play a major role in battling Iraqi tanks once the ground war was launched.

By concentrating more and more upon the massed Iraqi forces inside and near Kuwait as the ground war appproached, coalition fliers faced increased danger. Up north, the defenses around Baghdad were more or less neutralized, and the most the allied fliers had to contend with was the flak produced by indiscriminate firing. Iraq's long-range radar had been crippled and Iraq's SAM batteries were put out of action by F-4G Wild Weasels, which fired high-speed anti-radiation missiles (HARMs) that used specially designed shrapnel to disable the SAM's radar antennas. Coalition aircraft operating above 10,000 feet were out of range of most anti-aircraft weaponry. But attacking ground forces to the south meant flying low and sometimes slow in an environment where every enemy soldier with an automatic rifle was in a position to knock down an airplane or helicopter.

Fighter pilots considered small-arms fire to be the most deadly of all the defenses they faced in Desert Storm. Iraqi ground forces were also armed with shoulder-fired anti-aircraft missiles, a weapon designed especially for use against helicopters and slower moving, low-flying aircraft. Many of the fliers who were taken prisoner were shot down over Kuwait, often in slower-moving observation aircraft such as the OV-10. A U.S. Air Force AC-130 gunship crashed into the sea, with the loss of all 14 men aboard, evidently after being hit by a missile over Kuwait. It was this kind of threat that limited helicopter operations against the Iraqis during the first weeks of the air war.

Troops of Saddam's vaunted Republican Guard found themselves the object of attack after attack. Coalition forces used tactics held over from Vietnam and even World War II, including "carpet bombing" by B-52s: a single formation of three B-52s sowing a 1,000-by-3,000-yard swath of destruction, inside of which 300,000 pounds of high explosives created a moonscape. Colonel Ralph Cossa suggested that B-52 bombing methods over the deserts of the Gulf were not quite the same as the methods over

the jungles of Vietnam: "The venerable B-52s were looking at specific targets on the ground and bombing in football-field-size quadrants. This was not carpet bombing. However, it certainly wasn't precision bombing or laser-guided operations—but it wasn't indiscriminate either. It was militarily as well as psychologically significant. I'm thankful for the fact that I haven't had that experience. Anyone I've seen or interviewed who has been through a B-52 strike has been left with an indelible mark upon them. And I'm sure they've attributed the massive desertions, surrenders and defections to the B-52s."

The U.S. Air Force also resurrected another powerful weapon left over from Vietnam—the BLU-82 "Daisy Cutter." Developed in 1970 as a follow-on to ancient 10,000-pound bombs developed for use with B-36 bombers in the 1950s and then used in Vietnam to clear helicopter landing zones, the BLU-82 is essentially a 15,000-pound tank filled with a slurry mixture of TNT and propane. Dropped from C-130 transports, the Daisy Cutter is a highly effective weapon against troop concentrations. According to some news reports, BLU-82s were incorporated to detonate mines inside Kuwait, but it was not confirmed that they were used directly against troops.

In any case, the Iraqi troops had enough to worry about from heavily armed F-16s, called "killer bees." They repeatedly buzzed the terrain to destroy any moving targets. By scanning with infrared detectors at night, the pilots became efficient at finding the camouflaged and dug-in Iraqi tanks. Cautious Iraqi tank crews dug their tanks deeper into the sand—some of the fighting machines were buried so deeply that they were of no use when it came time for battle, and some crews reportedly suffocated inside after sandstorms. By the middle of February, enemy tanks were being killed at the rate of 100 per day.

The devastation of Iraqi ground weaponry was graphically described by Captain Mike "Disco" Beguelin, of Marine Squadron VMA-542, who flew an AV-8B Harrier: "It was the highway to hell! I refer to it as the Marianas Turkey Shoot of the Gulf War. There were two roads that left Kuwait and went into Iraq. One went due north and the other came out of the cloverleaf and went toward Bubiyan Island. The Iraqis' tanks had blocking positions at Al Jahrah and Al Salem.

"When I went up, it was sunrise and I was with my wingman, Greg Bogart. We had a fast FAC [forward air controller] with us, an F-18, who marked the targets by dropping some 'Willie Pete' [white phosphorus]. We went in and dropped some Rockeye on them. We returned to base, rearmed, and flew back. We had what

we call Alpha Points all over the country. It was just a designated spot they tell you to go to and await a mission. So you'd go to Alpha Point so-and-so, and hold."

American, British and Saudi C-130 crews were heavily involved in resupplying forward units throughout the campaign, in some cases landing on sections of highway that had been designated as forward airfields by engineers in order to deliver their cargo "as far forward as possible." Hundreds of dirt runways built to accommodate petroleum-exploration teams dot the landscape of Iraq and Kuwait. These runways were to play a major part in allied strategy for the invasion, each serving as a forward supply base into which the four-engine turboprop transports could operate.

When the much-feared ground war finally was launched in late February, American and allied troops entered Kuwait only to find an enemy whose will to fight had virtually disappeared. Certainly, there would be some ground battles, particularly when allied forces encountered units of the Republican Guard, but for the most part, the Iraqi forces were defeated before the ground war even began. Demoralized by six weeks of incessant bombing, Iraqi front-line soldiers surrendered in waves. The air campaign had effectively disrupted the enemy's lines of communication and rendered the weary Iraqi troops vir-

tually helpless. Without reconnaissance flights, Iraq never had a clear idea of the disposition of coalition ground forces until it was too late.

The start of Phase IV, the ground war, brought on a few new difficulties for coalition pilots such as Captain Beguelin.

"Once the ground war started, we had to fly low for our close air support missions," he said. "It made us more vulnerable to AAA, but that's our job—to support the ground troops. I think every Harrier that was hit got popped by a hand-held. They had SA-7s, SA-14s and SA-16s."

One illustration of the effectiveness of the air campaign is that more than 4,000 of the 4,200 tanks operated by the Iraqis were destroyed or captured. Evaluation teams, hoping to glean information from the tanks, found that in nearly every case the vehicles had been destroyed. Out of 4,000, only five were found to still be intact.

Clearly, the fiercest aerial bombardment in history—dozens of different warplanes ranging from the rapid, precise F-117 to the slow-flying but potent A-10 were flown in more than 100,000 sorties by a multinational cast of pilots—was necessary for the *swift* defeat of Saddam Hussein's forces. It is also certain that few political powers on earth today possess the technology and resources to withstand the kind of aggressive air war that was introduced to the world by Desert Storm. □

A Marine F/A-18 returns after a bombing mission on enemy targets on February 4, 1991, as the air blitz goes into its third week.

CHAPTER NINE

DIVERSION AT KHAFJI

COURTESY CAPTAIN JAMES R. BRADEN

Captain Mohammed of the 5th Battalion, 2nd SANG (Saudi Arabian National Guard), with U.S. Marine Captain D.R. Kleinsmith, in front of a Saudi V-150 Commando armored car.

AT NOON (Saudi time) on January 30, Nabila Megalli, an Egyptian reporter for The Associated Press stationed at Al Manamah in Bahrain, telephoned the Khafji Beach Hotel to inquire about an Iraqi claim that its missiles had set fire to oil refineries in the small coastal town. The answer she got on the other end of the line sounded like a joke: "We are Iraqi soldiers." Megalli laughed and got back to the business at hand.

"Fine, fine, can you please tell me if there is a fire at the refinery?"

The man at the other end, now joined by a comrade, replied by trying to recognize the accent of her Arabic. "Who are you? Who are you? Huh? Who? What, Egyptian?"

Megalli began to suspect that something was wrong. "Who are *you?*"

"We are with Saddam, with Arabism," shouted the Iraqi, who then added a few choice insults toward Egypt. Then, Megalli heard an out-of-breath voice in the background, and a man shout: "What fire? What fire? We don't see anything!"

His comrade said, "See you in Jerusalem," and then the line went dead.

Prior to January 29, 1991, it had seemed as if the coalition forces were having things entirely their own way. Air superiority over Kuwait and Iraq—even over Baghdad—had been achieved within 24 hours of the first air attacks, and the flying of first-line Iraqi aircraft to Iran for internment seemed to indicate that Saddam Hussein had conceded the air to the coalition forces.

Over the next 12 days, the Iraqi ground forces hunkered down in their underground revetments to endure an almost incessant pounding from the air. Meanwhile, General H. Norman Schwarzkopf and the allied staff laid their plans for the ground offensive to come, while military experts on television publicly speculated on what they *thought* the strategy would be.

Under those circumstances, it would seem that Saddam Hussein felt compelled to do *something* to give Iraq some say in these proceedings, to shore up the flagging morale of his troops and to awake his opponents from their complacency with a reminder from Winston Churchill: "However absorbed a commander

may be in the elaboration of his own thoughts, it is sometimes necessary to take the enemy into account."

The decision to assault Khafji could not have had any serious military objective in mind. The Iraqi forces involved were too small to follow up the attack with any significant flanking movement against the allied armies, and their equipment—T-54, T-55 and T-59 tanks, Soviet-built BTR-60 and Chinese-built Type 63 APCs (armored personnel carriers)—was not the latest in the Iraqi inventory. (The best equipment was farther behind the lines, with the Republican Guards, who were not committed to the thrust against Khafji, either.) If anything, it was evi-

dently hoped that this unexpected reminder that the Iraqi army still had teeth might throw the allied invasion plans off balance, and gain some political points with those parties still sympathetic to Saddam.

If Saddam had ordered the move on Khafji to achieve surprise for surprise's own sake, he briefly succeeded. On the night of January 29, four Iraqi battalions, comprising about 2,000 troops and 80 tanks, came out to fight over a 50-mile section of front and, by midnight, had occupied the abandoned city on the Saudi side of the border. Although there was no significant resistance awaiting them in town, their movement through thousands of mines and

Coming under Iraqi fire, U.S. Marines take cover behind and around their "humvee" multipurpose vehicle while one returns fire with his .50-caliber machine gun during the fight for Khafji, January 31, 1991.

Reacting swiftly to the Iraqi incursion into their territory, Saudi tankers move up to the border in their French-built, AMX-30 tanks on January 30.

other fortifications showed that the Iraqis possessed night-vision and infrared equipment, and were capable of coordinating complicated nighttime maneuvers. With Khafji's occupation a *fait accompli*, Radio Baghdad trumpeted: "Oh Iraqis! Oh Arabs! Oh Muslims who believe in justice! Your faithful and courageous ground forces have moved to teach the aggressors the lessons they deserve!"

Marine Captain Jim Braden of 1st ANGLICO (Air Naval Gunfire Liaison Company) was attached to the 2nd SANG (Saudi Arabian National Guard) on the night of January 28, when he observed two battalion-sized Iraqi units emerge from the Wafra forest area, north of the Kuwaiti border, and diverge in both an easterly and westerly direction. Air attacks were called in against them, and they withdrew.

"On the next night," Braden reported, "the exact same pattern of movement began to un-

fold. Again, we called in airstrikes on them but this time we received incoming artillery rounds and rockets on our border OPs [observation posts]. Then, more armored vehicles revealed themselves and additional rocket and artillery fire was taken in and around the Khafji area.

"At this time, we were working Recon, Special Forces, as well as our own ANGLICO teams in the vicinity of Khafji, about 20-25 kilometers in front of friendly lines. The call was put out for these advanced elements to pull back. The border OPs withdrew; the plan was for them to rejoin larger units and advance again.

"However, some units didn't get the word. At OP-7, one of my teams stayed on station because they had a great view of the battlefield and radioed in airstrikes on the Iraqi forces headed east, toward Khafji."

Inside Khafji itself, two reconnaissance teams suddenly found out that they had some unex-

a loss." He concentrated on "getting out of there so we can come back and do it again."

"The Saudi troops were two clicks back from the border, acting as a screening force," noted Captain Braden. "However, instead of staying on line, these units were moving back and forth all night. As the air slowed up, my team at OP-7 departed about 2:30 in the morning. One flight of Cobras did arrive from the 369th 'Gunfighter.' They started hunting the Iraqi armor using night-vision goggles. It was difficult—visibility was very poor. They only had a range of 500-700 meters. Unfortunately, these Cobras ran low on fuel and returned to base. Captain Kleinsmith, also with 1st ANGLICO, had to pull back. However, another four Cobras came on station and destroyed a platoon-sized mechanized force."

As the Iraqis entered Khafji, they encountered two U.S. Army trucks on a routine supply run. One of the surprised vehicles managed to escape, but the other crashed into a wall and its crew members, Specialists David Lockett and Melissa A. Rathbun Nealy, were captured by the Iraqis, along with its cargo. Although more than 100 American women have been taken prisoner in past wars, Rathbun Nealy was the first to be taken POW in an official combatant capacity.

Although General H. Norman Schwarzkopf dismissed the unopposed Iraqi incursion as insignificant, at least one senior Pentagon official was critical of the "obvious oversight" that had made it possible: "The Iraqis shouldn't have been in a position that they could waltz into that town, even if it was uninhabited."

Be that as it may, the coalition forces were not long in moving to correct that oversight. The Saudis mobilized three mechanized armored battalions, a tank battalion and a Qatari tank battalion to oust the Iraqis from their territory.

Captain Braden of 1st ANGLICO was witness to part of that counterattack on the morning of January 30:

"At 0400-0500, the Saudis realized the Iraqis were here in force. They started their rapid planning to cope with the situation. But this is something they do not excel at. They can grasp the general scheme of things pretty quickly, but they can't execute the plan. For example, they would say: 'This battalion go.' But they had no further orders beyond that. It was very confusing.

"When the battle kicked off, I was with the Saudi brigade commander of the 2nd SANG. We were bursting with ideas of how to attack and asked him what his plan was. He said, 'We must kill all the Iraqis and drive them out of Khafji.' And we said, 'Okay, but how are we going to drive them out?' He said, '5th

pected company. They spent the next 36 hours holed up in a four-story apartment building, calling in air and artillery strikes by means of coded radio messages while surrounded by enemy soldiers. At one point, Iraqis entered the building and searched the ground floor while the Marines hid on the roof, set up Claymore mines at the top of the stairs, and started burning their code books. "We could see their heads bobbing up and down," said Lance Cpl. Jeff Brown later. "They sure would have had a rude awakening if they had come up after us." But the Iraqis did not go above the ground floor.

"I'd be lying if I didn't say that dying hadn't crossed my mind," said Corporal Chuck Ingraham after escaping from the trap, "We were shaking for two days from cold and fear." Corporal David McNamee was worried about his family: "If I don't get out of here, not only am I going to be dead, my family's going to have

On January 30, the crewmen of a Saudi V-150 Commando keep their vehicle-mounted TOW missile ready for trouble as they approach Khafji, its skyline dominated by the water tower that the Iraqis—logically enough—used as an artillery observation post.

GREG ENGLISH, AP/WIDE WORLD PHOTOS

and 7th Battalions.' And we said, 'Okay, do you know where you want them to go?' He said, 'That is up to the battalion commander.' Then we turned to the battalion commander and said, 'What are you going to do?' He said, 'I will wait for orders from brigade.' It was a Catch-22 situation.

"We could find only two of the three SANG line companies. So, I attached one of my teams to one and Captain Kleinsmith attached one of his to the other. We then proceeded north and west of the city to cut off any Iraqis advancing into Khafji. My third team hooked up with another Saudi battalion heading in from the south.

"While this was transpiring, the Qataris, who were attached to the SANG, were quickly com-

prising a task force. They were equipped with about 21 AMX-30 French tanks. So, they married up seven tanks to each company of the 7th Battalion, 2nd SANG. To the west, about 18-20 kilometers, were the MODA (Ministry of Defense Aviation) of the regular Saudi army. They possessed M-60 tanks and were coming from the west to join up with us.

"As the Iraqi tanks were moving across the border, Colonel Knife, from the 5th Battalion, 2nd SANG, thought he could talk the Iraqis into surrendering because of the beating they were taking from the air. He took a loudspeaker with him to coax them into giving up, but the noise from the mechanized vehicles was deafening. The Iraqis did stop about a click out. We didn't know if they were going to surrender or not,

A veteran vehicle of the Vietnam era—as most of its Iraqi counterparts would prove to be—a Saudi M-113 armored personnel carrier advances on Khafji.

but an American military adviser attached to the SANG showed himself. I think this American lost his composure. And the Iraqis were not about to give themselves up to Americans because of the horror stories they heard. So—they started firing.

"There was a widely circulated story about the Iraqi tank turrets being turned around as if they were going to give up and then swinging them around to open fire. This is bogus! It never happened. Also, no Iraqi tanks entered Khafji. They were eliminated north of the city. Their APCs and other light armored vehicles did enter the city.

"A couple of my teams called in some Cobra gunships, Harriers and A-10 Warthogs. They must've wiped out between 30 and 35 tanks,

mainly T-54, T-55 and T-59 [the Chinese version]. One interesting note: Whenever we ran air on them, they would stop. This was great, because they became stationary targets. We used Rockeye, Hellfires and TOW [tube-launched, optically sighted, wire-guided] missiles, all of which worked very well.

"For most of that first day, whenever we engaged the Iraqis, the Saudis would pull back two to three kilometers. However, my team would remain and call in airstrikes on platoon and company-sized mechanized armor units and take out 10-12 vehicles. Near the end of the day, the Saudis fired some TOWs from their M-113 vehicles and V-150 armored cars. As they discovered that their TOWs outranged the enemy's AT-3s, their confidence grew. At night, it was Custer-circle-your-wagons—nobody fought. We were prepared to fight, but never had to. So, we took this time to resupply and coordinate the next day's movements.

"One of the problems we encountered with the Saudis was they didn't use their radios to talk to their higher echelon. The only way our higher echelon was getting a clear picture of the battle was from ANGLICO. We were telling our chain of command, and it was being passed on.

"Also, the Qataris weren't very good. They never were coordinated into the battle and were kept in reserve. In fact, the Saudis couldn't talk to them on their radios. Here's an attached unit you can't communicate with! It was extremely difficult."

Once they got the battle plan straight, the SANG members acquitted themselves with all the motivation that one might expect from men fighting to regain their own home ground.

Incoming! Members of the 1st Marine Division near Khafji on January 30, 1991, sprint for cover upon being notified that an Iraqi artillery barrage is on its way.

CHARLES PLATIAU, REUTERS/BETTMANN

One member of a TOW missile team aboard a V-150 armored car was credited with knocking out eight Iraqi tanks. Captain Braden continued his observations with an account of the fighting on January 31:

"On the second day, the Saudis fought much better. They found that their M-60s outgunned the T-55 by 900 meters or so and the TOWs were outdistancing the Iraqi weapons systems by 2,000 meters.

"By midday, we were tightening the ring on the Iraqis in Khafji. There was less and less chance for us to use close air support because we were fighting in close quarters. However, the fast movers were really accurate with their 20mm cannons.

"The Saudis began moving up to the south of Khafji with the 7th Battalion, 2nd SANG, the heavy gun sections of the 3rd Marines with them, and the Qataris in reserve. The 1st Battalion, 12th Marines, provided an excellent preparatory fire. The combat, as I said earlier, was close—we were shooting at each other face to face. Thank God there were no civilians. They had been evacuated around January 13. However, two Marine recon teams were trapped in the city. We didn't know they were there. They could easily have gotten out on the first night. They only had to move 700 meters to reach friendly lines. I know this may sound harsh, but it was more difficult for us with those two recon teams in there. We had to set up a restricted fire area so we didn't accidentally kill them. We finally established radio contact with them and they did call in one artillery mission."

One of the Marines in the trapped recon team, Lance Cpl. Jeff Brown, was directing allied artillery into an area where he had located some Iraqi APCs when he was hit in the left thigh by incoming shrapnel, thus becoming one of the earliest American candidates for a Purple Heart in the ground war. "It knocked me to the deck," he said later. "It's a weird kind of pain. It's more psychological than anything. You think, 'I'm hit!'

"We knew we had to take those vehicles out," he added, "If we hadn't, they could have caused us and everyone else a hell of a lot of trouble."

Some Iraqi FOs (forward observers) showed their share of professional coolness under fire, as Captain Braden conceded: "I will never forget the Iraqi FO in the water tower. It was shown on CNN. Their water towers are not like ours. It was solid and looked like a high-rise apartment building. Everybody took a shot at it—TOWs, Cobras, Hellfires and artillery. We actually had the Cobras land and have a face-to-face meeting with one of my teams to coordinate everything. In the end, most of the tower

CHARLES PLATIAU, REUTERS/BETTMANN

was still there—the Saudis said they counted five Iraqi dead around it, but I didn't see them.

"I can't say enough about the air support—it was tremendous! I felt bad because I had to turn away close air support missions due to the unavailability of targets. At one point, I had nine sections of F/A-18 Hornets stacked and we couldn't use them because the combat was so close.

"Funny thing—the Saudis don't clear a house like we do. If they're walking down the street and they take fire from a house...they blow it up! Crude, but effective, I guess."

Among other accomplishments at the end of the second day of fighting, Corporal Ingraham, Corporal McNamee, the wounded Lance Cpl. Brown and all nine other members of the two Marine reconnaissance teams that had been caught up in the Iraqi advance made their way out safely.

Thus far, the Iraqi soldiers had shown themselves to be every bit as tenacious on the defense as the reputation they had gained in their war with Iran had made them out to be. On January 31, however, the Saudis began making significant inroads into Khafji and, as they did, Iraqi morale began to take a significantly dramatic downturn. Outside the city, the Iraqi reinforcements to Khafji and attacking forces to the west continued to suffer from allied air attacks.

Captain Mike "Disco" Bequelin, an AV-8B Harrier pilot of Marine squadron VMA-542, recalled: "The last day of the battle for Khafji, I flew in. The Iraqis had a lot of armor and troop concentrations. We were under control of a FAC (forward air controller) on the ground, one of our ANGLICO people with the Saudis. We hit some APCs and they returned fire with SA-9s. Luckily they missed, or I wouldn't be here today. As the Iraqis were trying to flee Khafji, we hit a couple of the retreating columns. That area looked like a moonscape. When I went north to confront them, we went nose-to-nose. I dropped Rockeye on them and egressed back to the south and west, away from Khafji itself."

Elsewhere, tragedy struck during an engagement between U.S. Marine forces and an Iraqi armored battalion that made an abortive attack near Umm Hujul, about 50 miles west of Khafji. Missiles fired by a supporting American airplane—which possibly mistook the eight-wheeled Marine LAV-25s for Iraqi BTR-60s—struck a Marine vehicle and killed eight Marines. Although the Marines lost three LAV-25 armored cars during the fight, only four other Marines were killed in combat—half as many as fell victim to "friendly fire."

Over Kuwait itself, the U.S. Air Force lost an AC-130 gunship to anti-aircraft fire, with its entire crew of 14.

North of Khafji, Iraqi tanks, harried by the constant air attacks, gave up their attempt to reinforce the city and turned back for their underground revetments in Kuwait. As the realization that they were cut off began to sink in, Iraqi troops still in the city began to surrender en masse.

While Iraqi morale sagged, Marine Captain Braden saw the SANG troops' confidence grow:

"We [used] Saudi artillery on the third day. The first two days, Marine artillery supported us. However, the Saudis insisted it was their sector and their responsibility, so they wanted to fire their artillery. They had the M109A2 155mm self-propelled howitzer. They would hit the target all right, but when we asked for them to cease fire, they would send in another barrage. As I said, it was confusing, so when we were in doubt, we held our fire. I must say, the forward observer from 1/12 was invaluable, he did a great job.

"People thought that the Iraqi prisoners would be mistreated by the Saudis. We never saw any indication of that. In fact, the Saudis treated them very well. On the third day, we captured a big group and turned them over to the Saudis, and they marched them back. It looked like a homecoming parade—the Iraqis were cheering and waving. They felt that they had put up enough of a fight, so their honor was intact."

Qatari troops prepare to clear a building. Even after most Iraqis in Khafji had surrendered, a handful of holdouts and snipers continued to harass allied troops for some time.

127

Second-rate spearhead: A Saudi soldier picks up an Iraqi gas mask beside the burnt-out remains of an uparmored T-55 tank—one of 30 tanks and armored personnel carriers destroyed on the plain north of Khafji on January 31.

The third day of fighting in Khafji raged for more than 12 hours, from 2 a.m. to 2:30 p.m. By then, for all intents and purposes the battle was over, although intermittent sniper fire was reported the next day. In their first land battle, the Saudis had lost 18 men dead, 32 wounded and 11 missing.

Captain Braden appraised their performance: "We built the Saudi confidence. On Day One, they would always run; on Day Two, they would sometimes run; and on Day Three, they would hang in there with you. And, by Day Four, they were walking around 8 feet tall, saying: 'We bad! Yes, we bad!'

"Although the Saudis improved, they thought it was over. Their attitude was: We have demonstrated to the Iraqis we could fight—and that's it! You had to keep telling them it wasn't over and there were a whole lot more of them and we were going to have to go in there on the ground and get them. Air cannot do it all alone.

They just couldn't comprehend that. It's a child-like optimism you see in the Saudis."

Colonel Jack Petri, a U.S. liaison officer with the SANG, summed up the performance more concisely: "This was the first battle the Saudis had ever fought, and they acquitted themselves terribly well."

Most surprising was the fact that the SANG's performance at Khafji was—and thereafter would continue to be—superior to that of the regular Saudi army. The Guardsmen, mostly Bedouin volunteers trained by the Americans, were receptive to new ideas and weaponry—they learned fast and, when the Iraqi offensive began, they reacted fast. The regular army, which had not been opened up to training by foreign instructors (as had the Royal Saudi Air Force) was comparatively sluggish in its response to the crisis and would later struggle to keep up with the SANG during the coastal drive to liberate Kuwait City.

SANG troops look over the body of an Iraqi sniper, slain in an office in the central part of Khafji on February 2.

The Iraqis, for their part, had shown their share of courage during their short-lived offensive, especially when one considers the incessant bombardment they had endured in their front-line positions in the weeks preceding the attack. They had fought stubbornly in the first two days, but after that their morale deteriorated. Complete allied air superiority may not have been the only factor. The wrecked armor that the Iraqis left behind in Khafji and the desert 50 miles to the west consisted of T-55 tanks, Type 63 tracked APCs and BTR-60 eight-wheeled APCs, along with at least one French-built Panhard ECR-90 armored car. While quite capable of dealing death in the hands of skilled crews, none of those weapons were anywhere near state of the art. Clearly, the best vehicles and weaponry in the Iraqi arsenal had been reserved for the Republican Guard. The equipment given the front-line troops in Kuwait—including those committed to the attack on Khafji—were out-of-date and expendable. So, one would be logically led to infer, were the soldiers who manned them.

Total Iraqi losses in tanks and APCs during the three-day fight were estimated at anywhere from 24 to 80. Their casualties at Khafji came to 32 dead and 35 wounded, but an additional 463 Iraqi officers and men were taken prisoner. The mass surrenders on the third day presaged the future of the ground war.

"They lost 90 percent of their forces—hundreds of casualties and hundreds of equipment losses," said the Saudi commander, Lt. Gen. Khalid ibn Sultan, as he set his map against the charred remains of an Iraqi BTR-60 and surveyed the smoldering streets of Khafji. "It was a suicide mission for them. It's tragic that so many good people should be driven to death by their leaders. They can't gain anything, except politically, for the mission."

As far as any hopes on Saddam Hussein's part of throwing the allied invasion plan off schedule, General Schwarzkopf summed up its significance as being no more meaningful than "a mosquito to an elephant." The bottom line on Khafji's outcome was given by President George Bush after the battle, when he reiterated that any ground war in the Gulf would begin "on our timetable, not on Saddam Hussein's timetable." □

ESSAY

THE WORST FEAR

COURTESY RUSSELL A.C. SANBORN

ABOVE: Captain Russell A.C. Sanborn assumes a suitably "Top Gun" pose in the cockpit of his AV-8B Harrier II of VMA-231. His greatest test would come after a hand-held SAM grounded him on February 9, 1991.
RIGHT: Strategic error: Captured British Flight Lieutenant John Peters is displayed on Iraqi television. Exhibiting the POWs may have been meant by the Iraqis to undermine the resolve of the coalition forces, but had a diametrically opposite effect.

IT'S EVERY PILOT'S worst fear to be shot down behind enemy lines," said Captain Russell A.C. Sanborn, a Harrier pilot with Marine fighter squadron VMA-231 out of Cherry Point, North Carolina. "When the first allied POWs were displayed on Iraqi television, we were both angry and frustrated. Everybody was concerned for their safety. It was shaping up to be Vietnam all over again. It looked as if they were really being mistreated. We just wanted to go out there and kick butt!"

Little did he realize it then, but the 27-year-old Marine aviator from De Land, Fla., also would be shot down behind enemy lines.

On the afternoon of February 9, 1991, Captain Sanborn was over southern Kuwait, on his second hop of the day, strafing artillery positions. An F-18D Hornet, acting as a fast FAC (Forward Air Controller), marked the target with "Willie Pete" (white phosphorus) rounds. However, on his initial pass, Sanborn developed a computer "glich" and was unable to unload his ordnance. Coming back around, the leatherneck let loose his entire load.

"As I pulled off target, I rolled the wing over to see where my bombs had hit when I suddenly felt this loud thump on my left side," Sanborn remembers. "My plane immediately started spinning and inverting out of control. . . . However, I still struggled with the aircraft for a few seconds in hopes of saving her. But the fire light was on and I knew she was a goner. So, I got myself into a good body position and pulled the handle to eject—and out I

AP LASERPHOTO

went! I was on the ground no more than 10 minutes before the Iraqi welcoming committee reached me. They had rifles and I had a pistol. I was outmanned and outgunned. My heart was racing!"

Stripping him of his revolver and radio, the Iraqis led Captain Sanborn to a bunker. Once inside, an Iraqi rushed in and pointed at the stunned Marine and barked: "I shoot you down! I get two of you now!" With that, he relieved Sanborn of his name tag and shook his hand. "He had his arms over his shoulders, showing me that he had downed my plane with a hand-held SAM," Sanborn remembered.

Once darkness fell, Sanborn was blindfolded and had his hands tied behind his back. He

130

was thrown in the back of a truck and driven around for a short time. Stopping, he was taken off the vehicle and forced to run a gantlet of angered Iraqi soldiers. "They lined up and hit me with their fists, with sticks, and with their rifle butts," Sanborn explained. "For the last 18 or 19 days we had been bombing them. The guys I saw looked pretty tired and ragged. They needed somebody to vent their frustrations against. And I happened to be the unlucky one. They screamed insults at me in Arabic and broken English. I fell down a couple of times. They would quickly pick me up and push me forward. But I never lost consciousness. Then they placed me back on the truck, stopped, and repeated the procedure again. Then they did it a third time. By then, I was hurting."

During the first 72 hours, Sanborn was interrogated three times. The sessions were handled by professionals but the Marine's prior training in survival was extremely beneficial in helping him to adapt to his stressful situation. "I devised a way to protect myself during interviews," he says. "Again, I was tied up and blindfolded. Whenever they picked my chin up, I knew they were going to hit me. So...I would tuck my chin in and roll my shoulders forward to protect my face as much as possible. I would also feel what thumb they had pressed on me and brace myself. If it was the left thumb, then I knew it was the right hand coming around to strike me."

After a six-hour truck ride, Sanborn arrived in Baghdad. Here he was interrogated once more and thrown into his cell. "It was a typical 10-by-12 room with smooth cement walls about a foot-and-a-half thick," the Harrier pilot said. "My first cell had a single window, 18 inches high and about 24 inches long. There was a single steel-barred door to my room. The Iraqis draped a blanket over it to prevent us from seeing out."

Soon, Sanborn was communicating with other POWs, including some of the 20 other Americans who were captured. Unlike Vietnam, where prisoners were forced to use a tapping code to talk to each other, the inmates at the "Baghdad Hilton" would whisper in hushed tones. To his amazement, the captive found the adjoining cell occupied by Army Spc. 4 David Lockett. The young soldier had been captured near Khafji with a woman, Spc. 4 Melissa A. Rathbun Nealy, of Michigan. American concern about the young female soldier's fate at the hands of the Iraqis was widespread. Lockett told Sanborn that she had been treated remarkably well, however. The female prisoner was being held in the same prison but in a secluded location. Rathbun Nealy later said that only one

Iraqi officer had the key to her cell door, through which he delivered meals.

On the other side of Sanborn's cell was a room containing a British Commando who spoke some Arabic. "The Iraqi attitude was strange," Sanborn says. "An Iraqi doctor, who had been studying in London, came by to check on us every three or four days. The Brits told me he said...he had to return to Iraq when the war started and he hoped it would end soon so he could resume his studies. That seemed to be the prevailing Iraqi attitude: 'let's get this thing over with.'"

Then the Marine pilot was moved to another cell as a form of punishment. "I was caught talking," he explained. "My new cell had no window and it was very dark. The pilots were the bad boys anyway. The guards didn't like us— for obvious reasons. They were gruff and would shove, kick, or push us. We were never beaten by them though. From then on, we all became more cautious about talking. We needed that interaction with people. It was important to us. It definitely helped my mind."

Then one day the prisoners received uplifting news from Major Joseph Small, an OV-10 pilot who had been shot down and taken prisoner on the second day of the allied ground campaign: the ground offensive to liberate Kuwait had begun. Soon the prison network was buzzing. "Major Small told us how rapidly the troops were advancing and how the American people were still behind us. We were just peaking that day!" said Sanborn.

A few days later, a guard appeared and said: "Congratulations, the war is over!"

Sanborn was startled but kept his composure. "We didn't believe it at first," he said. "We didn't want our hopes dashed. Then there was no bombing in Baghdad that night. The next day I was allowed to shave for the first time since my captivity. On the third day they let me take my first bath since I had been there. I said to myself that this has got to be the real thing."

Taken to the Al Rashid Hotel in downtown Baghdad, the captives were turned over to the International Red Cross. Finally, Sanborn and the others were placed on a Red Cross plane en route to Saudi Arabia. "When we crossed the Saudi border and two F-15s pulled alongside of us as escorts, the whole plane just erupted in a loud chorus of cheers. There were Saudi soldiers on board and they began chanting: USA! USA! USA!"

Captain Sanborn and the other POWs returned to the United States and were given a hero's welcome. "I couldn't believe the reception we received," Sanborn said. "There were flags, yellow ribbons, and the people were incredible!" □

MARK FARAM, U.S. NAVY

Back from captivity, Captain Sanborn and Chief Warrant Officer Guy L. Hunter, Jr., receive the Purple Heart, the POW Medal and the National Defense Service Medal at Naval Medical Center, Bethesda, Md., on March 16, 1991.

CHAPTER TEN

BLOCKING THE CENTER

CARL DAVIS

"Scumdog," the pet M60 of Task Force Papa Bear, shows off its mine-detonating plow attachment and add-on armor.

BY THE BEGINNING of the ground war on February 23-24, 1991, the allied air offensive had dealt incalculable punishment to Iraqi forces in Kuwait and throughout Iraq. On the previous day, a Friday, teams of Saudi Arabian sappers—specialists in finding and disarming mines—had slipped six miles behind enemy lines, gently removed and defused 75 mines to clear a path through an Iraqi minefield, and gathered intelligence on troop deployment. At about the same time, coalition aircraft swept low over Iraq's defensive ditches, dropping napalm to burn off the oil that the Iraqis had hoped to fire at the right time to deter coalition ground forces. Allied air attacks blasted Iraqi supply lines, dug-in tanks and troop concentrations. Cross-border artillery duels became commonplace. For weeks, special operations units had been slipping back and forth along the Saudi border.

It was no secret that a ground war was imminent. In their bunkers along the Kuwaiti border, Iraqi troops were preparing for the onslaught as best soldiers can who have endured incessant aerial and artillery bombardment, shortages of food, little or no meaningful communication with Baghdad, and intelligence that largely was limited to what they could see coming their way.

For weeks, media commentators and military analysts had been speculating on the form the action would take: flanking movement, frontal attack, amphibious assault on Kuwait City itself—or perhaps some combination of all three.

The answer was known to few at that time, other than the top command and the mastermind orchestrating events from an underground command post at Riyadh, General Norman H. Schwarzkopf.

Affectionately known as the "Bear," Schwarzkopf was more widely known by another nickname, one he hated: "Stormin' Norman." He told television personality Barbara Walters that to him the "stormin'" adjective implied a man given to "raising hell all the time," a man of no sensitivity, while he personally felt that "any man who doesn't cry scares me a little bit." During the tragedy of the Vietnam War, Schwarzkopf had been one of many officers who had said—sometimes tearfully—that if they were in a position to do so, they would have done things differently.

Now he had that chance. Once he had assembled the means, in the form of military power, and could count on political support from the home front, Schwarzkopf was confident that the coalition forces he led would win. But he wanted to attain his goals without stressing enemy body counts and, more important, *at the smallest sacrifice in allied lives possible*. . .and it was to that latter goal that he devoted much of his energy. He hoped to make the Gulf War the antithesis of Vietnam.

Repeatedly, Saddam's army had tried to force the allied hand, most notably at Khafji, and with three other simultaneous Iraqi incursions near Umm Hujul during the last days of January. This sudden movement of Iraqi armor from

A leatherneck checks a bunker for any hostile stragglers as elements of the 1st Marine Division secure an abandoned Kuwaiti town on February 24, 1991.

CHARLES PLATIAU, REUTERS/BETTMANN

Members of the 1st Marine Division negotiate a tangled maze of barbed wire along the Saudi-Kuwaiti border.

CHARLES PLATIAU, REUTERS/BETTMANN

dug-in positions served only to trigger what one American pilot termed a "feeding frenzy" on the exposed and vulnerable vehicles. Meanwhile, allied aircraft played an earnest cat-and-mouse game to locate and destroy mobile Scud sites. During the course of the war, some 200 Scud sites would launch 81 attacks, about half of them against Israel. Satellites could spot the mobile firing points, and aircraft promptly would be dispatched to silence them.

In addition to airstrikes, however, it often became necessary to employ special means of eliminating Iraqi mobile Scud launchers before they fired. For this, Maj. Gen. Wayne Downing, commander of counterterrorist units, formed a "fusion cell" that combined the talents of the joint-military American commandos of Delta Force, the crack British Special Air Service and A-10

Thunderbolt II ground-attack planes. Over the next two weeks, the commandos went behind enemy lines to attack command-and-control centers and storage facilities serving the elusive mobile launchers, used laser target designators to pinpoint the launchers to the attack planes, and destroyed more than a dozen Scud sites.

On February 27, Saddam Hussein played his last gambit to goad Israel into entering the war by dispatching 26 more Scud launchers into western Iraq. By that time, however, the "fusion cell" had its mission down well enough to locate and destroy all 26 before they could do any damage. The cost included three Delta Force members—Patrick Hurley, Otto Clark and Elroy Rogriguez, Jr.—killed when their Blackhawk helicopter crashed into a sand dune during a low-level run into enemy territory.

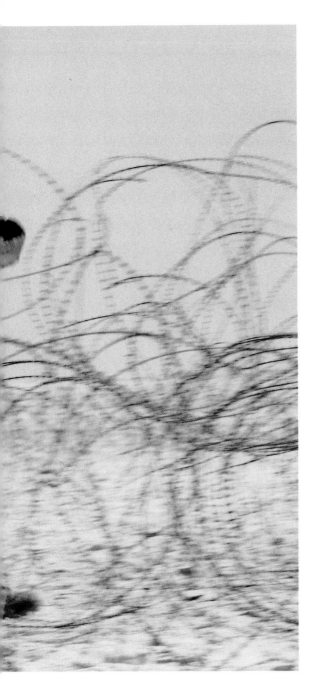

set for on or about February 21, less than two weeks away.

For years the United States had planned for likelihood of a war in the Persian Gulf region. An earlier scenario—even called Desert Shield—had been organized for in limited-scale rehearsals by Schwarzkopf's Central Command headquarters (Centcom) in Florida, coincidentally just prior to Iraq's invasion of Kuwait on August 2, 1990.

As the plan was modified, interservice rivalry surfaced. In September, General Michael J. Dugan, Air Force chief of staff, made his much-publicized statement that the war could be won by air power alone—a statement that led to his dismissal. And although the Army would not be ready until mid-February, it was repeatedly pointed out that the Marines had arrived early on in brigade strength, ready to sustain themselves in combat with sufficient arms and ammunition, if they could be committed before Saddam moved up his heavier armor. Yet the Marines had been initially put in logistic support of the 82nd Airborne, which could carry only a two-day supply of rations and ammunition. Despite the massive supply problem, however, the top allied command held firmly to its schedule.

During January, daily briefings had been held at Al Jabayl, Saudi Arabia, headquarters of General Walter Boomer, commander of the 1st Marine Expeditionary Force. Attending the briefings was Colonel H. Avery Chenoweth, a Marine reservist reactivated to head the Marine Corps Combat Art Program for the Marine Headquarters Historical Division. He had been sent to record the war on film and in sketches, for later painting. The Saudis provided him a very unmilitary-looking Honda Accord, but the briefings contained no hint of the unorthodox role he would ultimately play as a roving chronicler of the ground war to come. Instead, he watched the ground battle plan undergo a slow process of shifting and crystallization, while the coalition force continued its relentless air assault.

"Our strategy to go after this army is very, very simple. First we're going to cut it off, and then we're going to kill it," General Colin Powell had once said. The plan finally hit upon involved a very old tactical gambit on a new, epic scale: deceive the enemy into concentrating his defenses against a frontal assault, and then secretly move a large force around the enemy's flank and cut him off from the rear. Given the probability of having already partially, or even entirely, severed communications between Saddam Hussein and his field commanders, Schwarzkopf could regard such a move as a calculated risk worth taking. The element of surprise would not be in the flanking action

Another allied concern was the expected onslaught of behind-the-lines attacks by some 10,000 terrorists thought to be lurking in Saudi Arabia in various guises. Although the attacks never materialized, security had been tightened at installations and for all personnel in transit (lessons well-learned from the 1982 bombing in Beirut, Lebanon, of a U.S. Marine barracks, in which 241 Americans died).

Amid all these diversions and distractions, however, allied commanders had remained unruffled, holding to their agenda for the liberation of Kuwait. In early February, General Colin Powell, chairman of the Joint Chiefs of Staff, and Defense Secretary Richard B. Cheney met with Schwarzkopf in the Gulf as ground war battle plans were finalized. G-day, the day the ground war would start, was

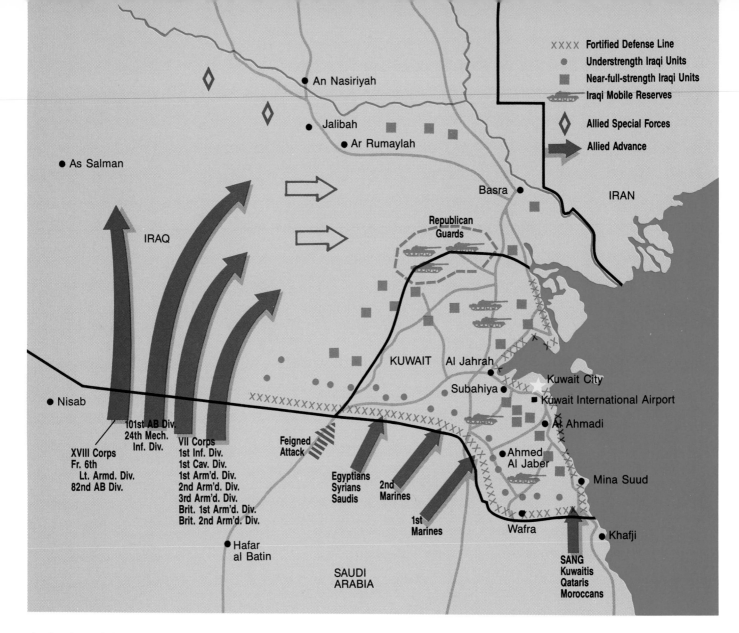

Legend (map):
- XXXX — Fortified Defense Line
- ● — Understrength Iraqi Units
- ■ — Near-full-strength Iraqi Units
- Iraqi Mobile Reserves
- ◇ — Allied Special Forces
- ➡ — Allied Advance

An Nasiriyah

Jalibah

Ar Rumaylah

As Salman

Basra

IRAN

IRAQ

Republican Guards

Nisab

KUWAIT

Al Jahrah

Kuwait City

Subahiya

Kuwait International Airport

101st AB Div.
24th Mech.
Inf. Div.

VII Corps
1st Inf. Div.
1st Cav. Div.
1st Arm'd. Div.
2nd Arm'd. Div.
3rd Arm'd. Div.
Brit. 1st Arm'd. Div.
Brit. 2nd Arm'd. Div.

XVIII Corps
Fr. 6th
Lt. Armd. Div.
82nd AB Div.

Feigned
Attack

Egyptians
Syrians
Saudis

2nd
Marines

Al Ahmadi

Ahmed
Al Jaber

Mina Suud

1st
Marines

Wafra

Khafji

Hafar
al Batin

SAUDI
ARABIA

SANG
Kuwaitis
Qataris
Moroccans

At the time of the allied ground offensive, the U.S. Army, British and French forces had accomplished a furtive shift to the west, while a pan-Arab force of Egyptians, Syrians and Saudis filled the gap. While the resultant ''Hail Mary'' play was spectacularly successful, the allied frontal assault breached the prepared Iraqi defenses with a speed that was equally remarkable.

itself—but in how far and how fast coalition troops could be deployed.

Between January 16, the commencement of the air campaign, and February 24, the day the ground war actually started, Schwarzkopf initiated his plan. On February 14, he sent the XVIII Airborne Corps and the VII Armored with more than 200,000 troops far to the west—all under an amazingly effective veil of secrecy. This end sweep he called the "Hail Mary" play or "Left Hook." Simultaneously, the "Saddam Line" of ditches and berms would be hit with a frontal assault. To further confuse the Iraqis, the Marines would appear to be preparing an amphibious attack on Kuwait City, and the 1st Cavalry Division under Brig. Gen. John H. Tilelli, Jr., would feint in the Wadi al Batin, along Kuwait's western border with Iraq. The division was ordered not to "decisively engage."

Initially, the Marines were to have been assigned a sector along the coast straight up to Kuwait City, but by early January their mission had been modified and their sector moved

westward, thus putting the SANG (Saudi Arabian National Guard), the Moroccans and the Qatari units in their place along the coast, with room left later for a Kuwaiti contingent.

As far back as January, before Desert Storm began, there were other adjustments in Marine positions. The Challenger-equipped British 1st Armoured Division (including the 7th Armoured Brigade, the "Desert Rats," which had been attached to the 1st Marine Division to add heavier armor to the Marines' own lighter M60 tanks, was transferred to the Army VII Corps in the west and replaced by the M1A1 Abrams tanks of the Army VI Corps' 2nd Armored Division. The Abrams tanks were later shifted yet again, this time to the 2nd Marine Division on the 1st's left flank.

Rumor had it that the westward shifts had been necessitated by the compromise of battle plans by a Saudi unit. Later, a coalition reconnaissance patrol further compromised the situation by losing a radio and cryptographic coding device, catastrophically affording the

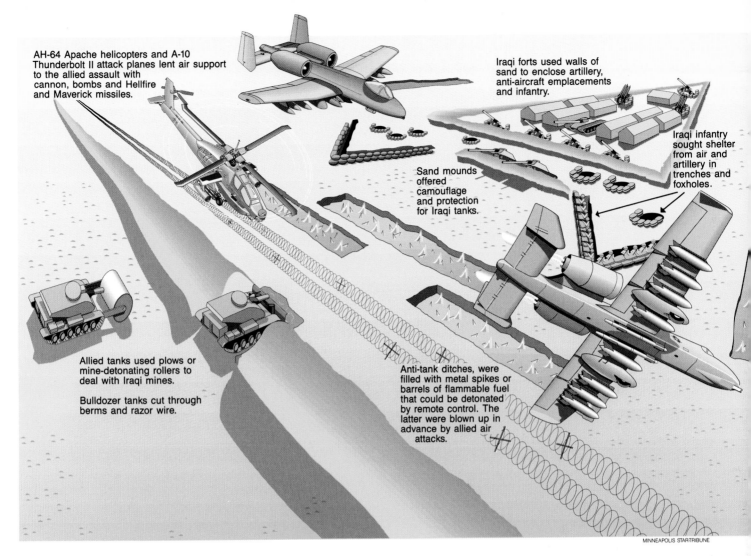

AH-64 Apache helicopters and A-10 Thunderbolt II attack planes lent air support to the allied assault with cannon, bombs and Hellfire and Maverick missiles.

Iraqi forts used walls of sand to enclose artillery, anti-aircraft emplacements and infantry.

Iraqi infantry sought shelter from air and artillery in trenches and foxholes.

Sand mounds offered camouflage and protection for Iraqi tanks.

Allied tanks used plows or mine-detonating rollers to deal with Iraqi mines.

Bulldozer tanks cut through berms and razor wire.

Anti-tank ditches, were filled with metal spikes or barrels of flammable fuel that could be detonated by remote control. The latter were blown up in advance by allied air attacks.

enemy the opportunity to listen in on all transmitted confidential radio traffic.

At the time, those seemed plausible reasons for sector adjustments—or they may have been deceptions and disinformation "plants." As Schwarzkopf later conceded, the press did print stories, especially about an alleged funding of the landing of the seaborne 4th Marine Expeditionary Brigade (MEB)—a landing which never actually occurred—that gave Saddam Hussein's forces a false picture of allied intentions. Without their own air power for surveillance, the Iraqis tuned in on Cable Network News (CNN), as did a good many allied troops in Saudi Arabia. There had been limited aerial reconnaissance by the enemy in the form of RPVs, or remote-piloted vehicles (small drones), which were spotted on occasion flying low over Al Kibrit. Clearly, coalition intelligence reasoned, the televised scenes of the coalition's buildup could only be demoralizing to the Iraqis.

Facing some 55 Iraqi divisions—or what was left of them—as G-day neared, the coalition battle forces were arrayed in the following order:

1) Aboard 31 ships in the Persian Gulf was the 4th Marine Expeditionary Brigade of 17,000, under U.S. Central Command, Naval Forces,

with the attack carrier USS *Nassau* as flagship. The 5th Marine Expeditionary Brigade was deployed ashore to create a screen between the easternmost Arab units on the coast and two Marine divisions farther to the west—the 1st and 2nd, poised between the "elbow," the lower junction of the Kuwait border where it abruptly turns north, and the "armpit," where it again abruptly turns west.

2) Positioned along a corridor of 20 to 30 kilometers along the Saudi coast were Arab forces consisting of the SANG as well as Qatari and Kuwaiti army units.

3) Along the southern Saudi-Kuwaiti border there was a 40-50 kilometer gap between the coastal Arab forces and the 1st Marine Division. This was quickly screened by the newly arrived 5th Marine Expeditionary Brigade, which had to come ashore still wearing non-desert green, or "verdant," camouflage uniforms to take up blocking positions. A successful ruse was staged to make the Iraqis just over the border believe that the main thrust of the allied effort would take place here: enormously powerful loudspeakers with a range of 10 miles were driven up and down the border for several days, playing recorded sound tapes of the noise of

Saddam Hussein's vaunted defense-in-depth, combining barbed wire, berms, mines and burning oil, proved to be embarrassingly ineffective in stopping—or even significantly slowing—the allies' direct assault into Kuwait.

Marines train in mission-oriented protective posture (MOPP) against the possibility that the Iraqis might resort to chemical warfare. Although the Iraqis did not use chemicals actively, at least one Marine vehicle was reported to have detonated a mustard gas mine.

Highly motivated: Soldiers of the Kuwaiti army-in-exile charge over a dune in M-113 APCs in a determined bid to make their way up the Kuwaiti east coast and liberate their capital.

mechanized vehicles, tanks, trucks and other appropriate sounds.

4) Stationed between the Marines and the westward-moving flanking force, made up of the U.S. Army VII and XVIII Corps with their British and French contingents, lay Joint Forces Command North, a pan-Arab force made up primarily of Egyptian, Syrian, Saudi and Kuwaiti units. Its objectives involved a direct assault against the Iraqi defensive line along the southwestern Saudi-Kuwaiti border, followed by a drive into Kuwait. The Saudi units, which had no NBC protection of their own, were equipped and trained by a chemical defense battalion fielded by the Czechoslovakian army, comprised of its volunteers under the command of Colonel Jan Valo.

The 1st Marine Division, under the command of Maj. Gen. James Myatt, utilized four special task forces, regiments comprised of various infantry battalions augmented by LAV-25s (light armored vehicles), amphibious tractors (amtracs), artillery and M60 tanks. These highly mobile air-ground task forces were designated Ripper, Grizzly, Papa Bear and Taro. An additional heliborne special company-sized group was named X-ray and was inserted as a right-flank screen. Finally, there was a unique unit comprised of fast-moving LAV-25s and—oddly—

Toyota four-wheel-drive pickup trucks. It resembled the flexible headquarters group used by German General Erwin Rommel in his *Afrika Korps* of World War II fame. This force would, as it turned out, tear through the desert past the other task forces and circle the Al Jaber air base, halfway to Kuwait City on the first day of the ground war. Combat art specialist Colonel H. Avery Chenoweth, seeing the advantages of a light, 4WD vehicle, soon wangled a trade—his Honda for a sand-camouflaged Jeep Cherokee. On Saturday, February 23, G minus 1, he was just inside the "elbow" not far from an abandoned Saudi police station which had been the site of the furious air and tank-on-tank battle weeks before. Stopping at the 1st Marine Division command post, he topped off the gas tank at a nearby fuel depot in preparation for the next day's battle. Nearby, a Ripper recon team scouted a jumping-off spot and scanned the horizon for the enemy.

"A 12-foot-high earthen berm had been bulldozed the entire length of the Kuwait border by the Iraqis and we were behind it," Chenowith said. "The sky over Kuwait on the other side was pitch-black from our aerial bombardment and the burning oil fields. One particularly enormous, bright flash lit up the entire night sky. I suspected it was from a 15,000-pound

CHRISTOPHER MORRIS, BLACK STAR

'Daisy Cutter' FAE [fuel-air-explosive] bomb which was delivered simply by rolling it out of the open back door of a Marine C-130 transport aircraft. I had seen one being loaded at Bahrain. The explosion was incredible! During that moonlit night, we could see other flashes and hear the long drawn-out rumble of a B-52 raid some 40 kilometers away. Two days later I was to descend by helicopter onto the B-52 target area, which was the Al Jaber air base, and witness the effect of that destruction—each of a dozen 30-foot-thick concrete hangars had a large crater right through its middle. The airfield had been a primary ground target, but after the B-52s hit it, there wasn't much reason in taking it, only to bypass and go on."

At the headquarters camp, Chenoweth huddled over a shortwave radio, waiting for the word that President Bush was, indeed, ordering the ground war to begin. When zero hour came, the radio was unnecessary: bombings and artillery barrages—some incoming—mingled with the noise of vehicles revving up. The task forces jumped off during darkness, equipped with night-vision devices and MOPP (mission-oriented protective posture) gear of mask, gloves and protective suit in case of chemical attack.

The spearhead assault unit of the entire Marine attack was the 1st Battalion of the famed

5th Marine Regiment in Task Force Ripper—the remainder of the regiment had stayed with the 4th Marine Expeditionary Brigade aboard ship. The regiment had distinguished itself in World Wars I and II. Chenoweth had served with the unit in the Korean War and, during Desert Shield, had been made an honorary member.

Shortly after dawn, Chenoweth learned that Ripper had streaked on through and breached the minefield barriers with tanks lobbing "giant vipers," or flexible explosive lines, over and in front of themselves to detonate the concealed mines. "The day of the ground war, President Bush had given Saddam Hussein a noon deadline to accept his terms for peace," said Colonel Carl Fulford, commander of Task Force Ripper. "That noon ultimatum was actually 2000 hours [8:00 p.m.] in Saudi Arabia. By that time, Task Force Grizzly, comprised of the 2nd Battalion, 7th Marines, and the 3rd Battalion, 7th Marines, on the left flank, began to move out. On the right flank, Task Force Taro, made up of elements of the 3rd Marines, also proceeded forward and began to infiltrate on foot across the obstacle belt to protect the flanks of Ripper.

"At 2200, we still had not received the word from the commander in chief to begin hostilities. Those two units that were infiltrating were

Having broken through Iraqi defenses, U.S. Marine amphibious personnel carriers take to the desert in a race to Kuwait City, while clouds from burning oil wells darken the daytime sky.

An abandoned Iraqi truck equipped to launch tactical missiles. Even the older Iraqi equipment could have been effective if Saddam Hussein's men had had more motivation to use it. Many an allied soldier was openly grateful that they had not.

given the go-ahead under the condition that they wouldn't do anything irreversible. I'm still not sure what that means. However, they began to put people through the breach. Then I got my orders from the commanding general to start movement into Kuwait but not to be surprised if we were told to turn around at some point. At midnight on G-day, we began our advance to assemble at attack positions 12 kilometers inside the Kuwaiti border. All told, we had 7,000 Marines and 1,000 vehicles of various types—everything from motorcycles to M60 tanks.

"The initial breach was relatively undefended with only a small skirmish on our left flank. Both Grizzly and Taro had done a good job of eliminating any organized resistance on Ripper's flanks. We did lose one M60 tank to a double impulse mine. Fortunately, no one was injured and we completed crossing four breaches in 1½ hours. At the second obstacle belt, we were getting some incoming artillery along our front. However, it wasn't very accurate nor was it sustained, which surprised me. The briefs we had been given had me fearing their artillery more than anything else. It was their most experienced combat arm and the most decisive during the Iran-Iraq War. Their ability to mass concentrations was highly touted. But they didn't do that. They fired 200-300 rounds at us but they landed on the periphery of our formation. Occasionally, though, a few shells would land inside the formation. Counterbattery was effective, but I think the air war had destroyed their command and control capabilities so that every time a plane went overhead it put the fear of God into them. They probably pulled the lanyard and ran. We did suffer four wounded, all minor, as the result of enemy artillery. When you have to concentrate a large force through a relatively narrow area, it can be dangerous. We were exposed."

Captain Ray Coia, Company C, 1st Battalion, 5th Marines, thought the first breaching "went like clockwork." The amtracs were equipped with 3-shot giant viper line charges. A line charge would detonate and clear a path. Then a plow moved forward, plowing through the furrow created by the line charge, detonating or "proofing" any unexploded mines. "You could actually see the mines," said Coia. "The Iraqis had sowed quite a few of them; it was really dense. They were surface mines and they weren't expertly done at all.

"We breached two minefield belts. The first wasn't defended. However, we encountered some artillery and mortar fire going through the second one. It was pretty well coordinated at first, until we responded with counterbattery and then it stopped. They had some older T-55s that were buried and used as stationary pillboxes, but they weren't very effective. They had

CHRISTOPHER MORRIS, BLACK STAR

Some Marines pause during their advance to disarm a group of surrendering Iraqis. Most EPWs displayed no liking for Saddam Hussein. One turned out to be an Iraqi-American pressed into service while visiting his family.

very little flexibility to move their turrets and were eliminated in short order."

With Task Force Papa Bear was a tank named "Scumdog" by its crew, part of the 3rd Battalion, 9th Marines. The vehicle roared into the lead of a wedgelike formation of eight "humvees," four of them equipped with machine guns, MK-19s and 40mm grenade launchers capable of firing 300 rounds per minute. "It's hard to explain the feeling," said Corporal Carl "Randy" Davis. "My stomach was all butterflies. I looked behind me and saw all these amtracs, tanks and Marines and thought: we are actually fixin' to do this." Scumdog, equipped with mine-detonating plows, started to enter the breach as the giant viper lines were fired. The tank behind Scumdog blew a track. "Every time we stopped," Davis said, "the mortarmen would pile out of the amtracs like ants, and set up to be ready to fire in the event we received ene-

my fire. During the second breaching, Sergeant White and our lieutenant were wounded by incoming mortar fire. That was when they were clearing out all the bunkers."

Some of the bunkers were well-stocked with arms. "The Iraqis had the equipment," said Davis. "They had a Sagger [Russian-made anti-tank missile] rigged to be fired remote. They stood a distance away and fired it by using what looked like a joystick. We went to a major Iraqi supply area. In one bunker, they had RPGs [shoulder-fired anti-tank weapons] from Jordan, stacked to the ceiling. Another had bayonets. Another held AK-47s. It was incredible! They could have put up a fight. We thought that if these holes were manned by Viet Cong or NVA soldiers, that the Marines and Army faced during the Vietnam War, we would have taken a lot more casualties."

When Davis had to take his humvee back to the motor pool for some work, he saw another

Egyptian troops guard Iraqis who surrendered to them on February 25. Although indoctrinated to expect torture and death from the Americans, most Iraqis knew of the Egyptian army's reputation for relatively equitable treatment of prisoners, and surrendered readily to them—often with brotherly embraces.

aspect of the war: "They had a wounded 16-year-old Iraqi soldier. Sixteen years old! Our lieutenant said, 'Do you see what kind of nut we're facing? He [Saddam] put a 16-year-old kid in the front lines.' And he hadn't retreated! He put up a good fight, I was told. But he got hit in the head. I stood there watching him die. And there was nothing I could do about it. That showed me what war is all about. It ain't pretty at all."

Papa Bear and the other task forces advanced so rapidly and resistance was so unexpectedly light that the ground-war timetable was advanced—the jump-off of the 2nd Marine Division by a day. Intermediate targets were reached well ahead of schedule. At this time, both BBC and Armed Forces Radio were reporting several amphibious landings on the coast—information which was false.

Farther to the west, the pan-Arab force assaulted the Iraqi line as planned, meeting with the same success as its allies did in the other sectors. The principle Syrian contribution came from their combat engineers, who assisted in clearing the minefields under fire with the same courage and efficiency that they had so often displayed in past conflicts against Israel. The Egyptian troops in particular found their Iraqi counterparts eager to surrender to them. Not that the Iraqis were especially choosy about to whom they surrendered—most of those in the pan-Arab sector were "not convinced of the war," as one Egyptian officer understated it—but, while the Iraqis had heard that the Americans would torture and kill them, they knew of the Egyptian army's past reputation for the humane treatment of prisoners. Besides, the Iraqis felt a measure of brotherhood with the Egyptians.

The next day, February 25, G-day-plus-1, the 1st Marine command post to which Chenoweth

had attached himself broke camp and moved out. The arduous drive in convoy halfway across Kuwait in perfectly flat but soft and deep sand, often whipped by strong wind gusts, led past heaps of wreckage, burned-out tanks which had been half-buried in position, and shallow bunkers that had collapsed. Along the route, EPWs (enemy prisoners of war) stood or walked, guarded by a handful of armed Marines with MOPP 2 gear.

One of the most sensational "catches" of the war was made by Company I, 3rd Battalion, 9th Marines. The incident occurred when Corporal Rob Detherow and his men jumped from a moving personnel carrier at a spot where some Cobra gunships were circling over a group of surrendering Iraqi troops. "An Iraqi approached one of my Marines," said Detherow. "He asked,

Marines examine wrecked Iraqi armor littering the road to Kuwait City. On February 27, Marine Task Force Ripper got into one of the last big armored encounters of the offensive, destroying about 100 Iraqi vehicles, including 60 tanks.

H. AVERY CHENOWETH

'Where the hell have you guys been? I've been waiting four months for you!' It seems this guy was from Chicago. He went to Iraq to visit family and they snagged him off the street and shipped him to the front lines! We rescued him. We processed about 700 EPWs. And there was only one platoon of us. A funny thing happened: the Iraqis thought we were going to eat them. And they also had been told that Marines had to kill a member of their family to be in the Marine Corps! They actually believed this propaganda."

The 1st Marine command-post convoy that Chenoweth was following threaded past elements of Task Force Grizzly, which was on foot, the men lugging heavy packs and weapons in the deep sand on a march that would extend for 23 miles—apparently on a mop-up mission. The 1st Marine command post bivouacked that

night halfway up Kuwait between the Al Jaber airfield on the left and the vast Al Burqan oil field to the right.

In Task Force Papa Bear's sector, the 3rd Battalion of the 9th Marines was also bedding down. "We prepared our defenses that night in the shape of a big sideways 's', said Corporal Rob Detherow. Then this thick fog rolled in. It was like the fog of war. That's what everybody was saying. I couldn't see a thing. Then all hell broke loose. Green tracers started flying everywhere. It was like a drive-by shooting—that's the only way I can describe it—a bunch of Iraqis in armored personnel carriers and BMPs [Russian-built infantry fighting vehicles], shooting at us as they drove by. On our left flank, two Marines ran up to another hole with an AT-4 and shot at the second BMP that drove by and

145

blew it up. They were just 15 or 20 feet from the enemy vehicle. Great shot, but it wasn't a mobilization kill—it didn't bother the Iraqis inside! The turret was still working, so the enemy swung it around and started shooting at these two Marines. That vehicle was finally eliminated by another AT-4."

As the fog started to lift, what Detherow and his fellow Marines had mistaken for a bush turned out to be an enemy tank—which was quickly eliminated. But then, five Iraqi APCs rolled out of the fog to Detherow's right. "The second vehicle was blown to hell by a Dragon round," said Detherow. When the shell hit the APC, the Iraqi who was hanging out of it fell and flopped around on the ground like a fish. The lead vehicle was destroyed by a Marine with an AT-4 from about 500 meters; the missile skipped along the ground, blowing the Iraqi vehicle apart. The third vehicle simply stopped and the Iraqis leapt out and fled. "We just picked them off. And the last two APCs were taken out by other Marines with AT-4s, I believe. This action lasted for some time. I honestly can't say how long though. In combat you lose track of time."

Near the 1st Division's mobile command post, Chenoweth, eager to absorb any experience he could expose himself to for later paintings and other illustrations, went up in a chase Huey on a "psy-ops" low-flying, loudspeaker-rigged mission to persuade bypassed Iraqis to lay down their weapons and surrender. The craft also flew over the forward task force positions, cautious of anti-aircraft dangers, and circled burning oil wells. When the Huey returned for a landing, it was waved off because of a reported gas attack. As the helicopter climbed, the crew donned masks and gloves. The source of the suspected "attack," Chenoweth was told later, occurred when a Marine vehicle hit a mustard gas mine. Chenoweth also learned that his head [latrine] had been built next to a small minefield and some booby-trapped bunkers.

During the night, the Iraqis fired the Burqan oil field to the command post's right, and the Al Gudair field to its left flank. "The roaring of the well-head fires sounded like a thousand freight trains were coming right at us," said Chenoweth, "and I counted 126 fires in a small 40-degree arc on the horizon. The night sky lit up with a red glow that you could read by." Soon, a battery of 155mm howitzers between the command post and the fires periodically fired "time-on-target" missions, in which every coalition artillery piece in an area fires on the same target, with the shells timed to land at the same time.

By February 26, it was clear that the coalition ground offensive was proceeding with greater

ease than expected, so the allied commander, General H. Norman Schwarzkopf, issued new orders to General Salah Halaby, the Egyptian commander of the pan-Arab force, specifying new targets that extended the distance of pan-Arab penetration into Iraqi-held Kuwait, after which his troops were to participate in the massive eastward turn toward Kuwait City, trapping the remnants of the Iraqi defensive forces and the Republican Guard. In effecting these changes in plan, the Egyptian army displayed great control and flexibility of maneuver with the combined-arms tactics it had first put to effective use during the October 1973 Sinai War with Israel. No small factor in this control was General Halaby himself; like Erwin Rommel

and many of his past Israeli counterparts, Halaby was a "fighting general" who believed in staying no farther than three kilometers behind the lines, understanding the importance of keeping in touch with the rapidly changing situation and the effect his closeness to his men would have on their morale. The overall success of the pan-Arab offensive was not to be the only reward for Halaby's aggressive leadership—after the war, he was promoted to lieutenant general.

By the morning of Wednesday, February 27, G-day-plus-3, the descending mist of oil and smoke had deposited an unremovable residue on vehicles, windshields, tents and anything else exposed in the open. When daylight belatedly broke through the eerie overcast, visi-

bility was scarcely a few feet—even then, the command post personnel could not see well enough to pack until after 0900.

As the convoy got underway, about noon, the smoke from the burning wells had so obscured the sky that vehicle headlights were turned on. At 1300, it was darker than midnight. Intermittent chill rain had turned the sand ruts in the roadway to muddy goo. Vehicles fish-tailed, and headlights only dimly picked up the taillights of the next in line. Other convoys, totally blacked out, suddenly came upon the command post column or passed by—often, the only indication being a sudden rocking from the wind of a racing 5-ton truck. Along the way sat the burned-out hulks of Iraqi tanks and personnel carriers.

Silhouetted by Saddam's nightmarish well-fires, Marines advance toward their objective.

PERRY HEIMER, U.S. AIR FORCE

A newly liberated Kuwait International Airport lies nearly in ruins, while the Magwa oil field burns in the distant background.

At the same time the convoy was headed toward Kuwait International Airport, Task Force Ripper engaged in a furious tank battle, the last big one of the war. The task force's M-60 tanks, TOW-mounted LAVs, humvees, and aircraft destroyed more than 100 Iraqi vehicles, including some 60 tanks.

Ahead of the 1st Marine headquarters' trucks, Task Force Papa Bear also was heading toward the airport. "We bypassed positions to stay in front," said Corporal Randy Davis. "The stay team behind us would take 'em prisoner. We were literally running right over them. I positioned myself on top of the humvee with my back against another Marine to cover him with my .50 caliber. It got kind of hard to concentrate—like when two Arabian horses came galloping by. Here are Fury and Black Beauty, with a dog following them, running all over the battlefield. Another time we arrived at an intersection. Here was chaos and combat: tanks, humvees, rounds going off everywhere. All of a sudden: 'Cease-fire! Cease-fire!' Down the road comes a Toyota car. The driver could have been going to work, for all I knew. As he passed, he waved to us. The war just stopped. He zipped by. Then the war continued.

"We went through a place we called Hell's Orchard. It was a fruit orchard near the Kuwaiti International Airport. Scumdog and all the other tanks knocked down the walls. It was like a maze that mice run through; zigzagging all over the place. We couldn't fire our heavy weapons in there because it was dark and real close quarters. This is where they lived. I emptied an entire magazine into one bunker when I received fire. We could only use M-16s and 9mm pistols. If we saw green or white tracers, we opened up. Luckily for us, they abandoned the area. It was a real scary lookin'

place. They could really have messed us up if they'd remained and fought. Thank God they ran!"

That night, the 1st Marine command post was set up on the tarmac of the all-but-destroyed airport and buildings. In the brilliant glow of the fires that lit up the horizon, Chenoweth sketched in colored pencil on black cardboard the silhouette of the wrecked buildings and parked and hovering helicopters. It was to be his last on-the-scene combat sketch.

The flood of prisoners continued to escalate. One of those assigned to guard them was Christopher Burnham of Connecticut (while on duty in the Gulf and wearing his desert camouflage, he had been sworn in as the Republican State Representative for the 147th District). The platoon he led was part of the 1st Battal-

JOHN GAPS, AP/WIDE WORLD

ion, 25th Marines; his platoon alone processed 2,000 prisoners. "It was interesting to note," he said, "that the defenders occupying positions on the first obstacle belts were comprised mainly of Kurds and Turks. As we neared Kuwait City, there were more Sunni Moslems. They were better clothed and better treated. In fact, a few were downright corpulent. Almost to a man if you mentioned the name of Saddam Hussein to them, they would spit on the ground and say: 'Saddam Hussein no good. It is his war—not our war.' Some Iraqis spoke very good English. There was one who even attended community college in New Jersey and worked in a pizza parlor there."

On Thursday, February 28, G-day-plus-4, there was a strange stillness in the air. President Bush had called for a cease-fire to begin at 0800.

Since the Marines had been ordered to stop short of Kuwait City, Chenoweth detached his team, which consisted of himself and a reserve gunnery sergeant, Gerry Sabatino, an artist and New York policeman in civilian life (another artist, Sergeant Charles Grow, was accompanying Grizzly), from the 1st Division. On the way to the coast and back down to Saudi Arabia, the Marine Combat Art Team drove into downtown Kuwait City and headed for the American Embassy. Thus, one of the most improbable units of the war—Chenoweth's Marine Combat Art Team—was the second American unit to enter the city. The first was a Marine 2nd Force recon team of 16 men and officers, who had sped to the structure during the night, securing it and making sure the Stars and Stripes were again flying. □

CHAPTER ELEVEN

HAIL MARY PLAY

82ND AIRBORNE DIVISION

The driver of an M-551 Sheridan light tank of the 82nd Airborne Division gives an optimistic "thumbs up" as Schwarzkopf's end run gets underway.

AS THEIR FELLOW countrymen waited for the expected allied ground offensive along the "Saddam Line" between the Kuwaiti border and Kuwait City, the soldiers of Iraq's Republican Guard also waited. Dispersed throughout the desert in the north of Kuwait, they, too, had had their morale sapped by the coalition aircraft that were constantly seeking them out in their camouflaged fortifications and hiding places. Those who had survived remained nervously at the ready, hoping somehow to receive news of the final allied ground assault—where it would come, to which part of the defensive line they would go as reinforcements, provided allied aircraft didn't annihilate them before they could get there.

By mid-January 1991, 300 helicopters of the 101st Airborne had inserted troops some 70 miles into Iraq along the Euphrates River. Special teams were hard at work adding to the vast pool of allied intelligence.

One of the more vital contributions made by the Green Berets was in the soil samples they took and sent back to allied headquarters in Riyadh, which indicated that the ground on which Schwarzkopf's "Hail Mary" play was to be conducted was solid enough for vehicles to traverse.

On a few occasions, the Green Berets were caught, but the results were invariably more hurtful to the Iraqis than to the Americans. Three, Master Sgt. Jeffrey Sims, Sgt. 1st Class Ronald Torbett and Staff Sgt. Roy Tabron, oper-

ating in the Euphrates Valley just 100 miles south of Baghdad, were detected on the morning of February 23 when a 7-year-old girl found their camouflaged spider hole. The Green Berets could not kill her, and almost paid the price when soon they found themselves surrounded by about 100 Iraqi troops. But Sims called in F-16 airstrikes, and an MH-60 Blackhawk helicopter from the 160th Aviation Regiment of the Special Operations Command raced in at 160 mph to extract the embattled trio. Despite heavy fire from the Iraqis, they managed to get away without a scratch to crewmen or Green Berets, leaving nine Iraqis dead.

On another occasion, an eight-man reconnaissance team fought off 150 Iraqis for six hours before being rescued by helicopter. Between the Green Berets and their air cover, more than 130 casualties were inflicted on the Iraqis, again without loss to the Americans.

Armed with the intelligence gathered from these recon units, the U.S. Army's mechanized

VII Corps, which had hitherto occupied the westernmost sector of the Saudi-Kuwaiti border, began secretly shifting farther west, beyond Kuwait, along the Saudi-Iraqi border.

With VII Corps went the British 1st Armored Division, consisting of the 4th and 7th Armored Brigades (together fielding 157 Challenger tanks, 135 Warrior infantry fighting vehicles and 24 M-109 self-propelled howitzers) and accompanying division troops.

Moving even farther west from its original position between the VII Corps and the U.S. Marines was the Army's XVIII Corps, made up of the 82nd Airborne and 101st Airborne Divisions, and the French 6th Light Armored Division. Taking their place along the border with Kuwait were the Pan-Arab forces, the Marines and the Saudis. Pounded by allied air attacks while deprived of their own air force—and the vital intelligence it could have provided—the Iraqis were unaware of the magnitude of these troop movements and continued to concentrate

their defenses against a direct allied assault into Kuwait that they still expected.

On February 24, while the first allied attacks battered the "Kuwait Line," the VII Corps began its thrust into Iraqi territory; the XVIII Corps, by a combination of air and ground advances, forged even farther afield into Iraqi territory, setting up fuel and supply stations deep in the desert. The farthest advance of the day was made by the 101st Airborne, which landed by air assault in the Tigris-Euphrates Valley, only 100 miles south of Baghdad.

The job of protecting the westernmost flank of the XVIII Corps' advance was assigned to General Bernard Janvier's French 6th Light Armored Division, which was to take and hold the town of As Salman, 95 miles inside Iraq. Despite its name, the 6th Light Armored Division was a land task force comprised of many diverse elements, including the 1st and 2nd Regiments and 6th Engineer Regiment of the Foreign Legion, totaling 3,200 Legionnaires;

An M-551 of the 82nd Airborne, its turret festooned with troops and their gear, advances past the burnt-out remains of an Iraqi T-54 tank on February 27.

Assured of allied air superiority, vehicles of the 82nd Airborne use bright orange identification panels to ensure that they are not targeted by their own planes as they prepare to thrust deep into enemy territory.

the 2nd and 3rd Overseas Infantry, 11th Overseas Artillery and Overseas Armored Infantry Regiments, together comprising 4,000 men; and elements of the Rapid Action Force—the 1st Regiment of Spahis (light armored cavalry), the 4th Regiment of Dragoons, the 1st Airborne Cavalry Regiment, and two combat helicopter regiments with a combined 120 helicopters. In all, the polyglot division totaled about 9,000 men.

The French actually got the offensive off to an early, unofficial start on February 23, though there had been other, small-scale crossings. In the interests of getting into a better position for the main attack, they crossed the border near the Saudi town of Rafhah. The next day, the French task force, bolstered by the 2nd Battalion, 82nd Airborne, moved out in earnest, and within a few hours had seized its intermediate

objective, a series of fortifications held by an Iraqi brigade, code-named "Rochambeau" by the French. By the evening of February 25, the French had moved on to secure their primary target, the airfield at As Salman, in the process of which they also engaged and destroyed the Iraqi 45th Division and took 2,900 prisoners, along with several hundred tanks and artillery pieces. French casualties came to three dead and about 50 wounded.

The overall result, despite the French positioning a day early, was to place the U.S. Army, British and French forces—250,000 troops backed by 3,500 tanks—in position to surprise Saddam Hussein's Republican Guard reserve before it could move forward to bolster the defenders in Kuwait—and also to prevent the Guard from retreating toward Baghdad.

by means of his most notable innovation: giant bladders of fuel suspended beneath CH-53 Chinook helicopters that set up forward refueling stations just behind—and often in front of—the advancing airborne and mechanized units.

Perhaps the most vital service in the Gulf was performed by the support cadre that proved to be the least needed—the NBC (nuclear biochemical) specialists, who were responsible for maintaining supplies of the protective masks and suits that made up MOPP (mission oriented protective posture) gear, chemical detecting equipment and antidotes for chemical agents, and who trained the troops on their effective use. Saddam Hussein's past record of using chemical agents against the Iranians and the Kurds imported a deadly earnestness to their activities. Some coalition troops kept live canaries as "early warning" of gas attack. At least one opted for a chicken—for warning and, eventually, a victory dinner.

Sergeant First Class Anthony Harper, of the 197th Infantry Brigade's Decontamination Platoon, described one aspect of NBC's role:

"When we first arrived in Saudi Arabia on Operation Desert Shield, we deconned [decontaminated] a company every other day for training until it became Operation Desert Storm. I have 15 years experience, so I felt pretty comfortable doing this. I could do it in my sleep. When we first got there, the heat was unbearable. It was pretty uncomfortable in our MOPP suits. But because of our training, we could have easily deconned at night. However, if the Iraqis had decided to use chemical agents against us then, it could have been pretty rough. They never did, though."

The payoff for all that bothersome NBC training in the sand came during the allied advance, when allied soldiers found stockpiles of artillery shells with chemical warheads and, in at least one case, written orders to use them. As the allies had feared, Iraq was indeed planning to keep open the option of bringing its chemical arsenal into play.

The very existence of chemical protection in the allied camp, however, removed the advantage of using chemical weapons—it would have gained the Iraqis little other than the possibility of the allies returning it in kind, in which case both sides would be miserable as they sweltered in their MOPP suits in the desert sun. Knowledge of how to counter the chemical threat—and the Iraqi army's knowledge that the allies had that ability—had served as a deterrent that undoubtedly influenced Iraq's front-line troops to disregard any orders from Baghdad to resort to their chemical weapons.

Schwarzkopf's plan came to its ultimate fruition on February 24, as the giant trap he had

82ND AIRBORNE DIVISION

Two 82nd Airborne members get their vectors straight. The NAVSTAR global positioning system (GPS) satellites and efficient communications eased allied navigation in the desert, even in sandstorms.

Backing up this effort were the essential services that the combat troops so often referred to by the derogatory acronym of "REMFs," but without whom they could not have pursued the greater program to come. In command of Army logistics was General Gus Pagonis, the son of a Greek-American short-order cook, who developed techniques of his own for providing the VII and XVIII Corps with more than just cheeseburgers on short order. Confident, like Schwarzkopf, that the allies had complete control of the skies, Pagonis had seen to it that the roads leading west from Kuwait were filled with trailer trucks, keeping the Army's combat units supplied daily with 5,000 tons of ammunition, as well as 555,000 gallons of fuel, 300,000 gallons of water and 80,000 meals. Once the XVIII Corps began its "leapfrogging," Pagonis kept up with it

Decorated with the famous jerboa emblem of the ''Desert Rats'' of World War II, FV432 and FV439 fighting vehicles of the British 7th Armored Brigade prepare to sally forth against an opponent much less formidable than the Germans in 1941.

so carefully laid sprang shut. Swinging east, the VII and XVIII Corps began systematically destroying the Republican Guard in detail. Cut off from their higher-ups, the Republican Guard units were still awaiting orders to move south when they found themselves under attack from a completely unexpected direction. Great numbers of their tanks were shot from the rear, their artillery crews caught with their guns pointing in the wrong direction.

Sergeant John Combs was with Headquarters Company, 3rd Battalion, 69th Armor, when the ground offensive got underway:

"What went through our minds when we got the word was: 'Oh my God, we're finally going to do this.' We moved fast and made no contact at first. I had a hard time seeing, because the dust was giving us thermal washout. We could see vehicles, but it was difficult to identify them because of the weather.

"My tank caught on fire about 70 kilometers short of Jalibah airfield. The rest of the battalion moved out and a maintenance crew changed the engine right there. That took about three hours. Not bad, considering the awful weather conditions."

Staff Sergeant William James of A Company, 3rd Battalion, 69th Armor, was more successful in keeping his M1A1 tank going: "We just took off! We crashed through the border about 1530 [3:30 p.m.]. We had to stop every two hours to clean air filters and change oil. The weather was real nasty. We had a 30-mph wind slapping us in the face while we were doing 20 mph in our tanks. To our front, the scouts were picking up contact and capturing EPWs."

Captain Stephen Sicinski, operations officer (S-3) of the 197th Infantry Brigade, described his unit's participation in VII Corps' advance:

"We were on the far left flank of the 24th Mechanized Brigade," he said. "We were the far-

thest west mechanized unit on the sweep. The French 6th Light Armor were on our left, but stopped and consolidated between the border and the valley. The 82nd Airborne had one brigade attached to the French, with the other two brigades behind them. The 82nd Airborne passed through us after we secured our objectives. The 101st Airborne was performing raids and interdiction between [As] Samawah and [An] Nasiriyah while we were doing the ground attack north into the Euphrates River valley.

"We did our attack in two phases. First was Objective Brown, about midway between the border and the valley itself. The second phase was the actual assault on the valley. We were located about 100 kilometers southeast from the town of Rafhah. We were between the Tapline Road and the border of Iraq, a very narrow area. We actually did our attack a little early on February 24. It was a very windy day with low visi-

Challenger tanks of the British 1st Armored Division attached to VII Corps make final preparations to move out. In addition to these giants, the Brits fielded 24 Scorpion and 24 Scimitar light tanks.

bility. We blew through the berm at about 25 to 30 mph. We tried to maintain that speed throughout the campaign. The Delta 4th Cavalry is a troop-sized element, reinforced with artillery and a MLRS [multiple launch rocket system] battery that was assigned to us for most of the operation. They acted as a recon and guard element about 10 kilometers to the front of us.

"We went north to Objective Brown, about 100 miles north of the border. We stopped to refuel our tanks and APCs [armored personnel carriers]. We had to refuel our tanks twice. The attack started late afternoon and lasted throughout the night. We dropped a lot of close air support on logistic sites and swept in with the battalion at first light. We captured 50 prisoners—guard troops and radar operators, mostly. We consolidated our positions and moved out to attack position Kelly. By the end of Day Two, we started our hooking movement, or right

wheel. And we were still the farthest unit north and left. And moving pretty fast!

"When we arrived at Kelly, a vicious sandstorm started that dropped visibility down to nothing. Winds were 40 knots or higher. It didn't affect us in terms of navigation, because of the GPS (global positioning system), and communications.

"The next day we began surprising smaller-sized units. They didn't know we were in the area. Then it started raining. The terrain got worse. Where it had been level, it was now hilly and rocky. We hit a bunch of dunes. Then we hit dry lake beds—which weren't dry anymore. The maps were pretty poor. Quite a few people got stuck—a lot of mud—tanks were stuck up to their road wheel. But we kept moving and we were able to recover better than 90 percent of our weapons systems and use them for the attack.

AMX-30B2 tanks of the 4ème Regiment de Dragons (Dragons de Mourmelon), *attached to XVIII Corps, raise dust as they storm their way toward As Salman to raise hell.*

JOEL M. TORRES, U.S. ARMY

SPC ELLIOTT, U.S. ARMY

TOP: M1 tanks of 3rd Brigade, 1st Armored Division, roll past a heap of burning scrap, which had once been a T-72 tank of the Republican Guard, a few kilometers outside of Kuwait on February 28. ABOVE: A defensive complex of the 2nd Battalion, 45th Iraqi Infantry Division, is overrun by troops of A Company, 1st Battalion, 327th Infantry Regiment, 101st Airborne Division.

"We ran into an Iraqi Special Forces regiment. They were slightly larger than us, about 7,000 to 8,000 people. They were completely disorganized. They didn't know we were there. We really surprised them. The attack wasn't like anything you could imagine. It all happened at high speed. We dropped a lot of air and artillery on them. That's where most of the destruction came from. The close air support was up north already. It was hard to get air in real close because of the poor visibility and because we operated mostly at night.

"Then we moved toward Objective Utah. This is just south of Highway 8 and Tallil airfield. This was a key area. Now every other armored unit was beginning to line up, although we were still the lead element. Two brigades of the 24th had already swung into the valley to the east. The 197th was oriented more to the west and north, covering our rear. And at this point we became the division reserve.

"We conducted a raid into Tallil airfield. It was pounded heavily with wave after wave of sorties. This was a combination of A-10 Warthogs, F-15s and F-16s. Two company teams went in and destroyed lots of personnel and equipment. We caught half a dozen planes on the ground, helicopters, air defense weapons systems, and APCs. It was real quick. The entire attack at Tallil lasted only 15-20 minutes. It was very violent and very quick. We had to go through the front gate because the airfield was surrounded by berms.

"After the attack on the airstrip, that raiding force rejoined the remainder of the brigade and we started moving east along Highway 8. We were taking lots of prisoners by this time; I'd say 1,000 or 1,500. They put up very little resistance. The 1st of the 18th was designated to cover our rear because of the unknown threat to the north.

"We later learned that the raid into Tallil had more significance than we first realized. What it did was unhinge the entire Iraqi defense. They thought we were going to attack north along the Euphrates River valley to Baghdad. This triggered a lot of movement by the Republican Guard and their heavy armored units. It enabled the VII Corps and the Air Force to close in and hammer them with Warthogs. And that was our main objective—to have the Iraqis pull out of their revetments so we could destroy them on the move. And it worked out well.

Sergeant Daniel Stice of 2nd Battalion, 69th Armor, 197th Infantry Brigade, described his view of the war as the tank commander of an M1 main battle tank:

"On the 25th, this screening force went along Highway 8, or 'Hardball,' as we called it. There were a lot of underpasses that we had to secure, and hidden under them were many Iraqis. We

158

ANTHONY SUAU, BLACK STAR

began firing our main-gun rounds at enemy trucks. You could actually see the Iraqis being blown from the vehicles. The EPWs thought we had airdropped our tanks and APCs into the area. That demonstrated to us that we definitely had the element of surprise on our side. They didn't realize what had hit them! That night we hit a mechanized infantry battalion about 15-20 miles away from Hardball. They were so disoriented! We fired about 2,000 coax rounds from our M-240 machine guns at them—and that's just our vehicle! Pretty soon the Iraqis would show their white flags and surrender. We processed EPWs all through the night of the 25th.

"The next morning, February 26, the ammunition trucks we had destroyed were still exploding. It was at this time that we received an operational order from brigade to seize Tallil airfield. This airfield was a threat to us because of its communication and radar equipment for the Republican Guard. I had nine tanks from Alpha Company, and Delta Company sent nine plus a platoon from the 2nd Battalion, 7th Cavalry. We lined up on the Hardball and moved out very fast—35 to 40 miles per hour. The air and artillery had prepped the area. When we got in there, we had to maneuver like an 'S' to avoid these massive berms. They had bunkers filled with RPGs [rocket-propelled grenades], AK-47s and other supplies.

"I fired the first main-gun round at a truck blocking the front gate and went right through with my tank. To our right, and to our front, there were probably 20 to 25 SA-60s [French-built helicopters]. We had main-gun rounds going off everywhere! Bore sight was great. The tanks hit everything we aimed at—SA-60s, MiG-23s, MiG-29s, Hind-D helicopters, a civilian plane and two radar discs. Plus we took out a lot of enemy soldiers there with our main gun as well as 7.62mm rounds from our machine guns. My tank alone fired 15 main-gun rounds and over 2,000 rounds of 7.62mm ammunition. We just leveled the place!

"We were on the road February 27, acting as a blocking force. We knocked out more trucks as far away as 1,800 to 2,000 meters. The EPWs we were capturing were so happy! They were patting us on the back saying: 'President Bush, good man!' I remember seeing one Iraqi who had had his legs blown off just sitting there smiling and telling me how grateful he was. That tells you what kind of life they had under Saddam Hussein."

Captain Matt Johnson, S-3 officer to 2nd Brigade, 24th Mechanized Infantry, described his unit's contribution:

"G-day for the French and other units was February 24," he said. "We were originally scheduled to move on the 25th. Later, I ascer-

AH-64 Apaches on the prowl. Although less rugged than the Air Force's A-10 Warthogs, the Apaches packed just as much tank-busting punch and provided the U.S. Army troops with formidable close-support capabilities while taking a heavy toll of Iraqi armor.

159

Artillery duel: Soldiers from the 101st Airborne Division in Saudi Arabia exchange shots with their Iraqi counterparts.

An Iraqi T-54 tank burns in the desert, one of hundreds knocked out by a variety of allied ground and air weapons.

tained that we jumped off early because of the tremendous success of the other assaults.

"The first 100 kilometers into Iraq, we encountered absolutely nothing. A sandstorm kicked up and impaired our vision. We could see no more than 200 meters to our front, so our formation had to be real tight. Our first objective, code-named 'Gray,' was about 10-15 meters west of [Makhfar] al Busayyah. This area was chosen to block any east-west travel. We reached Gray on the 25th and met one resistance which we quickly eliminated. They were primarily communication and light infantry units. About 90 Iraqis surrendered to us.

"On the 26th, we continued north to our new objective, Red Prime—just south and east of Objective Red. My brigade, the 2nd, was right behind the 1st Brigade. Securing that, we moved into Objective Orange to seize the Jalibah airfield. At 0400, we started our artillery prep consisting of MLRS [multiple-launch rocket system] and howitzers. The Iraqis began firing their air defense weapons, mainly the ZSU-23/4, mistaking our artillery barrage for an airstrike. They were just firing blindly with their air defense, and we were able to pinpoint them and our counterbattery took them out. In all, we destroyed between 12 and 14 tanks, some helicopters, and even a few aircraft, I believe they were MiG-23 Floggers, that were parked on the ground. It was like a shooting gallery.

running. Our artillery opened up near Jalibah airfield to prep it. Nobody told us and we thought it was incoming. Before you know it, I had three guys on top of me inside the turret.

"We had intelligence reports that said there was a company of T-55s and about 400 dismounts [infantry] at the airport. We crossed the Hardball and I stayed in the hatch to watch the whole thing. Charlie Company opened fire first, followed by Bravo Company, then Alpha. The Iraqi AA positions opened up with 14.5mm and 52mm. I saw their flashes. A MiG was destroyed, plus some tool sheds, and I saw a bunker destroyed with a TOW. That was impressive. The whole thing lasted probably 30 minutes after 3/15 and 1/64 swept across the airfield."

Back in Kuwait, there were virtually no defenses left for the embattled Republican Guard units to bolster. Allied aircraft, their efficiency honed by experience—including some sobering past tragedies in which allied troops had been killed in error by their own air support—now blasted a swath through minefields, flattened berms and swept-away barbed wire. The Egyptians, Syrians, U.S. Marines and Saudis who rushed into the resultant breach found thousands of demoralized Iraqi soldiers waiting to surrender to them. At least one Iraqi remarked to his allied captors that the only reason he and his comrades had not surrendered earlier was that they did not know how to get through their own minefields. These had been laid in staggered form by those who prepared the defensive positions in order to prevent just such desertions—many of the Iraqis had been waiting for the allies to clear a path through those minefields for them!

Farther north and east, the Republican Guard fought with somewhat more determination with the best tanks and artillery available—for all the good it did them. Many of Saddam Hussein's elite substituted mass slaughter for mass

An M109A3 self-propelled howitzer burns, either the victim of enemy resistance—which was intermittently sharp in the northern and eastern areas of Iraq—or allied error.

"The 1st Brigade ran into a whole convoy of Republican Guard forces on heavy equipment trailers, moving east to west along the Euphrates River valley, attempting to escape down Highway 8. They were quickly destroyed. They [the 1st Brigade] first ran into a light infantry commando unit, which is basically an execution squad, looking for deserters. After the engagement, the captured Iraqis informed the 1st Brigade they had no idea we had advanced that far. This was because we took out their command and control structure so quickly when the war started."

Staff Sergeant William James of A Company also helped overrun the airfield: "The Iraqi artillery was very inaccurate—when they weren't

A squad from the 82nd Airborne attached to the French 6th Light Armored Division takes position behind such cover as the desert can provide while armored vehicles advance.

An Iraqi bunker blows up as elements of the allied offensive turn eastward toward Kuwait City.

surrender—with as many as half of Iraq's 4,280 tanks already destroyed by allied air attacks and the rest being outmaneuvered and picked off almost as quickly as they emerged from their underground revetments.

Sergeant First Class Mike Bachand, serving in Headquarters and Headquarters Company of 5th Battalion, 16th Infantry, 1st Infantry Division, described one such encounter:

"We made the breach, and the Brits, together with VII Corps, shot through us. We had two tank companies, equipped with M1A1s, and two Bradley fighting vehicle companies, with M2s. The scouts had M3 Bradleys. We went east and became a blocking force in case the Iraqis decided to counterattack us.

"We had a night tank battle on the 27th of February with the Republican Guard. I can't tell how long the battle lasted—you lose track of time. We didn't lose any tanks or Bradleys in the fighting. We used the thermal sights which gave us the advantage over them. We could see them before they could see us. And we had the range on 'em...with our 120mm main guns. They had T-55s and T-72s. It was a 'hands down, see you later Jack' victory. We blew the hell out of 'em!"

Playing a more direct role in that night battle was Sergeant Brian Baker, the gunner of an M1A1 tank of 2nd Battalion, 34th Armor, 1st Infantry Division:

"When we first went through the breach, the Air Force had prepped the area pretty good. On February 27, we attacked elements of the Republican Guard at night. We had the advantage because our night sights are far superior to theirs. They didn't know we were there until we opened fire. And they couldn't fire back at us because, basically, they couldn't see us. We had two companies of scouts with us that came up on line and stopped. Then we just sat back and picked them off. Once the round hit, you could see the turrets just pop right off the enemy vehicles. They would burn for 35-40 minutes. The fuel and ammunition would keep it burning. And the rounds they stored in the tank would explode. They were trying to evade us, but the thermal sights we have picked them up. We had orders to fire at will. It was a free-for-all.

"We used the sabot round, which is like a giant, dartlike projectile. We also used HEAT rounds that have a shaped charge. I like the HEAT round because it could cause more destruction in my opinion, especially against the T-54s, T-55s and T-62s. The sabot was more effective against the T-72s.

"Once, we went into this area to secure it and my tank was in the lead. We had to cross a small wall the Iraqis had built. We found three T-55s. My platoon sergeant was in the other tank and he engaged one of the T-55s and destroyed it. However, they wouldn't let us fire on the other two because they were afraid we would have missed and maybe hit a friendly vehicle on the other side of the wall. I was scared because I

saw Iraqi crew members jump into these tanks just seconds before. We were lucky because I don't think they spotted us. When they finally did, a couple of Bradleys with TOWs mounted on them took out the other two T-55s."

"After that," continued Mike Bachand, "we made our way to the right and toward Kuwait. Our battalion defended the area where General Schwarzkopf met with the Iraqis at the peace conference. There was a Republican Guard tank brigade three clicks north of us. That's who we were guarding against. There were more helicopter gunships there than I ever saw in my life!

"I had three tours in Vietnam, but I never saw a war like this. It was fast and furious...."

The British had assigned three infantry battalions—the 1st Coldstream Guards, the Royal Highland Fusiliers and the King's Own Scottish Borderers—the job of handling the EPWs. Soon, however, there were so many that even the specialized units found their ability to accommodate them stretched to the limit.

"The EPWs were amazing," added Sergeant Baker. "We'd come across hundreds walking through the desert, just waving, smiling and giving us thumbs up. That's where Saddam was wrong—he wanted to fight, but his army didn't."

By February 28, as all allied units converged on a liberated Kuwait City, there was no longer a question of where the U.S. Army had been. It had applied the *coup de grâce* to a coalition victory already preordained by a month of

preparatory air attacks, and it had done so with results that had done its commander proud. It had annihilated the fourth-largest army in the world, inflicting as many as 100,000 deaths upon it, while losing less than 150 men.

On March 2, Republican Guard troops fired on a U.S. Army platoon. In response, the Americans destroyed 23 T-72 tanks and numerous other vehicles. The next day, General Schwarzkopf met with the Iraqi field command to spell out conditions for a permanent cease-fire. With him was Saudi commander Lt. Gen. Khalid Ibn Sultan. The American wore desert camouflage, while the Iraqis had donned more formal uniforms, including shoulder boards. Schwarzkopf had to give the skeptical generals assurances that he was, indeed, the American who would meet with them. The Iraqis further showed their ignorance of the strategic situation when they told the coalition side that they had 45 allied prisoners, then asked how many Iraqis had been captured. "About 60,000," quipped Schwarzkopf. The Iraqis' stunned surprise was eloquent testimony to how uninformed they really were of the overall situation.

In Iraq, Captain Matt Johnson and the 24th Infantry reacted in their own way: "When we got word of the cease-fire, all the American flags went up. In Saudi Arabia, we weren't allowed to fly our flag out of respect for their customs and religion. However, when the shooting stopped, all the flags came out!" □

Members of the 101st Airborne Division take a breather over the ruins of an Iraqi bunker complex. The man at left carries an AT-4 anti-tank missile launcher in case the Republican Guard still cares to dispute their presence.

CHAPTER TWELVE

AFTERMATH AND ANALYSIS

H. AVERY CHENOWETH

Marine combat artist Colonel H. Avery Chenoweth makes it to the U.S. Embassy in Kuwait City. His was the second American unit to reach the compound.

ON FEBRUARY 28, 1991, two-thirds of the Marine Combat Art Team, Colonel H. Avery Chenoweth and Gunnery Sgt. Gerry Sabatino, drove their Jeep Cherokee into Kuwait City. The non-military-looking vehicle wound down wreckage-lined streets. Debris was strewn everywhere—wrecked cars, stores, buildings, hotels—and there was no water or electricity. . .a ghost town, but one of breathtakingly modern architecture.

People slowly began to appear when they saw the combat artists, who had taken off their combat gear, put aside their weapons, and were down to plain desert camouflage and floppy hats. Civilians ran up or drove past, flashing the "V" for victory sign and yelling: "Thank you! Thank you, Marines! Thank you, President Bush!" The two artists waved back, and fell into an impromptu motorcade.

The team found numerous abandoned Iraqi Russian-made T-62 and T-55 tanks littering the roadways along the bay. One had live rounds all around it, along with a varied assortment of clothing, plus some baby things—dolls, a teddy bear and a juvenile walker—presumably stolen from stores to take back to Baghdad.

The defenses left behind by the Iraqis were amazingly crude: a few strings of barbed wire, some sandbagged trenches, and some mines along the beach where the amphibious assault that never happened had been expected. Saddam Hussein's troops seemed to have an equally primitive concept of air defense—a few unprotected British Bofors 40mm ack-ack guns

of World War II vintage sitting out on the sidewalk, and other relics such as quadruple-mount .30-caliber machine guns, seldom seen except in reruns of 1940s movies. Another feeble defense consisted of piles of tires and other trash, which had been set afire to create a smoke-screen—of sorts—against air attack.

The art team also found the American Embassy and the 2nd Marine Expeditionary Force recon team of 16 men and officers who had sped to it in the middle of the night. "We told them about the cease-fire," said Chenoweth, "and discovered that we were the second Marine—American, for that matter—military unit to reach the embassy. Us! The Marine Corps *Combat Art Team*! The press reported an Army 'commando' team helicoptering to the American Embassy. However, that occurred three days later."

DENNIS BRACK, BLACK STAR

Caught in an allied air attack while in the act of flight, a devastated convoy of Iraqi military and "appropriated" civilian vehicles litters a highway north of Kuwait City, March 1.

An Army soldier's account varied somewhat—his claim was that a Special Forces unit had slipped in earlier and that "[members] of the 3rd Special Forces had stormed the U.S. Embassy eight times. After the initial assault, they did it again for the ambassador, the press, for training purposes and other various reasons. They would speed-rope in and do it again."

One of the later arrivals, Spc. 4 Tim Moss, said: "When we finally went into the city itself...the Kuwaitis were having parties everywhere. The city resembled New Orleans at Mardi Gras time or Times Square in New York City on New Year's Eve....I was kissed by more men than women. It was so crowded with people and cars, you couldn't walk the sidewalks. Kuwaitis were firing M-16s, AK-47s and even M-60 machine guns in the air. It looked like a light show with all the tracer rounds going skyward. Tragically, 30 or so people died as a result of these indiscriminate rounds."

For months after the liberation, the Iraqi occupation continued to take its toll. Kuwaitis continued to lose limbs to hidden Iraqi "shoe mines." The search went on for more than 3,000 Kuwaitis who had either simply disappeared or been taken out of the city by the fleeing Iraqis. Residents struggled to breathe against suffocating toxins from the fires of February that still blotted out the sun. Reports of Iraq's summary executions of civilians and suspected deserters continued, along with sporadic exchanges of shots between Iraqi and coalition forces—including the downing in March of two Iraqi Su-22 fighters by U.S. F-15s in separate incidents. By mid-June, 1991, there were reports that Saddam had hidden and preserved some of his nuclear warfare capability.

CHARLES PLAIAU, REUTERS/BETTMANN

Saddam's man-made oil spills posed hazards of another type. John Walsh, director general of the Boston-based World Society, said that animal-rescue teams from the world over would attempt to undo whatever harm they could. Uncounted wild birds were found to be dying from the toxins spewed by the fires. Some birds and fish—long a staple commodity in the Persian Gulf—were particularly vulnerable to the oil spills. Thousands of gulls, cormorants, grebes and other seabirds fouled by oil lay dying or dead, littering beaches, rocks and coastal grasses. "If the birds are dying like this, it must also be affecting humans," said biologist Walsh.

Walsh and his volunteers scrambled to help the handful of zoo animals (out of an original 442) still alive after the Iraqis fled. A mine detector was used to locate bullets in a wounded elephant. Among the other animals they treated were seven monkeys, five lions and two tigers.

For Kuwaiti health officials, the postwar chapter of the country's ordeal promised to prove most harrowing of all. The long-term effects of the oil-fire fumes were of special concern. In mid-March 1991, more than 600 fires still raged, blanketing the Gulf with more than 35 million cubic yards a day of methane, ethane, propane, butane, copper and arsenic, along with acid sulfides of hydrogen and sulfur. No one knew how to deal with the long-term effects—not Kuwait's specialists, not foreign experts, not the U.S. Environmental Protection Agency nor its international counterparts. "The trouble, you see, is the scale of the thing," observed Mohamad Bakr Amin of King Fahd University. "No matter what the computer models show," he said, "the catastrophic effects are for the people who live in the immediate region...for others, the impacts of the events will be far away; it will be some time before the effects are felt."

Desert Storm's political environment was murky as well. The international trade embargo and Iraq's staggering losses in the war triggered open revolt within more than 20 Iraqi cities. On March 4, less than a week after the cease-fire, Kurdish and Shiite rebels were being hunted down and killed by Iraqi helicopter gunships. In April, the plight of the Kurds and Shiites prompted the United States Holocaust Memorial Council to issue a statement saying that the council, "concomitant with its mandate to educate the American public about the slaughter of millions of innocent victims by the Nazis 50 years ago, recognizes that although the scope and nature of events in Iraq are different, the suffering of the victims is not. The council condemns the slaughter and calls for the international community to assist the hundreds of thousands of Kurdish and Shiite civilians at risk of massacre, torture and forced expulsion from Iraq."

Despite such pleas and many appeals for armed intervention, the Bush administration at first declined to become involved in Iraq's internal strife, though coalition forces did construct and maintain camps to provide sanctuary for thousands of refugees fleeing from Iraq's civil war.

Meanwhile, reconstruction of ravaged Kuwait began slowly—and expensively. The U.S. Army Corps of Engineers spearheaded the effort in assessing damage and preparing to return basic services. The rebuilding itself was projected to take five years, at a cost of more than $60 billion. Although the country lay in ruins after the war, its wealth remained considerable. Even during the war, Kuwaiti agents were reported to be stockpiling drilling equipment for later shipment to the war-torn country. In addition, some of the cost could be extracted from Iraq: "There are Iraqi government assets which are locked and frozen," said Sheik Saud Nasir Al-Sabah, Kuwait's ambassador to the United States. Further, he said, most of the rebuilding contracts would go to U.S. companies "in recognition of the immense sacrifice of the people of the United States in liberating Kuwait."

The task of controlling the hundreds of oil-well fires alone was considerable. Putting out the fires, which were burning more than 6 million barrels of oil a day, required the expertise of three companies, two American and one Canadian. To extinguish an oil-well blaze, explosives must be lowered into the well, under a covering spray of water. The explosives then are detonated, drawing off oxygen and suffocating the fire. The crews experienced long delays in getting the proper equipment and in building special water pipelines to the Gulf.

Formidable as the physical rebuilding appeared, political reconstruction was even more daunting. Although a U.S.-style democracy seemed unlikely—perhaps even undesirable—to a country with a ruling emir, there were signs of movement toward a change in direction for Kuwait's form of government. In April, a new cabinet was named. Only a little more than a month after the Iraqi invasion the previous August, Kuwait's ruling Al-Sabah family had backed a "National Kuwaiti People's Congress" meeting in Saudi Arabia that was attended by more than 1,300 prominent Kuwaiti exiles. One of them, Hassan Al-Ibrahim, former rector of Kuwait University, later told an Arab-American journal: "I have no doubt that Kuwait will emerge from this period of trial with a strengthened social and political fabric. Kuwait has learned many lessons relating to its own people and the behavior of other states. . .it can be assumed that in the future Kuwait will have a pronounced democratic character and that together

American General H. Norman Schwarzkopf and Saudi Lt. Gen. Prince Khalid discuss cease-fire terms with Iraqi commanders Lt. Gen. Mohammed Abdez Rahman al-Dagitistani and Lt. Gen. Sabin Abdel-Aziz al Douri, on March 3, 1991. The astonishment of the Iraqis at the disparity involved in prisoner exchange demonstrated how ignorant they still were of the magnitude of their own defeat.

Darkness at noon: Marines disembark from their helicopter to the roof of the U.S. Embassy on February 28, amid the haze caused by burning oil fields. There will be work ahead, putting the embassy back in working order—and much more work to restore the ravaged nation of Kuwait.

with its neighbors will manifest a much stronger. . .self-awareness."

In the wake of Desert Storm, the United States assumed leadership in trying to hammer out a peaceful solution to a wide range of political ills in the Middle East, including differences between Israel and its Arab neighbors. Although Israel was drawn to the brink of war during the Iraqi Scud attacks, its restraint won the Jewish state some credibility among the Arab members of the coalition, notably Egypt and even Syria—though the latter technically remained in a state of war with Israel. Israel's Yitzhak Shamir government refused to budge on two points: 1) the fate of the West Bank, where continued Jewish settlement made the possibility of its being returned to Jordan or becoming part of a separate Palestinian state slimmer; 2) Israel's refusal to meet with representatives of the Palestinian Liberation Organization (PLO) in any talks with Palestinians. The Palestinians, meanwhile, pressed to have the PLO represented in any such talks, but PLO leader Yasser Arafat—along with Jordan's King Hussein—had lost worldwide credibility for taking a pro-Saddam stance during Desert Storm.

An unacknowledged force during Saddam's invasion and occupation of Kuwait had been Palestinian "freedom fighters" living in Kuwait, who, with the Kuwaiti Resistance, had provided valuable intelligence to coalition forces (ironically, during the war, a great number of Palestinians in Jordan had demonstrated in support of Saddam). Instead of recognition, many Palestinians in Kuwait were looked upon as probable collaborators with the Iraqis. "Nobody trusts them," said one coalition soldier. "Two Palestinian women told me that people would spit on them as they walked by. I just don't understand that."

While the United States struggled on the political front, the coalition was busy partially dismantling the wartime machinery left behind. In the waters of the Gulf, free-floating mines remained a hazard to navigation. British Secretary of State for Defense Tom King reported in March that the Iraqis' main minefield ran in a crescent along most of the length of the Kuwaiti coast. He said that smoke from burning oil wells had helped screen early clearing operations, but that the "worst of it" had been cleared.

American forces gathered enough live ammunition to fill about 15,000 flatbed trucks, according to Donna Mikles in *Soldiers* magazine. As the VII Corps prepared to return to bases in Germany, trucks were repainted—woodland camouflage replacing the familiar desert sand color scheme. Helicopters were packaged in plastic for shipboard loading.

Meanwhile, thousands of troops began coming home to Stateside ports and air bases. They

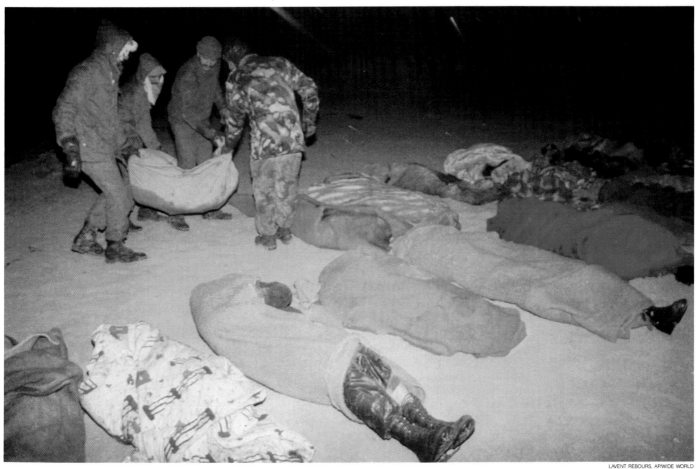

were greeted by an outpouring of public support not seen since World War II. General H. Norman Schwarzkopf personally welcomed allied prisoners returned by the Iraqis, embracing Spc. 4 Melissa Rathbun Nealy as though she were a long-lost daughter.

At Hampton Roads, the venerable battleship *Wisconsin* navigated the channel toward Virginia's Norfolk Naval Base. Scores of sailboats, powerboats, launches, and even a cruise ship escorted her upriver. The sun glistened on the saluting jets of water being sprayed high by the horn-tooting fireboats. A few miles away, at Langley Air Force Base, Jim Drewke, an aircraft service technician with the 1st Tactical Fighter Wing, stood on the flight line near rows of F-15s. He admitted some concerns about how he would be received. "But when I saw all those hundreds of people waiting on the strip when we landed I was prouder of being an American than I've ever been in my life," he said.

"It's a proud day for Americans, and by God, we've licked the Vietnam syndrome once and for all," said President George Bush when Desert Storm drew to its spectacular close. On June 8, 1991, some 800,000 people attended a national victory parade of troops led by a somber Schwarzkopf in Washington, D.C.

Few would deny that, strategically, the roots of the victory in the sands of the Persian Gulf lay in the jungles of Vietnam, for the one unifying force that bound all the senior commanders in Desert Storm—from Chairman of the Joint Chiefs of Staff General Colin Powell to General Schwarzkopf, the U.S. commander in the Gulf, to the senior Army, Navy, Air Force and Marine generals, to the commanders of the divisions, combat brigades and regiments—was their combat experience in Vietnam.

Following Vietnam and the confusions of counterinsurgency, there was movement back toward fundamental conventional war missions. As early as April 1972, the basis for the Marine Expeditionary Force that performed so well in the Gulf was laid. "We are pulling our heads out of the jungle and getting back into the amphibious business," said General Robert E. Cushman, then the commandant of the Marine Corps. "[We] are redirecting our attention seaward and re-emphasizing our partnership with the Navy and our shared concern in the maritime aspects of our national strategy."

And the other services followed suit. By 1979, the newly formed Army Training and Doctrine Command had begun work on a new "warfighting" doctrine. Called "AirLand Battle," it was first published in 1982 in an Army field manual called *Operations.* Instead of attempting to win a war by wearing down and destroying the enemy's armed forces, the new doctrine

Iraqi EPWs carry the body of a dead comrade to a collection point for Iraqis killed during the brief fight for Kuwait City on February 28. Thousands of them had paid with their lives for Saddam Hussein's ambitions, but he survived, leaving the war's ultimate legacy in continuing dispute.

Kurdish insurgents drive through Arbil during the civil strife in Iraq that followed the coalition victory. Through the ruthless use of the military resources he had managed to conserve, Saddam Hussein managed to hold on against the Kurds, Iraqi Shiites and contingents of his own disillusioned soldiers.

called for rapid maneuver to disorient and confuse the enemy. It had three main components: deep operations, primarily by the Air Force, to disrupt the enemy's command, control and communications and destroy his war-making facilities; rear operations involving the buildup and protection of supplies; and "close operations" to break through enemy defenses and destroy his armed forces in the field.

For the next decade, AirLand Battle doctrine was the basis for the Army's organization, equipment and training, and for joint Army-Air Force training exercises. Rehearsed repeatedly over the ensuing years by every Army infantry and armor battalion and armored cavalry squadron at the National Training Center in the Mojave Desert and at the combined Military Training Center at Hohenfels in Germany, it would serve as the blueprint for the highly successful Desert Storm air and ground campaigns.

When American reserves were activated, the war effort received more widespread support as many communities now had a stake in the conflict. Also, in winning congressional approval in December 1990, President Bush clearly defined the war's objectives. The support did not waver, even in the face of peace-movement protests in such cities as Washington, D.C., San Francisco, New York City and Atlanta.

As soon as Operation Desert Shield began, a U.S. Army think tank at Fort Leavenworth, Kan., titled the Center for Army Lessons Learned (CALL), started assembling data for analysis. Information covered aspects such as equipment maintenance in the desert, tactics and deployment.

The war gave civilian and military analysts the world over much to ponder. "There was a weakness on the part of the Iraqi army in general to put the combined arms battle together," said Lt. Gen. Bernard E. Trainor, U.S. Marine Corps (Ret.), ABC-TV's military analyst during Desert Storm. "They were fine in set-piece battles, as, for example, the Fao Peninsula campaign during the Iran-Iraq War, and the invasion of Kuwait, both of which did not require much flexibility on their part. To fight a battle that demanded greater maneuverability was not in their doctrine, which was primarily defensive in nature.

"While the air war had tremendous impact, I don't think their final collapse was due to air power. The air campaign concentrated on command and control facilities, supplies and equipment, as primary targets. The troops, being spread out and dug in, while taking heavy casualties, were not broken."

Did Saddam Hussein misunderstand the awesome firepower and tremendous maneuverability of the coalition forces? "Well, I can't an-

NODA BAKHSHANDAGI, BLACK STAR

swer for Saddam Hussein," said Trainor. "However, his senior officers could not have. They were very professional and of the highest quality. They were educated overseas in schools operated by military personnel from British, French, Soviet and Communist Bloc countries. . .Maybe they didn't have it down to a discreet level of understanding of what our weaponry was capable of—but I don't think we did either. I think they were simply afraid to tell Saddam Hussein the truth.

"Basically, in the final analysis, he overrated his own forces and actually thought they would fight like tigers. And nobody was going to tell him anything to the contrary."

The soldier on the ground confined analysis to a narrower, more pragmatic focus: the need for a better desert boot, rations in a rough-textured package that wouldn't slide off everything one set it on, and the like, but Corporal Carl "Randy" Davis of Heavy Guns, Dragon Section, 3rd Battalion, 9th Marines, Task Force Papa Bear, offered a telling summation of the Iraqi force he and his fellow "Scumdog" tank crewmen confronted: "In my opinion, you can't force people to fight. Yes, Saddam had a million-man army. And yes, he put them in uniform. And yes, they went through the motions. But when we hit 'em, they didn't have the heart to fight." □

DAN HULSHIZER, AP/WIDE WORLD

U.S. NAVY

TOP: Returning troops march down Fifth Avenue in New York City on June 10, 1991. LEFT: Kimberly Mongralla of Fort Dodge, Iowa, follows the flag-draped casket of her husband, Marine Sergeant Garratt Mongralla, killed during the Battle of Khafji. ABOVE: U.S. Navy personnel receive the best welcome of all, from waiting family and friends.

175

CONTRIBUTORS

ED BAILEY, U.S. NAVY

Kuwaitis and allied soldiers celebrate following the withdrawal of the last Iraqi troops from Kuwait, completing the country's liberation.

H. Avery Chenoweth: *Personal observations of the ground war and its aftermath.* A three-war veteran and Marine reserve colonel, Chenoweth was recalled as a combat artist, covering Desert Shield–Desert Storm at sea, in the air, and with the 1st Marine Division in the ground war. He was one of the first to enter Kuwait City.

Robert Dorr: *Air buildup, Desert Shield and analysis.* Dorr, a retired career diplomat, is a well-known lecturer, historian and political analyst. After returning from Saudi Arabia, he wrote *Desert Shield: Trial and Triumph in the Persian Gulf.*

John Gresham: *Smart Weapons.* Gresham is a military systems analyst who was involved in the development of such weaponry as the Sidewinder, Harpoon and Tomahawk missile systems. He is currently working on a book in collaboration with Barrett Tillman.

Jon Guttman: *Allied members of the coalition forces, Battle of Khafji, and the Army's end run in the ground war.* Guttman is senior editor, research director and frequent writer for Empire Press publications. He has also been published internationally on such topics as military aviation and naval history. He is a sergeant in the Virginia National Guard.

Michael E. Haskew: *Naval buildup, War at Sea.* Haskew is an expert on naval history and tactics. He has written for several Empire Press publications, and is currently a contributing editor for *America's Civil War* Magazine.

Albert Hemingway: *Forging an Alliance.* Hemingway also conducted numerous interviews providing the basis for many of the first-hand accounts used throughout the book. A Marine Corps veteran of Vietnam, he is a contributing editor for *Vietnam* Magazine and writes frequently for all Empire Press magazines.

C. Brian Kelly: Editor of *World War II* and *Military History* Magazines, a lecturer in journalism at the University of Virginia and a former award-winning newspaper reporter. Kelly's most recent book is *Best Little Stories of World War II.*

Eric Lee: *Aftermath and strategic analysis.* An Israeli journalist, Lee has contributed to Empire Press publications in the past. He also served as a reservist in the Israeli Defense Force during the Gulf War, helped in the distribution of gas masks to the civilian population, and witnessed a Scud attack.

Sam McGowen: *Aerial Avalanche.* McGowen is a corporate pilot for Ashland Oil. As an Air Force forward air controller in Vietnam, he flew missions over North Vietnam and Laos. He is the author of a book on the C-130 tactical airlift and has written numerous articles as a contributing editor for Empire Press magazines.

Robert Need: *Homecoming of the troops and return of the battleship* Wisconsin. Need, a former Air Force sergeant major, spent much of his military career as an historian in the military personnel branch. His 1967-68 tour of duty in Vietnam was with the Combat News Team.

Craig Roberts: *Intelligence.* Roberts, an internationally published author, is a major in the U.S. Army Reserve, serving as ground liaison officer in the intelligence section of a tactical fighter squadron. He is a Marine Corps Vietnam veteran and frequent contributor to Empire Press publications. He is co-author of the book, *One Shot, One Kill.*

Colonel Harry G. Summers, Jr. (U.S. Army, ret.): *Strategic analysis and Media.* Summers is editor of *Vietnam* Magazine; he covered Desert Storm as a television network military analyst. He began his military career as an enlisted man and ever since has been a spokesman for the soldier.

John H. Waller: *Battlefield of Sand.* Waller first encountered war in the Middle East when he arrived in Cairo with the Office of Strategic Services (OSS) just as the British Eighth Army defeated the German *Afrika Korps* in the epic desert battle of El Alamein. His later career as a foreign service officer took him to Iran and the Persian Gulf, where he witnessed many of the tense events leading to Desert Storm.

David Walsh: *The Rape of Kuwait and Aftermath.* Walsh is a Washington, D.C.-based freelance writer whose specialty is Middle Eastern affairs. His writings include articles published by *The Washington Post*, U.S. Naval Institute, Air and Space Museum and Empire Press.